PAPAL AUTHORITY AND THE LIMITS OF THE LAW IN TUDOR ENGLAND

CAMDEN MISCELLANY
Volume XXXVI

PAPAL AUTHORITY AND THE LIMITS OF THE LAW IN TUDOR ENGLAND

CAMDEN MISCELLANY
Volume XXXVI

Edited by
Peter D. Clarke and Michael Questier

CAMDEN FIFTH SERIES
Volume 48

CAMBRIDGE
UNIVERSITY PRESS

FOR THE ROYAL HISTORICAL SOCIETY
University College London, Gower Street, London WC1 6BT
2015

Published by the Press Syndicate of the University of Cambridge
University Printing House, Shaftesbury Road, Cambridge CB2 8BS, United Kingdom
32 Avenue of the Americas, New York, NY 10013-2473, USA
477 Williamstown Road, Port Melbourne, VIC 3207, Australia
C/Orense, 4, Planta 13, 28020 Madrid, Spain
Lower Ground Floor, Nautica Building, The Water Club,
Beach Road, Granger Bay, 8005 Cape Town, South Africa

© Royal Historical Society 2015

First published 2015

A catalogue record for this book is available from the British Library

ISBN 9781107130364 hardback

SUBSCRIPTIONS. The serial publications of the Royal Historical Society, *Royal Historical Society Transactions* (ISSN 0080-4401) and Camden Fifth Series (ISSN 0960-1163) volumes, may be purchased together on annual subscription. The 2015 subscription price, which includes print and electronic access (but not VAT), is £168 (US $280 in the USA, Canada, and Mexico) and includes Camden Fifth Series, volumes 47 and 48 and Transactions Sixth Series, volume 25 (published in December). The electronic-only price available to institutional subscribes is £141 (US $235 in the USA, Canada, and Mexico). Japanese prices are available from Kinokuniya Company Ltd, P.O. Box 55, Chitose, Tokyo 156, Japan. EU subscribers (outside the UK) who are not registered for VAT should add VAT at their country's rate. VAT registered subscribers should provide their VAT registration number. Prices include delivery by air.

Subscription orders, which must be accompanied by payment, may be sent to a bookseller, subscription agent, or direct to the publisher: Cambridge University Press, University Printing House, Shaftesbury Road, Cambridge CB2 8BS, UK; or in the USA, Canada, and Mexico: Cambridge University Press, Journals Fulfillment Department, 100 Brook Hill Drive, West Nyack, New York, 10994-2133, USA.

SINGLE VOLUMES AND BACK VOLUMES. A list of Royal Historical Society volumes available from Cambridge University Press may be obtained from the Humanities Marketing Department at the address above.

Printed in the UK by Bell & Bain Ltd.

CONTENTS

EDITORS' PREFACE

The current volume brings together contributions from two separate editors. The first is a collection of texts edited by Peter Clarke that evidence Cardinal Thomas Wolsey's legatine powers to grant dispensations and other papal graces and his exercise of these powers during the 1520s in Henry VIII's realm. The second is a text edited by Michael Questier. It takes the form of glosses on and suggested readings of the Elizabethan statute law which imposed treason penalties on Catholic clergy who exercised their office in reconciling to Rome (i.e. absolving from schism and heresy) and on those who availed themselves of this sacramental power. The rationale for linking these contributions in a single volume is threefold. First, both generally concern Catholicism in Tudor England, especially the authority of Catholic clergy there both before and after the break with Rome. Secondly and more specifically, they regard the role of these clergy as agents of papal authority in Tudor England. Wolsey was appointed as a papal legate in 1518 and obtained legatine powers from successive popes on a scale unparalleled in pre-Reformation England, notably to grant dispensations, and he exercised these dispensing powers there extensively; he was thus the papal agent *par excellence* in Tudor England on the eve of the Reformation. The Elizabethan 'tolerationist' text, by contrast, seeks to deny that Catholic clergy necessarily functioned as agents of papal authority. They were not, therefore, all without exception traitors to the queen, even though one literal reading of the statute book might give the impression that this was what the State had meant. Instead, so this manuscript claimed, the statutes themselves could be read in such a way as to imply that the legislators themselves accepted that the Catholic clergy's priestly functions did not depend exclusively on papal supremacy (unlike Wolsey's legatine status) or even a malign anti-popish understanding of the papacy as a legal and ecclesiastical entity. Therefore the exercise of their faculties could not automatically be interpreted as treasonable. Coincidentally Wolsey's activity as a papal agent led to him being attainted him with treason, and although the charge did not relate to his dispensing powers, four years after Wolsey's fall Henry VIII forbade his subjects to petition Rome or its agents for the kinds of graces Wolsey had issued. He established the Faculty Office to issue such graces instead, and its authority depended on royal, not papal, supremacy. Both contributions, therefore, concern the relationship between Catholic clergy and supreme authority in the English Church, wherever this was deemed to lie. Thirdly, both contributions illuminate the limits of the law and flexibility in interpreting and applying it. Wolsey's graces in effect limited the operation of canon law: his dispensations suspended it in specific instances, notably regarding marriage and ordination; and he also granted licences permitting activity that it normally forbade, such as clergy not residing in their benefices. The 'tolerationist' text implies, although with arguments which at times seem rather specious, that the Elizabethan State was, even in its more draconian utterances, to some extent drawing in its horns. Both contributions, therefore, concern apparently binding law which might be relaxed in Tudor England with regard to Catholic clergy (as well as laity in the case of Wolsey's papal graces).

Peter Clarke presented earlier versions of the introduction to his texts at conferences at the Carlsberg Academy (Copenhagen) and the University of Sussex, and at research seminars in Yale University and the University of Connecticut; he is grateful to his hosts and audiences on these occasions, in particular for their comments and questions, which helped improve this essay. A final draft of it further benefited from close reading by Patrick Zutshi, Peter Gwyn, and George Bernard; Peter Clarke is grateful to all three. He also thanks the Harry Ransom Center in the University of Texas at Austin for the volume's cover image and authorizing its reproduction. He drafted his contribution while his wife Barbara was pregnant with their son Matteo, now a delightful one year-old, and he dedicates it with love to her.

Peter D. Clarke,   Michael C. Questier,
University of Southampton   Queen Mary, University of London

ABBREVIATIONS

BCL	Bachelor of Civil Law
BCnL	Bachelor of Canon Law
BCn & CL	Bachelor of Canon and Civil Law
Beds.	Bedfordshire
Berks.	Berkshire
BRUC	A. B. Emden, *A Biographical Register of the University of Cambridge to 1500* (Cambridge, 1963)
BRUO	A. B. Emden, *A Biographical Register of the University of Oxford to A.D. 1500*, 3 vols (Oxford, 1957–1959)
BRUO, 1501–1540	A. B. Emden, *A Biographical Register of the University of Oxford, A.D. 1501 to 1540* (Oxford, 1974)
BTh	Bachelor of Theology
Bucks.	Buckinghamshire
BVM	Blessed Virgin Mary
Cambs.	Cambridgeshire
Cardigans.	Cardiganshire
Carmarth.	Carmarthanshire
Ches.	Cheshire
Co.	county (of)
Cornw.	Cornwall
CPL	*Calendar of Entries in the Papal Registers relating to Great Britain and Ireland: Papal Letters*, ed. W. H. Bliss et al., 20 vols to date (London, 1893–1960; Dubin, 1978–)
Cumbd.	Cumberland
Decretum	*Decretum Gratiani*, printed in *Corpus iuris canonici*, ed. E. Friedberg (Leipzig, 1879), Vol. I (cited by *distinctio* (D.) and canon (c.) in Part I, and by *causa* (C.), *quaestio* (q.) and canon (c.) in Part II)
DCL	Doctor of Civil Law
DCnL	Doctor of Canon Law
DCn & CL	Doctor of Canon and Civil Law
Derbys.	Derbyshire
dioc.	diocese
DM	Doctor of Medicine
dom.	dominus
DTh	Doctor of Theology

E. Yorks.	East Yorkshire
Eubel, *Hierarchia catholica*, III	C. Eubel, *Hierarchia catholica medii aevi, sive summorum pontificum, S. R. E. cardinalium, ecclesiarum antistitum series*, III: *Saeculum XVI ab anno 1503 complectens* (Münster, 1910)
Fasti, viii	*Fasti Ecclesiae Anglicanae 1300–1541*, VIII: *Bath and Wells Diocese*, comp. B. Jones (London, 1964)
Fasti, x	*Fasti Ecclesiae Anglicanae 1300–1541*, X: *Coventry and Lichfield Diocese*, comp. B. Jones (London, 1964)
Fasti, xi	*Fasti Ecclesiae Anglicanae 1300–1541*, XI: *The Welsh Dioceses*, comp. B. Jones (London, 1965)
Glamorg.	Glamorganshire
Glos.	Gloucestershire
Hants.	Hampshire
Heads of Religious Houses, III	*The Heads of Religious Houses: England and Wales*, III: *1377–1540*, ed. D. M. Smith (Cambridge, 2008)
Herts.	Hertfordshire
Houlbrooke	R. Houlbrooke, *Church Courts and the People during the English Reformation 1520–1570* (Oxford, 1979)
Knowles & Hadcock	D. Knowles & R. N. Hadcock, *Medieval Religious Houses: England and Wales*, 2nd edn (Harlow, 1971)
Leics.	Leicestershire
Letters and Papers	*Letters and Papers, Foreign and Domestic, of the Reign of Henry VIII*, ed. J. S. Brewer, J. Gairdner and R. H. Brodie, 23 vols. in 38 (London, 1862–1932)
LPL	Lambeth Palace Library (London)
M.	*Magister*
MD	Doctor of Medicine
Monmouth.	Monmouthshire
MTh	Master of Theology
N. Yorks.	North Yorkshire
Norf.	Norfolk
Northants.	Northamptonshire
Northd.	Northumberland
OCarm	Carmelite Order
OCist	Cistercian Order
OESA	Order of Austin Friars
OFM	Franciscan Order (Order of Friars Minor)
OPrem	Premonstratensian Order
OSA	Order of St Augustine
OSB	Order of St Benedict

Oxford DNB	*The Oxford Dictionary of National Biography*, ed. H. C. G. Matthew & B. Harrison, 60 vols (Oxford, 2004)
Oxon.	Oxfordshire
par. ch.	parish church
Reg. Blythe	Register of Geoffrey Blythe, bishop of Coventry and Lichfield (1503–1531); Lichfield Record Office, B/A/1/14i
Reg. Bothe ed.	*Registrum Caroli Bothe, episcopi Herefodensis, A.D. MDXVI–MDXXXV*, ed. A. T. Bannister, Canterbury and York Society, Series 28 (1921)
Reg. Campeggio	Register of Lorenzo Campeggio, bishop of Salisbury (1524–1534); Wiltshire and Swindon Record Office (Trowbridge), D1/2/15
Reg. Clerke	Register of John Clerk, bishop of Bath and Wells (1523–1541); Somerset Record Office (Taunton), D/D/B. Reg. 12
Reg. Clerke ed.	*The Registers of Thomas Wolsey, Bishop of Bath and Wells 1518–1523, John Clerke, Bishop of Bath and Wells 1523–1541, William Knyght, Bishop of Bath and Wells 1541–1547, and Gilbert Bourne, Bishop of Bath and Wells 1554–1559*, ed. H. Maxwell-Lyte, Somerset Record Society 55 (1940), 27–89
Reg. Fisher	Register of John Fisher, bishop of Rochester (1504–1535); Kent History and Library Centre (Maidstone), DRb/A/r/1/13
Reg. Fox, 5	Fifth register of Richard Fox, bishop of Winchester (1501–1528); Hampshire Record Office (Winchester), 21M65/A1/21 (covering the years 1522–1528). Fox's first four registers (21M65/A1/17–20) contain no letters of Wolsey.
Reg. Ghinucci, 1–2	Registers of Geronomo de' Ghinucci, bishop of Worcester (1522–1535): 1. Worcestershire Record Office (Worcester), b.716.093-BA.2648/8(ii); 2. Worcestershire Record Office (Worcester), b.716.093- BA.2648/9(i)
Reg. Longland	Register of John Longland, bishop of Lincoln (1521–1547); Lincolnshire Archives (Lincoln), Episcopal Register XXVI
Reg. Nykke, 4	Fourth register of Richard Nykke, bishop of Norwich (1501–1535); Norfolk Record Office (Norwich), Reg/10/16. Nykke's first three registers (Reg/8/13; Reg/9/14–15) and his fifth (Reg/11/17) contain no letters of Wolsey.
Reg. Tunstall	Register of Cuthbert Tunstall, bishop of London (1522–1530); Guildhall Library (London), MS 9531/10

Reg. Veysey, 1: see *Reg Veysey, 2*

Reg. Veysey, 2   Second register of John Veysey, bishop of Exeter
                               (1519–1551); Devon Record Office, Exeter
                               diocesan records, Chanter catalogue 15.
                               Veysey's first register (= *Reg. Veysey, 1*; ibid.,
                               Chanter catalogue 14) contains no letters of
                               Wolsey but records institutions related to his
                               letters in the first register.

Reg. West   Register of Nicholas West, bishop of Ely
                               (1515–1533); Cambridge University Library,
                               Ely Diocesan Records, G/1/7

Reg. Wolsey (York)   Register of Thomas Wolsey, archbishop of York
                               (1514– 1530); Borthwick Institute (University
                               of York), Reg. 27

Reg. Wolsey (Winchester)   *Registrum Thome Wolsey, cardinalis ecclesie*
ed.   *Wintoniensis administratoris*, ed. F. T. Madge and
                               H. Chitty, Canterbury and York Society
                               Series 32 (1926)

Rut.   Rutland
Staffs.   Staffordshire
STP   *Sacrae Theologiae Professor*
Suff.   Suffolk
TNA   The National Archives (Kew, London)
Venn   *Alumni Cantabrigienses: A Biographical List of All
                               Known Students, Graduates and Holders of Office at
                               the University of Cambridge, from the Earliest Times
                               to 1900*, Part 1: *From the Earliest Times to 1751*,
                               ed. J. Venn and J. A. Venn, 4 vols (Cambridge,
                               1922–1927)

VCH (London)   *The Victoria History of London*, Vol. I, ed. W. Page
                               (London, 1909)

VI   *Liber Sextus*, printed in *Corpus iuris canonici*, ed. E.
                               Friedberg (Leipzig, 1879), II. 933–1124 (cited
                               by book, title and chapter; e.g. VI 1.1.1 =
                               Book 1, title 1, chapter 1 of the *Liber Sextus*)

W. Yorks.   West Yorkshire
Warwicks.   Warwickshire
Westmor.   Westmorland
Wilts.   Wiltshire
Worcs.   Worcestershire
X   *Liber Extra* (or *Decretales Gregorii IX*) printed in
                               Corpus iuris canonici, ed. E. Friedberg (Leipzig,
                               1879), II. 2–928 (cited in the same way as VI)

I

RIVALLING ROME: CARDINAL WOLSEY AND DISPENSATIONS

Edited by Peter D. Clarke

INTRODUCTION

Cardinal Wolsey, archbishop of York and Henry VIII's chancellor, was appointed as papal legate *a latere* by Pope Leo X on 17 May 1518.[1] Wolsey was to exercise legatine powers in the English realm until his fall from grace in October 1529. As the pope's representative in Henry VIII's realm he was to wield almost unprecedented authority over the English Church, including the power to conduct visitations of religious houses, convene legatine councils and intervene extensively in the jurisdiction of bishops. This activity is well known to historians, but a neglected aspect of his legatine authority is his power to grant dispensations.[2] The aim of the present edition is to assemble documents evidencing Wolsey's dispensing powers and his exercise of them.

Dispensations formed an important part of ecclesiastical jurisdiction by Wolsey's time. The rules of canon law then bound all members of the Catholic Church, and dispensations were important because they relaxed some of these rules, expressly those which were man-made and not divine in origin. Hence canon law derived from scripture was not dispensable,[3] but that introduced by popes and councils might be. The human law that dispensations relaxed largely concerned marriage, ordination, and ecclesiastical benefices. Marriage dispensations were the main kind sought by laity, naturally, and most dealt with impediments arising from kinship, principally the prohibited degrees of consanguinity (kinship by blood) and affinity

---

[1] T. Rymer, *Foedera . . .*, 3rd edn (London, 1739–1745), VI. 140–141 (XIII. 606–607).

[2] e.g. A. F. Pollard, *Wolsey* (London, 1929), omits dispensing from its lengthy treatment of his legatine powers in ch. 5. Cf. P. Gwyn, *The King's Cardinal: The Rise and Fall of Thomas Wolsey* (London, 1990), ch. 8, which in its similar survey at least treats this briefly on pp. 284–285.

[3] This, of course, was the grounds for Henry VIII's request for a papal divorce from Catherine Aragon, namely that Julius II's dispensation for their marriage and hence the marriage itself were invalid since they went against divine law in Leviticus 18:16 and 20:21, which was understood to ban marriage to a brother's widow (Catherine was the widow of Henry's brother Arthur when she married Henry). In this particular case, however, the papal dispensation was supported by divine law in Deuteronomy 20:5, which permitted marriage to a brother's widow if the brother had died childless; this exception exactly fitted Henry's circumstances (Arthur and Catherine had no issue); see J. J. Scarisbrick, *Henry VIII* (London, 1968), chs 7–8.

(relationship through marriage) not covered by Leviticus 18–20.[4] Other marital impediments, from which dispensations were less commonly sought, included public honesty and *cognatio spiritualis*. The former arose where one marriage partner was betrothed to someone related to the other partner within the prohibited degrees, but the betrothal had been broken off without consummation.[5] *Cognatio spiritualis*, or spiritual kinship, usually applied in instances where the parent of one spouse had presented the other for baptism, or less commonly confirmation. Most couples sought marriage dispensations before marrying, but they might also do so retrospectively, especially if they had only learned of the impediment in question after marrying.[6] Other, non-marital, kinds of dispensation were largely sought by clergy. Many of these dealt with impediments to ordination, notably: illegitimate birth (*defectus natalium*), which might also debar religious, including women, from appointment as head of their order or one of its houses without a dispensation; being under-age (*defectus aetatis*), which for ordinands to the priesthood meant being below the age of twenty-five; ordination on Sundays or feasts outside of the four general ordination days in each year (*extra tempora statuta a iure*);[7] and physical deformity (*defectus corporis*), principally affecting ordinands' hands or eyesight. Clergy also requested various dispensations regarding the holding of benefices, particularly two or more together. This was pluralism, and canon law expressly forbade this where the benefices were 'incompatible', generally meaning that each had 'cure of souls' requiring the incumbent to administer the sacraments to his parishioners, notably confession. Pluralism clearly involved non-residence in at least one of the benefices held; dispensations might also free clergy from obligations to reside in their benefices, and not only where held in plurality, but also in other

---

[4] The degrees of kinship within which canon law prohibited marriage were seven by the late 11th c.; in 1215 the Fourth Lateran Council reduced them to four (X 4.14.8). Leviticus 18–20 covered most instances in the first and second degrees, thereby largely restricting dispensations for kinship to the 'outer', man-made degrees.

[5] According to canon law, consummation would have turned the betrothal into marriage and the impediment into affinity. Affinity usually arose from sexual relations, even outside marriage, i.e. where one marriage partner had had extra-marital sex with someone related to the other within the prohibited degrees.

[6] Couples seeking retrospective dispensations for impediments known to them when they married further needed papal absolution, for they incurred automatic excommunication through their conscious violation of canon law. Marital impediments normally became known as a result of reading the banns, which canon law required from 1215 before all marriages, therefore most of these couples had probably contracted 'clandestine' marriages, also condemned and penalized by canon law (X 4.3.3).

[7] These were the so-called 'Ember days', i.e. the Saturdays after the first Sunday in Lent, Pentecost, Holy Rood Day (14 September), and St Lucy's Day (13 December).

permitted circumstances, notably for study-leave at university.[8] Male religious might likewise seek dispensations, known as 'capacities', allowing them to leave the religious life and obtain secular benefices. Other more miscellaneous dispensations and related graces, such as special licences, notably to eat meat and dairy produce in Lent and other fasting-periods, also existed and will be discussed later.

Authority to grant these various dispensations and other graces largely resided with the pope, who issued them by virtue of his *plenitudo potestatis*; canon law further reserved to the pope absolution from certain grave sins, known as 'reserved cases', notably assaults on clergy and apostasy.[9] Petitioners solicited dispensations from the papal curia by at least the late eleventh century, and penitents' requests for papal absolution go back even earlier. The origins of this system of papal graces has even been traced back to the Early Church though it was probably only with the growth of papal power from the late eleventh century and the development of a universal body of Western canon law from the twelfth century that such graces were granted in significant numbers.[10] Letters conferring these graces were issued by the papal chancery initially and many were copied in its registers. These testify to rising demand for such papal favours across Western Europe, and the system of papal graces, though it would be attacked as an abuse later by Protestants, largely seems to have expanded in response to this popular demand, since people found such graces useful. Consequently, just as the papacy increasingly delegated cases appealed to its judgement to lesser churchmen in response to growing judicial business at the curia from the mid twelfth century, it likewise began at about this time to delegate to other clergy powers or 'faculties' to grant dispensations and other papal graces. Much of this delegated authority passed to curial officials, notably the cardinal or 'major' penitentiary, who, along with the minor penitentiaries subordinate to him, received ever expanding faculties from successive popes, so much that by the mid thirteenth century his activity was discharged through a growing new department of papal government, also called

---

[8]Sanctioned in 1298 by Boniface VIII's constitution 'Cum ex eo' (VI 1.6.34); see L. E. Boyle, 'The constitution "Cum ex eo" of Boniface VIII: Education of parochial clergy', *Mediaeval Studies*, 24 (1962), 263–302.

[9]The canon 'Si quis suadente' (*Decretum*, C.17 q.4 c.29) made anti-clerical violence a 'reserved case' in 1139; apostasy, the canonical crime of religious leaving their houses without a superior's consent, became one in 1298 (VI 3.2.24). Offenders in both cases incurred automatic excommunication reserved along with the offence to papal absolution.

[10]R. A. Aronstam, 'Penitential pilgrimages to Rome in the early Middle Ages', *Archivum historiae pontificiae*, 13 (1975), 65–83, esp. 67–70 on penitents seeking absolution from the pope in person. On the origins of the system see W. J. Sparrow Simpson, *Dispensations* (London, 1935), 1–6.

the penitentiary.[11] By the fifteenth century it expedited many of the same graces as the papal chancery, except dispensations for plurality, which the chancery continued to issue. In addition popes conceded faculties to papal agents, including legates *a latere*, nuncios and even cameral collectors, to exercise in those provinces where they were sent from the curia. Bishops might also possess faculties, notably those enjoying the status of *legatus natus* such as the archbishop of Canterbury, and could even concede certain graces *ex officio*, but their dispensing powers were generally limited.[12]

Wolsey was, therefore, not unique in having delegated papal authority to issue dispensations even in the English realm. Papal officials visiting the kingdom had long enjoyed faculties as part of their commission, and several graces they granted to English and Welsh beneficiaries survive.[13] Even if such papal agents were more conveniently accessible than the distant curia, they were transient and intermittent sources of papal graces, however, and their faculties were often restricted to dispensing small numbers of people.[14] Consequently, Wolsey's position as a permanently resident legate *a latere* in the English kingdom was remarkable; only Cardinal Beaufort had paralleled this a century earlier and even his legatine powers had been stymied by the English Crown and episcopate.[15] Nevertheless, Wolsey's legatine authority had to be carefully built up over many years of lobbying

---

[11] See *Supplications from England and Wales in the Registers of the Apostolic Penitentiary, 1410–1503*, ed. P. D. Clarke and P. N. R. Zutshi, 3 vols, Canterbury and York Society 103–105 (2013–), esp. the introduction in Vol. I, xiii–lviii, and other scholarship on the penitentiary cited there.

[12] For example, in 1298 Boniface VIII limited episcopal dispensations for *defectus natalium* to allowing men of illegitimate birth to receive minor orders and a benefice without cure of souls; anything more required a papal dispensation (VI 1.11.1). As to the archbishop of Canterbury's faculties, these are not well understood and need investigation; see I. J. Churchill, *Canterbury Administration: The Administrative Machinery of the Archbishopric of Canterbury Illustrated from Original Records* (London, 1933), I. 506–507.

[13] See, for example, the faculties conceded by Innocent VIII to James of Imola, legate *a latere* to the English and Scottish realms, in 1485: *CPL*, xiv. 23–26. Original examples of graces issued by such agents comprise: Bangor University Archives, Penrhyn MS 6 (papal nuncio, 1386); London, Lambeth Palace Library, Papal Documents 129b (papal chamberlain, 1506), 130 (nuncio, 1514); Archives départementales du Nord (Lille), B429–16141 (papal orator, 1468), edited by P. D. Clarke 'English royal marriages and the papal penitentiary in the fifteenth century', *English Historical Review*, 120 (2005), 1014–1029, at 1026–1029. Others were copied in English episcopal registers, e.g. Lichfield Record Office, B/A/1/13 (Register of Coventry and Lichfield diocese, 1490–1502), fols 124v (papal nuncio, 1491), 161v, 164r–v (papal collector, 1495), 249v (papal orator, 1502); etc.

[14] For example, James of Imola (see n. 13) might only dispense twelve persons from *defectus natalium* and the same number to hold two benefices in plurality.

[15] See, e.g., Pollard, *Wolsey*, 168–169.

the papacy, not least for amplification of his faculties.[16] Wolsey had sought the legation along with the cardinalate since at least 1514, but whereas Leo X conceded the latter in 1515, he long proved reluctant to grant the former, in particular because it would set a precedent for a ruler's minister holding extraordinary power over a national church, especially at a time when national monarchies were increasing their control over churches in their realms. Leo only yielded in 1518 by making Wolsey co-legate with Cardinal Campeggio, largely to facilitate the latter's entry to England, which Henry VIII had resisted. The pope sent Campeggio to further plans for a crusade against the Turks, which he had long sought to finance by taxing the English church; Wolsey had promised to raise the money without result, and Leo intended the joint legation to induce Wolsey to deliver.[17] This inducement was not enough to satisfy Wolsey, however. Leo's initial commission made him legate only for the duration of Campeggio's stay in England and for the sake of the crusade. On 27 August 1518 Leo issued a further bull authorizing both legates to reform monasteries, but not secular clergy too as Wolsey had hoped. The Italian curialist Silvestro Gigli, bishop of Worcester, who was lobbying for Wolsey at Rome, relayed to Leo Wolsey's complaints about the 'prohibitions to his legatine authority'.[18] Leo apparently considered his demands for a fuller commission 'importunate', because it would impinge too much on the authority of the English bishops and because Wolsey had still not fulfilled his promise about clerical taxation. The pope was also unmoved by Wolsey's assertion that he sought more faculties 'not for the sake of extorting money but to do some good in the Lord's vineyard and reform the clergy'.[19] His actual motivation for seeking greater legatine authority is a matter of debate, and will be addressed later on. What is clear, however, is that Wolsey was preoccupied by the potential expiry of his legation on Campeggio's departure; he had sought a separate fuller commission for himself even as the joint

---

[16]Pollard, *Wolsey*, 179–182; M. J. Kelly, 'Canterbury jurisdiction and influence during the episcopate of William Warham, 1503–1532', PhD dissertation (University of Cambridge, 1965), 164–173; W. E. Wilkie, *The Cardinal Protectors of England: Rome and the Tudors before the Reformation* (Cambridge, 1974), 83–5, 105–106, 113–114, 129–131, 133–135, 142–144, 168–169.
[17]W. E. Lunt, *Studies in Anglo-Papal Relations during the Middle Ages*, II: *Financial Relations of the Papacy with England, 1327–1534* (Cambridge, MA, 1962), 160–168.
[18]Pollard, Wolsey, 179; *Letters and Papers*, III, no. 149 (Gigli's letter to Wolsey, 29 March 1519).
[19]*Ibid.* no. 298 (Gigli's letter to Wolsey, 10 June, 1519); E. Martène and U. Durand (eds), *Veterum scriptorum et monumentorum historicum, dogmaticorum, moralium amplissima collectio*, Vol. III (Paris, 1724), col. 1289 (Wolsey's letter to Leo, 25 March 1519).

legation was being conceded.[20] Nevertheless, before Campeggio left England on 24 August 1519, Wolsey had only managed to secure a papal bull on 10 June empowering him to reform the monasteries on his own after his co-legate's return to the curia.[21] Leo's dissatisfaction at Wolsey's failure to raise the crusade tax remained the chief sticking-point, as Kelly observed: 'Whereas the pope displayed obstinacy in extending the legateship in the hope of attracting a subsidy, the cardinal was using the prospect of taxation to extort amplification of his powers'.[22] Wolsey indeed continued to petition Leo, and with support from Campeggio and Henry VIII he had secured the promise of a bull by December 1519 extending his legation. This would only be for a year dated from Campeggio's departure, that is until 24 August 1520, but on 6 January 1521 Wolsey obtained another extension for a further two years beyond this deadline.[23] Wolsey had still not delivered the long-promised taxation, which continued to irritate Leo, but the pope's concern to deter England from an alliance with France had apparently persuaded him to be more conciliatory toward Wolsey, prime mover in Anglo-French relations.[24] This doubtless also accounts for two more bulls issued respectively on 1 April and 27 June 1521, which not only further extended Wolsey's legation to ten years in total but also conceded extraordinary faculties to issue dispensations and other favours.[25]

The April bull allowed him to appoint forty apostolic notaries, fifty 'golden knights', and the same number of counts palatine and papal chaplains, and any amount of papal scribes, within the realm and his own household. As Kelly suspects, Wolsey probably saw these papal titles as largely a means to attract and reward familiars. Additional concessions included powers to legitimize bastards, normally the prerogative of temporal rulers, and confer degrees in canon and civil law, theology, arts, and medicine. No evidence has been found for Wolsey's exercise of any of these powers, except the latter and only in

---

[20] *Ibid.* col. 1284 (Wolsey's letter to Leo, 11 April 1518): he requested the withdrawal of Campeggio's *de iure* legatine faculties and their transfer to him, asserting that Campeggio could never enter England but for him.

[21] *Letters and Papers*, III, no. 475; Pollard, *Wolsey*, 180.

[22] Kelly, 'Canterbury jurisdiction', 165; cf. Lunt, *Financial Relations*, 165–166.

[23] *Letters and Papers*, III, no. 557 (Campeggio's letter to Wolsey, 19 December 1519); Rymer, *Foedera . . .*, VI. 191 (XIII. 734–735).

[24] Pollard, *Wolsey*, 181; Kelly, 'Canterbury jurisdiction', 168–169.

[25] Rymer, *Foedera . . .*, VI. 193–194 (XIII. 739–742), which added a second two-year extension; Appendix 1a, which added a five-year extension beyond this (making ten years). Discussed by Pollard, *Wolsey*, 180–181; Gwyn, *The King's Cardinal*, 278; and Kelly, 'Canterbury jurisdiction', 169–171, who quotes the remark of John Clerk, the English ambassador in Rome, that the April bull contained 'such faculties as I thinke the like hath not byn seen in englond theis many yeris'.

one case: a commission on 30 September 1525 to award Richard Foxford a doctorate in both Roman and canon law.[26] The other faculties conceded were arguably more significant, and certainly his use of them is better documented. He might grant dispensations from *defectus natalium*, *defectus aetatis* and other 'irregularities' (impediments to ordination or the use of orders already conferred), allowing promotion to all, even holy orders, including the priesthood; ministry in such or existing orders even at the altar, that is celebrating mass; and tenure of any kind or number of benefices with or without a cure, in effect pluralism. Wolsey might also dispense secular clergy to study and graduate in civil law,[27] and religious to preach anywhere; and grant absolution from excommunication and other spiritual sanctions imposed by ecclesiastical judges or canon law (i.e. in 'reserved cases') or to anyone failing to say their required hours. Above all, Wolsey obtained the long-coveted power to reform secular clergy, even bishops, and punish them himself or through a deputy. His use of this power, and of his existing authority to visit monasteries and correct religious, has attracted much attention, not least because of the reaction it supposedly provoked among the English episcopate, including Archbishop Warham of Canterbury, although recent historiography suggests that this was not as negative as has often been assumed.[28] Though it is not the intention here to revisit this issue, Wolsey's dispensing powers were relevant to reform, as we will later see, and his bull of June 1521 was to extend these even more dramatically.

It confirmed the April bull's concessions regarding clerical reform, absolution from spiritual sanctions, and the awarding of degrees and papal titles, except that Wolsey might now confer any number of the latter. It defined his faculty to dispense from *defectum aetatis* in greater detail, as permitting ordination to the subdiaconate, diaconate and priesthood at 17, 18 and 23 respectively for secular clerks and 16, 17 and 22 for religious, as well as tenure of a benefice with a cure at 18. He might further license under-age clergy to seek ordination to two of these grades on the same day, *extra tempora a iure statuta* and from all Catholic bishops; albeit any bishop might issue letters dimissory

---

[26] Appendix 2. **38** below.

[27] Honorius III's constitution 'Super speculum' (1219) banned beneficed clergy from studying civil law on pain of excommunication (X 3.50.10).

[28] For the older view see Pollard, *Wolsey*, esp. 178–179, 190–196, who even characterizes Wolsey's exercise of legatine authority as 'ecclesiastical despotism' that allegedly contributed to the break with Rome. Cf. the more measured, 'revisionist' views of Houlbroke, 10, and Gwyn, *The King's Cardinal*, 267–299. See also K. Brown, 'Wolsey and the ecclesiastical order: The case of the Franciscan observants', in *Cardinal Wolsey: Church, State and Art*, ed. S. J. Gunn and P. G. Lindley (Cambridge, 1991), 219–238.

allowing clergy in his diocese to seek ordination outside of it. The bull did not elaborate upon his other existing faculties but added many new ones, several likewise concerning ordination and benefices. He might dispense clergy holding benefices with a cure so they were not obliged to take holy orders for up to seven years, provided that they became subdeacons within the first two years of that period. He might dispense male religious, except friars, to hold a secular benefice with a cure, that is issue 'capacities'. He might also absolve any religious, including mendicants, from the reserved sin of apostasy and its canonical penalties, and dispense them from irregularity; (which regular priests could incur by celebrating divine offices while excommunicated as apostates).[29] Penitent apostates often sought to return to the religious life, but not always to their original house or order, indubitably repelled by the same reasons which had prompted them to flee it in the first place. These might include the severity of its rule, as Wolsey might dispense the transfer of apostates to laxer orders, even permitting mendicants to enter non-mendicant orders: a dilution of the canonical requirement to license transfers to another house or order 'of equal or stricter observance'.[30] He might concede some graces only to certain clergy, notably those in his household. He might dispense his familiars, graduates, and noblemen to hold up to four incompatible benefices in plurality, and any man living at his expense, up to three; and authorize his familiars to unite two of their benefices into one, even parish churches. Other faculties regarded graces mainly requested by laity. He might dispense marriages in the third degree of consanguinity or affinity, and the third and fourth degrees combined, and from an impediment of *cognatio spiritualis* or public honesty, recognizing their issue as legitimate. His marriage dispensations could be retrospective, since he might also absolve couples who had married knowing of such impediments without a prior dispensation.[31] He might not, however, concede a dispensation for the 'levirate', that is marriage between a man and his childless brother's widow, coincidentally what Henry VIII had needed in order to marry Catherine of Aragon. Wolsey might, nevertheless, license solemnization of marriages without reading of the banns (as any bishop might do within his own diocese),[32] or during Lent and other forbidden times. Further graces more often sought by laity than clergy and which he might concede released from religious

---

[29] In common with the 1298 ruling in n. 9, the bull chiefly defined apostasy as abandoning the habit (implying a return to the secular life).

[30] As stipulated by Innocent III's decretal 'Licet quibusdam' (1206); X 3.31.18.

[31] See n. 6, and also, on the next sentence, n. 3.

[32] See the ruling in n. 6, which required priests to read the banns in the couple's parish church on three Sundays preceding the marriage.

obligations. He might 'commute' pious intentions in wills into some other pious duty (*alia pietatis opera*), and license consumption of eggs, butter, cheese and other dairy produce during Lent and other fasting periods when this was forbidden, even meat if the beneficiary's doctors advised it. Finally, Wolsey might concede graces designed to facilitate popular piety. These included licences for laity or clergy to appoint a personal confessor, secular or regular, which relaxed the obligation to confess to their parish priest. He might extraordinarily empower the confessor to commute vows to go on long-distance pilgrimages to Rome or Compostella (but not vows of perpetual chastity or for entering the religious life) and to absolve from observing oaths; this was important for it was usually reserved to the pope and oaths formed a major part of ecclesiastical jurisdiction. Violators of oaths as solemn promises before God were often sued for perjury in English church courts by Wolsey's time, even if their promises were of a worldly nature (most cases regarded non-payment of debts). The confessor might also grant absolution in all but reserved cases and a plenary indulgence at the point of death (*in mortis articulo*).[33] Wolsey himself might grant indulgences too, for ten years each and forty in total, as he saw fit. He might also license nobles, priests or graduates to have a portable altar, where masses and other divine offices might be celebrated for them and their households anywhere, even before day-break or in places interdicted by 'ordinary' authority, which canon law did not normally allow.[34]

This wide range of faculties was significant because it enabled Wolsey to confer many of the same graces which petitioners sought from the papal curia, notably the penitentiary, and thus potentially to rival Rome as a source of these favours for English and Welsh supplicants, as I have argued elsewhere.[35] Indeed, his powers to grant dispensations, absolutions, and licences were broadly comparable with those of the cardinal penitentiary, especially on marriage, and even exceeded them in some respects, notably concerning dispensations for uniting benefices and pluralism, which the chancery might issue but not the papal penitentiary. Admittedly, he might not issue the full range

[33] The Fourth Lateran Council (1215) had imposed an obligation on all adult Christians to confess their sins at least once a year at Easter to 'their own priest', generally understood to mean their parish priest (X 5.38.12). The subsequent popularity of friars as confessors encouraged growing demand for such papal licences from the mid 13th c.

[34] The interdict was a spiritual sanction suspending religious rites in certain places; it could be imposed by local ecclesiastical judges or 'ordinaries', notably bishops, and beneficiaries of these licences still had to observe it if they had occasioned it or it was imposed on them personally.

[35] Peter D. Clarke, 'Canterbury as the new Rome: Dispensations and Henry VIII's reformation', *Journal of Ecclesiastical History*, 64 (2013), 20–44, esp. 23–25.

of graces in the penitentiary's gift, and the June bull expressly excluded some of them, particularly commutation of vows for the religious life and chastity.[36] Certainly the bulls of 1521 were still not enough to satisfy Wolsey: he continued to press for fuller legatine authority, doubtless conscious of the more extensive faculties other cardinals enjoyed.[37] Leo X's successor, Adrian VI, agreed in 1523 to confirm the five-year extension of Wolsey's legation (till 24 August 1524), but hesitated to renew it for life and refused any further faculties.[38] But Giulio de' Medici's election as Clement VII on Adrian's death in late 1523 raised Wolsey's hopes, for de' Medici had been cardinal protector of England and they had collaborated on allying England with the papacy and empire against France from 1522; in January 1524 Clement indeed confirmed his legation 'with all faculties' for life. Even this did not fully please Wolsey, who 'thought his bull of faculties somewhat restrained'. In particular he sought that his faculties to grant graces to familiars be extended to include non-familiars.[39] Although Clement VII issued further letters concerning Wolsey's legation, none are known to have added to his faculties of 1521.[40] Two of Wolsey's surviving letters of dispensation from the mid 1520s would claim to exercise new faculties granted by Clement, but no independent evidence supports this.[41] And Clement VII was reluctant to increase his powers, for he feared that they might deprive the curia of business and income from English or Welsh petitioners, a position that Wolsey's exploitation of his faculties would justify, as we will later see. Indeed, English agents reported that the curia opposed his demands in 1524 as it was 'in great misery' and 'totally impoverished' since its revenues from France and Germany had declined

Wolsey's ambition for greater legatine power remained unabated, however, if the curious text in Appendix 1b is at all indicative. It takes the form of a *breve*, a kind of papal document that originated by 1389 'as an alternative to the traditional *bullae* of the chancery' and was

---

[36] On these and other graces issued by the penitentiary see *Supplications from England and Wales*, ed. Clarke and Zutshi, I. xxvi–xlvi.

[37] See the examples noted by Kelly, 'Canterbury jurisdiction', 169 n. 3. In 1519 Gigli had informed Wolsey that he pointed out to Leo X on Wolsey's behalf 'the ample legatine authority granted to Cardinal de Bussi' in France (*Letters and Papers*, III, no. 149).

[38] *Letters and Papers*, III, no. 2771 (letter of Thomas Hannibal, English ambassador in Rome, to Wolsey, 13 January 1523).

[39] *Letters and Papers*, IV, nos. 14, 15, 252 (letters to Wolsey, the first two dated 9 January and the third, 16 April 1524, from John Clerk, the first with two other English diplomats in Rome). Such faculties were doubtless those to dispense for plurality and unions of benefices noted above.

[40] e.g. his bull of 21 August 1524 edited by Rymer, *Foedera* . . ., VI. 9–10 (XIV. 18–20); on what follows see n. 39.

[41] Appendix 4. **31** and **56**, to be discussed below.

drawn up by papal secretaries, who first appear under Benedict XII (1334–1342) and came to form new curial departments by the fifteenth century.[42] The text's format as a *breve* is signalled by its brief *intitulatio*, simply naming the pope as Clement VII, and by the address 'Dilecti filii'.[43] Though the addressee is omitted along with the greeting, it has long been supposed that Wolsey was the intended recipient.[44] First, the text occurs in a Cotton manuscript comprising a collection of letters and papers concerning Anglo-Papal relations in 1527. The text's date is omitted, but its references to the pope's captivity allude to the 'Sack of Rome' by imperial troops in May 1527, after which Clement VII and his cardinals remained captive in the Castel Sant'Angelo for months. Second, its addressee was apparently a legate whom the text appointed as papal vicar with unprecedented delegated authority during this crisis ('ut in inaudito casus eventu insolitam potestatem per delegacionem exerceas') and within the bounds of his legation ('infra terminos legationis tue'); in an English context Wolsey is the obvious candidate. But, several features of this text make its authenticity doubtful. It lacks the external appearance of a papal *breve*, being written not as a single-sheet parchment document sealed with the papal fisherman's ring but over six paper folios unsealed. It is probably not a copy of a *breve* either, even though its truncated address and dating clauses might suggest this, but appears more like a draft and a rather clumsy one at that. Passages of the text are crossed through, but this reads more like redrafting than correcting copyist's errors, notably on fol. 236r–v, where statements are deleted as redundant since they merely rephrase previous ones.[45] Its author was striving to imitate the curia's humanistic Latin and formulae but not always successfully, for example in the superfluous repetition of 'non obstantibus' at the end. Much more suspect than the text's style is its content, which purported to delegate power to concede all dispensations and other graces both within and beyond papal authority, even relaxing divine law, as if the pope could grant divine power outside his Petrine commission. This is all the more remarkable given that in 1527 Henry VIII began to seek

[42] K. A. Fink, 'Die ältesten Breven und Brevenregister', *Quellen und Forschungen aus italienischen Archiven und Bibliotheken*, 25 (1933–1934), 292–307; M. J. Haren, 'Papal secretariate and datary correspondence relating to Great Britain and Ireland in the fifteenth and early sixteenth centuries: Summary report of a survey in the Vatican Archives', *Analecta Hibernica*, 33 (1986), 1–14 (quotation on p. 3). I am indebted for advice here to Dr Patrick Zutshi and Professor Michael Haren, especially for the latter's detailed diplomatic and linguistic observations on this purported *breve*.
[43] Cf. G. Battelli, *Acta Pontificum*, fasc. III (Vatican City, 1965), nos. 28c and 28d.
[44] *Letters and Papers*, IV/2, no. 3401.2.
[45] Notably the passage '~~diuinas humanasve leges~~ remittendo, relaxando, limitando ~~aut moderando~~', though even here, as Prof. Haren has pointed out to me by email, the failure to omit 'remittendo, relaxando, limitando' upsets the syntax and sense.

a divorce from Catherine of Aragon on the basis that their marriage and the papal dispensation permitting it contradicted divine law.[46] Presumably this text seeking unlimited dispensing power was drafted at Wolsey's request, with the aim of gaining papal approval for it, or a redrafted version, at the curia, and the drafter's imagination overcame his judgement. Certainly it is incredible that Clement VII issued such a commission, and there is no evidence that Wolsey received one or acted as if he had.

Even if we take this as proof of his continuing dissatisfaction with his dispensing powers, the evidence for Wolsey's use of them is, in fact, extensive; and what I have traced is collected in Appendices 2–4. This evidence comprises some of Wolsey's original letters of dispensation,[47] and copies of many others, all but one found in English episcopal registers.[48] The letters, over ninety altogether, date from between 12 August 1521 and 7 September 1529, which indicates that Wolsey began exercising his faculties soon after receiving them in the bulls of April and June 1521 and continued to do so until at least a month before his fall from grace in October 1529, which effectively ended his legatine activity. This body of evidence also suggests that he issued on average about a dozen such letters a year, but in fact it only represents the tip of the iceberg. A list survives, edited in Appendix 2, which records 110 graces that he issued in one year alone, between 10 July 1525 and 4 July 1526. And letters have been traced for only seven of these 110 graces,[49] which implies that the total number of his letters of dispensation was well over ten times higher than the ninety or so known to survive, that is over one thousand letters. The actual total was probably even higher than this, since the list of 1525–1526 appears to record only graces for which Wolsey had received payment. It is certainly incomplete since it omits as many as seventeen graces from the same year known from extant letters.[50] Likewise, another list, edited in Appendix 3, records some 174 graces which Wolsey issued in the three years to 23 October 1529, but this includes only those for which he was still owed payment

[46]See n. 3. Prof. Haren characterizes this as a 'dispensatory blank cheque' representing 'wishful thinking on the part of Wolsey or those close to him'.

[47]I have traced five, calendared in Appendix 4. **7, 51, 63, 77, 90**.

[48]These comprise the remaining calendar-entries in Appendix 4 not noted in n. 47, including **37**, which occurs in a diocesan visitation book (identified *pace* Houlbrooke, 185) rather than a bishop's register. Doubtless similar material can be found in other English visitation and church court records, but the sheer volume of these records and their distribution across many repositories made it impractical to gather such material systematically for this edition. All episcopal registers for England covering the 1520s were, however, searched for Wolsey's letters of dispensation; (no such registers survive for Carlisle, Durham or the four Welsh dioceses).

[49]Appendix 2. **9, 14, 18, 20, 35, 61, 88**.

[50]Appendix 4. **30, 31, 35, 36, 41–43, 45–52**.

at his fall.[51] Speculative as it is to extrapolate the full extent of his dispensing activity from such incomplete evidence, this activity was evidently substantial.

Its scale far exceeded, for example, the papal penitentiary's dealings with English and Welsh petitioners. Under Pope Alexander VI (1492–1503) the office approved about sixty petitions a year from England and Wales, according to its registers, but this figure had declined to only four in 1525–1526,[52] the same year when Wolsey approved at least 110 graces. Of these four two came from petitioners who were apparently visiting the curia, but it is less clear why the other two supplicants did not turn to Wolsey instead.[53] In any case most petitioners in England and Wales clearly found it more convenient to approach him rather than a distant curial office for favours that he and the penitentiary were equally competent to grant. It is harder to gauge the effect of Wolsey's activity on papal chancery business, since the calendar of entries for Great Britain and Ireland in its registers has not yet been published for the 1520s. However, English bishops' registers provide some indication, since papal dispensations were often copied there. When such registers record papal graces that the chancery issued during Wolsey's dispensing activity, these are largely favours which Wolsey was not competent to grant. Most authorized unions of benefices,[54] which Leo X had empowered him to grant only to certain beneficiaries. Moreover, episcopal registers generally contain many more graces issued by Wolsey than the chancery in this period;[55] clearly,

[51] Only four of these 174 graces have been identified, and only tentatively, with extant letters: Appendix 3. **132, 144, 153, 166**. Some thirty-six other letters survive which Wolsey issued in the same period: Appendix 4. **55–64, 66–82, 84–90, 92, 93**.

[52] Rome, Penitenzieria Apostolica, Registra Matrimonialium et Diversorum, 74, fols 101r–v (Exeter dioc.), 224r–v (Bath and Wells dioc.), 244v (St David's dioc.), 246r–v (Bath and Wells dioc.). The register relates to the third year of Clement VII's pontificate; a second register should exist for this year, recording supplications for marital dispensations, but does not survive. Thus the number of supplications from England and Wales approved by the papal penitentiary was probably higher than four that year.

[53] The second and fourth petitions noted in n. 52 came from apostates who had doubtless fled their houses to the curia, since the penitentiary committed their absolution to bishops resident there. The first petition concerned a dispensation from *defectus natalium*, which Wolsey was competent to grant, but, as we will see, some suspected that his power to do so was restricted. The third regarded a runaway Benedictine who asked to be freed from the religious life and apostasy charges on the grounds that his profession was forced and under-age and thus invalid; it is unclear whether Wolsey made such grants under his faculty to absolve apostates.

[54] For example the three papal bulls for unions issued between 1522 and 1524 in *Reg. Veysey*, 1, fol. 26v; 2, fols 40v–41r, 49r–50r. Cf. *Reg. Blythe*, fols 11v–12r, 16v–17r, 114v: two bulls for unions and two others for plurality, where Wolsey's dispensing powers were similarly restricted; all four date from between 1522 and 1526.

[55] For example, *Reg. Blythe* contains twelve graces of Wolsey in contrast to the four contemporary bulls in n. 54.

where Wolsey might issue the same graces as the chancery, English suppliants preferred to seek them from him. And such registers depict more starkly the effect of Wolsey's dispensing activity on English business at the papal penitentiary, even compared with the office's own registers. In fact, penitentiary letters virtually disappear from English bishops' registers, having appeared there in considerable numbers before his activity. Wolsey's own register as archbishop of York records numerous penitentiary letters sought by petitioners in his diocese from 1513 onward, but they stop dead early in 1521 and only copies of his own graces appear there from 1522 to 1528. The same pattern occurs in other episcopal registers, where penitentiary letters generally only reappear after Wolsey's fall forced English petitioners to turn back to Rome for most graces.[56] Nonetheless, Wolsey's dispensing activity during the 1520s rivalled that of Rome in Henry VIII's realm, and even eclipsed it in the case of the papal penitentiary. And this situation arguably became even more acute after the 'Sack of Rome' in May 1527 effectively paralysed papal government for months, if not years, after; the penitentiary, in particular, does not appear to have resumed normal activity until the early 1530s.[57] Indeed, Appendix 4 indicates the extent of Wolsey's activity in the aftermath of the 'Sack'. Even if Wolsey never obtained the unlimited dispensing powers which he appears to have coveted in these circumstances (see Appendix 1b), in effect he had replaced the curia as the source of dispensations in the English realm by the late 1520s, when chancery graces also all but vanish from English episcopal registers.

This development is all the more remarkable in that his dispensing activity penetrated into all twenty one English and Welsh dioceses, despite the alleged clerical resistance to his legatine authority. At least one grace was obtained from him in each diocese, and many more in most dioceses.[58] Admittedly, the evidence is too patchy to give a complete picture, but the regional pattern that emerges is perhaps not altogether surprising. The larger dioceses understandably account for

[56] e.g. *Reg. Bothe ed.*, 93–94, 273–273: two penitentiary letters, one issued before Wolsey's activity, in March 1521, the other after, in 1533. *Reg. Veysey*, 2, fol. 12r–v, nevertheless records a penitentiary letter dated 7 August 1521 but it was probably requested before Wolsey's dispensing powers were generally known in England.

[57] See my 'Canterbury as the new Rome', 26–28.

[58] Entries in Appendices 2 and 4, but not Appendix 3, indicate the dioceses of his graces' beneficiaries, except for six entries in Appendix 2 which omit the beneficiaries' location. The entries for each diocese are indicated in the index, and the consolidated figures based on it are: Bangor (1); Bath and Wells (7); Canterbury (3); Carlisle (3); Chichester (1); Coventry and Lichfield (33); Durham (1); Ely (2); Exeter (9); Hereford (3); Lincoln (20); Llandaff (14); London (11); Norwich (11); Rochester (5); St Asaph (1); St David's (4); Salisbury (26); Winchester (12); Worcester (9); York (23). These figures count Wolsey's marriage dispensations twice where they concern partners from different dioceses, such as the five instances in Appendix 2.

more of Wolsey's known graces than the smaller, notably the extensive Coventry and Lichfield, Lincoln and York dioceses compared with the tiny Ely and Rochester dioceses. Certain dioceses may be well represented because of their ecclesiastical wealth. Salisbury and Winchester dioceses were noted not for their size but their rich benefices; many of Wolsey's numerous graces for beneficiaries in these dioceses were indeed dispensations for plurality.[59] The number of graces in bishops' registers also partly depends on varied diocesan registration practices. The York archiepiscopal chancery had a long tradition of enregistering many of the papal graces obtained by petitioners in its diocese.[60] The large number of Wolsey's graces in his York register probably owes more to this, and the diocese's size, than the fact that he was the diocesan; he only spent significant time in York diocese after his fall, when his dispensing activity effectively ceased. By contrast, contemporary registers for Canterbury and Chichester record no graces secured from any source by petitioners in these dioceses. The small number of Wolsey's graces for Canterbury diocese might also reflect the fact that its archbishop held his own dispensing faculties as *legatus natus*, but even the exercise of these went unrecorded in Archbishop Warham's register (1503–1532). Nevertheless, Wolsey's activity does not appear to have been limited by others with papal faculties elsewhere; other episcopal registers record graces issued by papal agents before and after Wolsey's dispensing activity but virtually none during it:[61] further proof of how he dominated English trade in dispensations in the 1520s.

It remains to be seen how Wolsey exercised his dispensing powers: what kinds of graces did he grant, and how far were these within the limits of his known powers? The question matters not least because historians disagree on how he used his legatine authority generally. Pollard spoke of the 'ruthless vigour with which he used his legatine powers',[62] but Kelly and Gwyn have instead portrayed Wolsey as careful not to overstep the bounds of his legatine authority. In order to test the validity of such interpretations in relation to Wolsey and

---

[59] e.g. Appendix 4. **2, 3, 7, 15, 18, 34, 51, 56, 58, 62, 65, 84, 86.**

[60] P. D. Clarke, 'Central authority and local powers: the apostolic penitentiary and the English Church in the fifteenth century', *Historical Research*, 84 (2011), 416–442, at p. 419.

[61] e.g. *Reg. Fisher*, fol. 160r–v (cameral collector, 9 March 1530); *Reg. Veysey, 2*, fol. 9r–v (nuncio, 25 May 1521); *Reg. Nykke, 4*, fols 117r–v, 120v–121v (both of cameral collector, 27 November 1529 and 6 July 1530).

[62] Pollard, *Wolsey*, 215. Cf. Kelly, 'Canterbury jurisdiction', 201: 'The cardinal may have felt hamstrung by the undoubted limitations to his faculties – all the more so since he interpreted his powers conservatively and took no large moves without papal or episcopal acquiescence'; also Gwyn, *The King's Cardinal*, 338: 'It is important to grasp just how cautious and circumscribed was Wolsey's approach to the exercise of his legatine powers.'

dispensations, we need to compare his dispensing activity with his faculties. In practice he granted a wide range of graces, both to clerical and lay beneficiaries, even if we do not have evidence for his use of each of his faculties. One of his major categories of business was marriage, hardly surprising given that roughly half the supplications approved by the penitentiary concerned marriage by Leo X's pontificate (1513–1521).[63] Indeed about half of Wolsey's graces from 1525–1526 listed in Appendix 2, that is 53 out of 110, regard marriage. Only eight graces relating to marriage feature among his letters of dispensation in Appendix 4, but his graces for clergy are generally better represented in episcopal registers than those for laity. None of Wolsey's graces from 1526–1529 listed in Appendix 3 are said to concern marriage, but the nature of most of these graces was unspecified, and it recorded 31 graces (out of 174, i.e. over a sixth of this total) issued to pairs of men and women, which most likely regarded marriage.[64] Most of his matrimonial graces in Appendices 2 and 4 were dispensations for the third and fourth degrees of consanguinity and, less often, affinity in various permutations (including the third and fourth degrees combined); several others dispensed from *cognatio spiritualis*; and a few were licences for solemnization without banns.[65] Almost all had been requested before marriage; only two were retrospective, but the couples in question claimed that they had been unaware of the impediment concerned and hence the need for a dispensation prior to marrying.[66] All of these graces, even these two, broadly fell within the terms of Wolsey's bull of June 1521. But two other graces did not, for both dispensed from the second degree of affinity.[67] One of them is known as a letter, and its preamble describes Wolsey's faculty to issue marriage dispensations as granted by Leo X and confirmed by

[63] This is evident from the office's system of registration, which changed under Leo from one annual register to two, one of which was devoted exclusively to marriage.

[64] Appendix 3. **15, 16, 18, 20, 22–24, 34, 36, 37, 41, 46, 49, 63, 65, 66, 71, 84, 89, 90, 98, 100, 112, 114, 120, 147–150, 154, 157**.

[65] Fourth degree of consanguinity: Appendix 2. **6, 10–12, 17, 41, 43, 51, 53, 73, 74, 78, 81, 95, 99, 100, 108**. Third degree of consanguinity: Appendix 2. **52**; Appendix 4. **16, 92**. Third and fourth degrees of consanguinity: Appendix 2. **7, 33, 39, 76, 94, 106, 109**; Appendix 4. **81**. Fourth degree of affinity: Appendix 2. **34, 58, 70, 75, 79, 102, 107**. Third degree of affinity: Appendix 2. **63, 64**. Third and fourth degrees of affinity: Appendix 2. **3, 48, 77**; Appendix 4. **14**. Other, more complex permutations: Appendix 2. **13, 25**; Appendix 4. **8, 49**. *Cognatio spiritualis*: Appendix 2. **8, 45, 46, 50, 55, 80, 97, 101, 105** (unusually arising from confirmation); Appendix 4. **92**. Solemnization without banns: Appendix 2. **21, 44, 71**. The bull also authorized him to grant dispensations for public honesty, but none issued by Wolsey are known.

[66] Appendix 2. **3, 72**.

[67] Appendix 2. **47** (combined with the fourth degree); Appendix 4. **53** (combined with the third).

Clement VII, but even this does not mention the second degree and conforms to the terms of the bull.[68] Dispensations from the second degree were rare, and even the cardinal penitentiary often sought express papal approval for such grants since they apparently did not lie within his ordinary faculties.[69] Perhaps Wolsey had done likewise in these instances, but it is odd that his letter does not say so, as the penitentiary's letters normally do, especially given the disjunction between the faculty which it describes and its grant exceeding that.

Another major part of Wolsey's dispensing activity regarded *defectus aetatis*, which displays similar anomalies. Thirty-three such graces are known.[70] Twenty-five of them concern under-age ordination in most cases specifically to the priesthood but in a few others also to deacon's or even all holy orders.[71] Of this twenty-five, seven allowed such ordination at 24, seventeen at 23 and one at 22, the lowest age at which clergy might be dispensed by Wolsey to enter the priesthood, according to the bull, but provided that they were religious, which in this instance the ordinand was not.[72] Some of these dispensations made further concessions in relation to ordination, including promotion to two orders on the same day, *extra tempora statuta a iure*, or by any Catholic bishop, all of which also lay within the bull's terms.[73] In addition, two of Wolsey's dispensations for under-age ordination along with his eight other graces concerning *defectus aetatis* permitted tenure of a benefice with cure of souls. Half of these allowed this at ages ranging from 19 to 24, all above the youngest age of 18 at which Wolsey might

---

[68]Appendix 4. **53**; cf. **8**, **14**, **16**, **49**. The latter letters in describing this faculty also distinguished that Wolsey might dispense marriages retrospectively whether couples had prior knowledge of the impediment or not; this distinction is not made explicit in the bull, but implied.

[69]*Supplications from England and Wales*, ed. Clarke and Zutshi, I. xxviii.

[70]Appendix 2. **1**, **5**, **9** (= Appendix 4. **29**), **14** (= Appendix 4. **32**), **15**, **18** (= Appendix 4. **33**), **19**, **20**, **28**, **57**, **62**, **82**, **98**, **104**; Appendix 4. **12**, **21**, **25**, **27**, **30**, **31**, **35**, **42**, **47**, **61**, **64**, **66**, **68**, **71**, **72**, **75**, **82**, **88**, **89**.

[71]Deacon's and priest's orders: Appendix 4. **72**, **82**, **88** (understandably all three beneficiaries were subdeacons). All orders: Appendix 2. **104**.

[72]Priesthood at 24: Appendix 2. **19**, **20** (with benefice), **57**, **62**, **98**; Appendix 4. **71**. Priesthood at 23: Appendix 2. **1**, **9** (= Appendix 4. **29**), **14** (= Appendix 4. **32**), **15**, **18** (= Appendix 4. **33**), **28**, **82**, **104**; Appendix 4. **30**, **35** (with benefice at 20), **41**, **60**, **63**, **65**, **67**, **81**, **88**. Priesthood at 22: Appendix 4. **25**. He might dispense seculars to become priests only at 23.

[73]Two orders on the same day: Appendix 4. **42**, **66**, **68**. *Extra tempora statuta a iure*: Appendix 2. **62**; Appendix 4. **66**, **68**, **72**. Any bishop: Appendix 2. **82**; Appendix 4. **25**, **29** (= Appendix 2. **9**), **30**, **32** (= Appendix 2. **14**), **33** (= Appendix 2. **18**), **42**, **61**, **64**, **72**, **82**, **88**, **89**. In the case of the latter concession, about half of the beneficiaries are known to have taken advantage of it by receiving ordination outside of their home diocese (Appendix 4. **25**, **29**, **30**, **32**, **33**, **61**).

dispense for this according to the bull.[74] The other half, however, allowed such benefice-holding below this age-limit, at 17 and even 16.[75] An incomplete letter of Wolsey, which must have granted a similar grace and probably in late 1525 (Appendix 4. **31**), includes a preamble claiming that Wolsey held a faculty from Clement VII to dispense men from the age of fifteen to obtain an incompatible benefice. This would have justified Wolsey's graces for benefice-holding below the age-limit set by Leo X in 1521, and they date from mid February 1525 onwards (i.e. from Clement VII's pontificate), but none of them invoke this faculty. Hence, it cannot be verified on the available evidence, and, as we will later see, more than one English petitioner doubted by Clement VII's time whether Wolsey possessed all the dispensing powers he asserted.

He also interpreted his dispensing powers broadly and likewise claimed that Clement VII had extended them in another key area: pluralism and unions of benefices. The bull of April 1521 authorized him to grant graces in these matters as part of his dispensations from 'irregularity'; but in practice he does not appear to have done so. Nonetheless, the bull of June 1521 further permitted him to dispense graduates, noblemen, and his familiars in these matters. He certainly used this faculty extensively; forty of his dispensations for plurality are known, and eighteen for unions of benefices. It is less clear that he restricted these favours in accordance with the faculty's terms. Of the forty recipients of his dispensations for plurality, sixteen are known to have been graduates, but it is unclear whether any of the other twenty-four were his familiars or noblemen, though it seems doubtful that all of them were.[76] Admittedly, it has not proved possible to identify these recipients fully, particularly those listed in Appendix 3 because of the minimal information which this provides about them, but graduates listed in Appendices 2 and 4 are generally specified as such in the sources edited there, which implies that others not so specified were not graduates. Wolsey did at least limit himself to dispensing for a plurality of two incompatible benefices in all but

---

[74]Appendix 2. **20** (at 24); Appendix 4. **12** (at 19), **30** (at 24), **35** (at 20), **75** (at 23). Two of these also dispensed the benefice-holders for seven years from the obligation to seek ordination as priests, provided that they became subdeacons within two years; which the bull had also authorized (Appendix 4. **12**, **75**).

[75]Appendix 2. **5** (at 16); Appendix 4. **21** (at 17), **27** (at 16), **47** (at 16), **71** (at 17). Four of the ten dispensations for under-age benefice-holding also comprised licences for non-residence (Appendix 4. **21**, **47**, **71**, **75**), to which we will return later.

[76]Graduates: Appendix 2. **49**, **54**, **88** (= Appendix 4. **44**); Appendix 4. **4**, **7**, **10**, **11**, **15**, **39**, **45**, **48**, **51**, **55**, **60**, **65**, **83**. Others of uncertain 'status': Appendix 2. **2**, **4**, **83**, **83**, **96**; Appendix 3. **3**, **5**, **6**, **8**, **10**, **11**, **167**, **169**; Appendix 4. **2**, **3**, **6**, **17**, **18**, **57**, **59**, **67**, **76**, **77**, **86**, **87**. For 'trialty' discussed below: Appendix 2. **54**; Appendix 4. **83**.

two cases, which regarded three benefices, a 'trialty'; the bull of June 1521 actually permitted him to dispense for up to four. In the case of unions, eleven of the eighteen beneficiaries are known to have been graduates, and one of these was also a familiar of Wolsey's.[77] Their graduate status is again specified in most cases, doubtless because it mattered under the bull of June 1521. Those of uncertain status are mainly listed in Appendix 3, admittedly, but two of Wolsey's letters for unions implied that recipients of such graces were less restricted than the June bull stated in any case. The first letter was issued in April 1523 allegedly by virtue of a faculty granted by Leo X and confirmed by Adrian VI for uniting benefices, without specifying its restrictions. The second from November 1526 instead referred to a faculty of Clement VII to unite benefices for anyone in Wolsey's legation, even non-familiars provided that they were noblemen or graduates.[78] Certainly Wolsey had supplicated Clement in 1524 to extend his faculties for familiars to non-familiars; if Clement overcame the curia's reluctance to concede this, it seems on this evidence that Wolsey obtained nothing more than confirmation of Leo's original faculty in terms designed to make it sound wider than it really was. However, in practice Wolsey seems to have dispensed non-familiars not covered by the confirmed faculty. He also licensed non-residence in many of his dispensations for plurality, which Leo X's bulls did not explicitly authorize either.[79] Chancery bulls dispensing plurality routinely included a clause permitting non-residence, and Wolsey's dispensations may simply have followed this practice. But a few of them expressly omitted the clause, and Wolsey also issued some licences for non-residence separate from any dispensation.[80] Moreover, Wolsey permitted non-residence for the canonical reasons of university study or residence in another benefice held in plurality, in common with chancery bulls, but in a few cases he also allowed it for the worldly purpose of serving the King, Queen, or high nobility.[81] This seems contrary to canonical prohibitions against clerical involvement in

---

[77] Graduates: Appendix 2. **29, 56, 68, 86**(?); Appendix 3. **166** (? = Appendix 4. **83**), **170, 171**; Appendix 4. **13** (also Wolsey's familiar), **50, 56, 70**. Others of uncertain status: Appendix 2. **87, 90**; Appendix 3. **2, 4, 7, 9, 173**.

[78] Appendix 4. **13, 56**. Ironically both letters were addressed to graduates, one of them also Wolsey's familiar.

[79] Appendix 2. **83, 86, 96**; Appendix 4. **3, 6, 7, 10, 11, 15, 17, 18, 39, 44, 45, 48, 51, 55, 57, 59, 60, 67, 76, 77, 83, 86, 87**.

[80] *Absque clausa non residendi*: Appendix 2. **2, 4**. Separate licences: Appendix 2. **22, 27, 35** (= Appendix 4. **37**), **37, 84, 85, 103**; Appendix 4. **4, 43, 58** (for 2 benefices), **62** (with absolution for breaking oath of residence), **69**.

[81] Appendix 4. **37, 39, 45, 51**. Canonical reasons: Appendix 4. **3, 4, 6, 7, 15, 17, 18, 21, 44, 47, 48, 55, 57, 59, 60, 63, 71, 76, 83, 84, 86, 87**.

secular affairs, but bishops had long disregarded these in England by entering royal service, as Wolsey himself demonstrated.[82]

Wolsey also seems to have interpreted his powers creatively in granting other kinds of graces. For example, the bull of June 1521 allowed him to license ordination *extra tempora statuta a iure*, by any Catholic bishop or to two orders on one day within his dispensations for *defectus aetatis*, but he also issued such graces, often in combination with one another, separate from these dispensations.[83] Indeed, he rarely appears to have granted these graces in the context of such dispensations.[84] Ironically, he attached them to at least three dispensations for *defectus natalium*, which Leo's bulls did not specifically allow either.[85] Indeed a recipient of one such dispensation later petitioned the chancery, since 'some' doubted whether Wolsey's faculties might authorize the ordination of illegitimate men *extra tempora statuta a iure* (Appendix 4. **40**); the petitioner obtained papal confirmation by January 1525 that he might still enjoy the benefits of his dispensation despite these doubts. Even Wolsey's own letters do not suggest that Clement VII had extended his faculty for dispensing from *defectus natalium*. One of his dispensations for this from mid 1525 simply states that Clement VII had confirmed Leo X's faculty to dispense men of illegitimate birth to receive all holy orders and two incompatible benefices, which defined more precisely but did not significantly add to Leo's concession in his bull of April 1521.[86] Though Wolsey clearly pushed his faculties to the limits and beyond on occasion, his dispensations for *defectus natalium* are remarkably few, especially compared with those for *defectus aetatis*; (and both had been major categories of Anglo-Welsh business at the papal penitentiary).[87] Maybe English and Welsh clergy perceived Wolsey's faculties in this area as restricted in more ways than one.

The only other graces that he conceded in significant numbers were capacities, and even here he exceeded the terms of his faculties. The bull of June 1521 authorized Wolsey to dispense non-mendicant male religious to hold a secular benefice. But Wolsey issued at least

---

[82] See, for instance, M. Gibbs and J. Lang, *Bishops and Reform, 1215–1272, with Special Reference to the Lateran Council of 1215* (Oxford, 1934; repr. 1962), 164–167.

[83] *Extra tempora statuta a iure*: Appendix 2. **31, 32, 42, 60, 91**. With ordination by any bishop: Appendix 4. **24, 36, 54, 79**. With promotion to two orders on one day: Appendix 2. **26, 92, 93**. All three combined: Appendix 4. **38** (= Appendix 2. **61**), **46, 74, 80, 91**. Two orders on one day: Appendix 2. **30**.

[84] Appendix 4. **66, 68, 72**.

[85] Appendix 4. **40, 84, 90**.

[86] Appendix 4. **28**.

[87] Appendix 2. **24**; Appendix 4. **28, 40, 41, 84, 90**. Cf. *Supplications from England and Wales*, ed. Clarke and Zutshi, I. xlii–xlv.

five such dispensations to mendicants out of twenty-one which he is known to have granted.[88] The only other religious who apparently obtained more of these from Wolsey were regular canons. No doubt, the long-standing involvement of both the friars and regular canons in lay pastoral care made them especially predisposed to entering the parochial ministry. Wolsey dispensed some of them to go even further, however, by being non-resident from their benefice, wearing their habit under secular priest's dress, or even both, which again Leo X's bulls had not explicitly authorized.[89] He doubtless interpreted his power to issue such graces widely since he saw it as part of his mandate to reform regular clergy. Indeed he granted at least three capacities, and a licence to transfer to another order, to religious from houses which he suppressed in the mid 1520s.[90] Whether reform motivated Wolsey's pursuit and exercise of dispensing powers more generally will be discussed later.

As for his other graces, these were few and miscellaneous. Most were only loosely related to his faculties granted by Leo X, if at all. They included licences for religious bodies to collect alms and sell indulgences,[91] which might be associated with his faculties to license preaching and grant indulgences. Wolsey also dispensed from *defectus corporis* at least once (Appendix 4. **78**), which the April bull's faculty to dispense from all 'irregularities' might have covered. He used his faculty to license consumption of forbidden foods during fasting periods but in a way that the June bull did not intend, not for specific individuals but everyone resident in his legation.[92] Wolsey, moreover, licensed at least one priest to celebrate mass twice on Sundays (Appendix 2. **40**), which none of his known faculties authorized. Nevertheless, evidence has not been traced for Wolsey's use of several of his faculties, notably those to license personal confessors and portable altars, absolve apostates, and commute intentions in wills.

---

[88]Friars: Appendix 4. **52** (OCarm), **63** (OESA), **73** (OFM), **85** (OFM Observant), **93** (OFM). Regular canons: Appendix 2. **16** (OSA), **23** (OSA), **36**, **59** (OSA); Appendix 4. **1** (OSA), **19** (OSA), **20** (OSA), **26** (OPrem). Monks: Appendix 2. **69** (OSB), **110** (Cluniac); Appendix 3. **161** (OCist). Unspecified religious: Appendix 3. **12**, **28**, **30**, **31**, **32**.

[89]Habit under priest's garb: Appendix 2. **16**, **36**; Appendix 4. **19**, **20**, **52**. He also granted this favour outside of capacities: Appendix 4. **22** (OSB), **26** (OPrem). Non-residence: Appendix 4. **19**, **20**, **26**, **52**, **63**.

[90]Appendix 4. **19**, **20**, **22**, **23** (transfer). The June bull indeed authorized him to license transfers.

[91]Appendix 2. **65**, **66**; Appendix 3. **60** (cf. *ibid.* **163**).

[92]Appendix 4. **5**. The faculty described in this letter indeed specifies 'certain persons' as the intended recipients; the papal penitentiary normally granted such licences to individuals: *Supplications from England and Wales*, ed. Clarke and Zutshi, I. xxxvi. The June bull also authorized Wolsey to permit meat-eating in such licences only on medical advice, a qualification this letter ignores.

But it does not mean that Wolsey never employed such faculties. More likely it reflects the nature of the evidence. The tenor of most of Wolsey's graces recorded in Appendix 3 is unspecified, while episcopal registers, the main source for Appendix 4, traditionally recorded only certain kinds of papal graces, principally marriage dispensations and dispensations regarding ordination or benefices.[93] The recipients of these graces doubtless had them copied into episcopal registers, in the case of married couples to prevent local church courts dissolving their unions because of the impediments requiring dispensation, and in the case of clergy to secure ordination and admission to benefices from local bishops. These beneficiaries probably had to pay for such copies, particularly because they were often made by notaries in Salisbury and other dioceses in order to guarantee their legal authenticity.[94] Doubtless to avoid such costs some clergy did not have dispensations from Wolsey copied but simply presented them on seeking ordination, hence these graces are only known from references to them in ordination lists.[95] This may be one reason why other graces of Wolsey's, notably many of those listed in Appendix 2, do not appear in bishops' registers. Another explanation is that Wolsey's graces do not seem to have required 'execution' by bishops. This was a procedure associated with letters of dispensation issued by the curia: these letters were issued in response to petitions, and petitioners receiving these had to present them to a commissary; the letters summarized their petition and required him to verify its claims; if he found these to be true, the letters authorized him to 'execute', or put into effect, the grace requested, but not otherwise.[96] The commissary, to whom the letters were addressed, was usually the petitioners' bishop or his vicar; hence such letters were often copied into bishops' registers, normally with the record of their execution, but no such record has been found alongside Wolsey's letters in episcopal registers. Not all papal graces required execution, admittedly, notably licences for personal confessors, but many of Wolsey's would have done if the curia had issued them. Nonetheless, his graces did not wholly escape official scrutiny. Some were shown at visitations, notably in 1537 when royal confirmation had to be sought for them lest they

[93]Clarke, 'Central authority and local powers'.

[94]Notarized copies: Appendix 4. **20, 24, 27, 30, 42, 43, 46, 57–60, 62, 64, 66, 69, 71, 73, 80, 82–6, 89, 92**. The notaries who signed these copies were: P. Wyverne (**83**); Gregory Stonyng (**59, 66, 71, 92**); Thomas Candell (all other copies above except **73**). Stonyng was a notary public by August 1517 and had studied civil law at Oxford (*BRUO, 1501–1540*, 543).

[95]Appendix 4. **25, 32, 33**. Likewise on admission to benefices: *ibid.* **50**.

[96]See Clarke, 'Central authority and local powers', esp. 430–431 regarding a case where the bishop refused to execute the grace since he found the petitioners' claims incorrect.

were deemed void as papal graces following the break with Rome.[97] One dispensation issued by Wolsey on 1 June 1527 was even subjected to judicial inquiry in the same month.[98] Richard Pescod exhibited it before Winchester Consistory Court to justify his retention of a fellowship at Winchester College and rectory at Shaw (Berks.) in plurality, but the judge objected to the dispensation's implication that his fellowship was a compatible benefice when, as Pescod confessed, it required continual residence, and thus ordered Pescod to explain why he should not incur the canonical penalty on this account. No final judgement on the dispensation's validity was recorded, but Pescod had clearly erred by failing to ask for the right sort of dispensation, that is one specifying his benefice as incompatible and including a non-residence clause as Wolsey had given to others.[99] Gwyn goes too far in attributing failure here to Wolsey's legatine administration rather than Pescod,[100] but if the former had required execution of its graces, doubtless such errors would have been more systematically detected.

Little is known about Wolsey's legatine administration, but the documents edited below refer to the personnel concerned with his dispensations. The first known scribe to engross Wolsey's letters of dispensation was 'R. Toneys' (or 'Toneys'); between May 1522 and June 1526 his signature appears under the plica of two original letters on the right and his name is recorded below nine others in bishops' registers. He also kept a register of Wolsey's graces; this does not seem to have survived, but the list of 1525–1526 in Appendix 2 refers to it and was doubtless based on it.[101] He was probably Robert Toneys, a Cambridge graduate in civil law who held canonries at Salisbury and Crediton while in Wolsey's service.[102] Two other names regularly appear at the foot of Wolsey's dispensations from November 1526 (by which time Toneys had apparently died). One was a William 'Claiburgh' (or 'Claiburn'), who signed under the plica on the right in letters down to December 1528 as Wolsey's 'datarius', a title borrowed from the papal curia, which originally designated

---

[97] Appendix 4. **7**, **51**, **62** and **76** were exhibited for this purpose, at least one of them to royal visitors (**62**); cf. my 'Canterbury as the new Rome', 40. Appendix 4. **37** was presented at an episcopal visitation.

[98] Appendix 4. **65**. Hampshire Record Office (Winchester), 21M65/C1/3 (Winchester Consistory Court, Office Act Book, 1526–1528, 1529), fols 63v, 68v, 69v, 73v.

[99] e.g. Appendix 4. **3**; etc. On similar failings by penitentiary petitioners, see Clarke, 'Central authority and local powers', 421–422, 430.

[100] Gwyn, *The King's Cardinal*, 285. See also Houlbroke, 185–186.

[101] Appendix 2. **110**: 'cuius nomen remanet in registro magistri Toneys'. For letters signed by him, see under 'Robert Toneys' in the index.

[102] *BRUC*, 591. Toneys was also Wolsey's registrar of the joint-prerogative court (Gwyn, *The King's Cardinal*, 279, 301).

the official who dated and sealed chancery documents.[103] His duties were doubtless similar and apparently included collecting taxes for Wolsey's graces.[104] He was doubtless William Claybrook or Clayburgh, another Cambridge graduate who was a doctor of canon and civil law by 1522–1523 and held various benefices from 1519, including the Worcester archdeaconry from 1531 until his death in 1534.[105] By May 1529, Edmund Bonner, DCL of Oxford, had replaced him as Wolsey's 'datarius', at least down to July and probably till the latter's fall in October; Bonner was also Wolsey's chaplain by 1529 till the cardinal's arrest in November 1530.[106] The other name that regularly appeared beside the datary's (and sometimes on its own) was John Hughes, who signed under the plica on the left in letters until mid 1529 as Wolsey's 'actuarius et registrarius'.[107] He succeeded Toneys not only as registrar of Wolsey's graces but probably also their scribe. Moreover, as his title 'actuarius' implies, Hughes kept accounts of taxes charged for Wolsey's dispensations, even before Toneys's death, as early as May 1525, and until Wolsey's fall.[108] After this event, his financial records as 'former receiver' (*receptor*) of income from Wolsey's 'faculties' served as the basis for the list edited in Appendix 3. He is presumably the John Hughes who was an Oxford graduate in both laws by 1514 and DCL by 1528.[109] Indeed all those involved in administering Wolsey's graces had relevant legal expertise, which is clearly why Wolsey engaged them. It also seems that they formed part of his household and travelled around with him, as Wolsey's graces are normally dated at his residence near Westminster but occasionally at others.[110]

The growing division of labour that this prosopography illustrates was doubtless necessitated by increasing demand for Wolsey's graces and the income which these generated. Some idea of the volume of business can be gained from the sources in Appendices 2 and 3, which were compiled primarily as financial records. The list in Appendix 2 recorded an income totalling £209 13s 4d from the 110 graces issued by Wolsey in the year following July 1525. Another account for a

---

[103] Only one original thus signed by him survives (Appendix 4. **77**), but his name is consistently recorded on the right below copies in bishops' registers (listed under 'William Claiburgh' in the index). He was also an official of Wolsey's legatine court of audience (Gwyn, *The King's Cardinal*, 282).

[104] Appendix 3. **161–64, 172–74**.

[105] Venn, i. 350; Appendix 3 styles him 'Doctor'.

[106] Appendix 4. 88, 89, 91; his name similarly appears on the right below these letters. *BRUO, 1501–1540*, 57–58.

[107] On three originals: Appendix 4. **63**, **77**, **90**. His name normally appears on the left below copies (listed under 'M. John Hughes' in the index).

[108] *Letters and Papers*, IV, no. 4592.

[109] *BRUO*, II. 925.

[110] Hampton Court: Appendix 4. **35–7**. The More: *ibid.* **93**.

longer, unspecified period circa 1525 refers to £334 received by John Hughes for Wolsey's dispensations.[111] By 23 October 1529 the arrears alone, recorded in Appendix 3, for Wolsey's graces granted in the previous three years amounted to £822 7s 5¼d. It is hardly surprising then that Clement VII complained of his curia's falling income from dispensations when resisting Wolsey's demands for greater faculties in 1525. It is, nevertheless, remarkable that Wolsey deprived it of business despite charging more for graces than its own offices. As I have noted elsewhere,[112] a comparison between the list of Wolsey's graces from 1525–1526 and a contemporary tax-list of the papal penitentiary shows that his fees were usually higher. Wolsey's charges for some graces may even have increased in the late 1520s; for example a licence for uniting benefices cost £4 in his list of 1525–1526, but between £5 and £15 in the list compiled in late 1529.[113] Despite such fees, English and Welsh petitioners still found it more convenient to approach Wolsey than the curia: its distance made the process of petitioning lengthier and arguably dearer given the hidden costs involved in engaging proctors and other intermediaries to relay requests to Rome.[114] The 'Sack' made the curia even less accessible in the late 1520s, leaving little choice but to petition Wolsey. However, whether his administration deliberately profiteered in raising its fees for some graces at this time is hard to judge.

This leaves the question of Wolsey's motives and intentions in seeking and using dispensing powers. One interpretation is that Wolsey exercised his legatine powers for the sake of 'self-aggrandizement'.[115] This is chiefly Pollard's view. It belongs to a 'Protestant' historiography which perceived the pre-Reformation church as corrupt; and, for Pollard, Wolsey epitomized this corruption. Revisionist scholarship has challenged this opinion of both the late medieval church and Wolsey as its nadir. Nevertheless, Wolsey always

---

[111] *Letters and Papers*, IV, no. 4592.

[112] 'Canterbury as the new Rome', 28–29.

[113] Appendix 2. **29**, **87**; Appendix 3. **2** (£5 5s 4d), **4** (£9), **7** (£8 10s), **9** (£13 6s 8d), **169** (£5), **170** (£15), **173** (£9). But comparison of fees in each list shows no similar inflation for capacities and dispensations for plurality: the former cost between £5 and £6 in Appendix 2, and between £3 15s 8d and £6 19s in Appendix 3; the latter, between £6 and £8 6s 8d in Appendix 2, and between £4 13s 4d and £6 15s 8d in Appendix 3 (though this might seem a price decrease, the average fee was around £6 in both lists). Fees for similar graces clearly varied even in the same list, and did so according to each grant's specific nature: dispensations for plurality cost more if they included a non-residence clause (Appendix 2. **49**(?), **83**, **88**) or concerned a 'trialty' (*ibid.* **54**; Appendix 3. **8**).

[114] P. D. Clarke, 'Petitioning the pope: English supplicants and Rome in the fifteenth century', in *The Fifteenth Century XI: Concerns and Preoccupations*, ed. L. Clark (Woodbridge, 2012), 41–60, esp. 48–49; 'Canterbury as the new Rome', 29–31.

[115] Houlbrooke, 10. See n. 28 on what follows.

yearned for greater legatine authority than the papacy was prepared to concede, and the alleged *breve* in Appendix 1 hints at the scope of his ambition; there is little doubt that he strove to rival other contemporary cardinals in this regard. But, it is unlikely that the aim of Wolsey's dispensing activity was to dominate the English Church; its bishops had few if any dispensing powers, so dispensations had to be sought outside their jurisdiction in any case. And if Wolsey exceeded his dispensing powers on occasion, this was most likely in reaction to popular demand, since Wolsey, like the curia, conceded graces largely in response to petitions. Indeed popular anticipation of his legatine powers and their benefits existed as early as 1516.[116] Wolsey possibly lobbied for faculties to meet this popular expectation. It cannot be denied that he profited financially from granting dispensations, charging even higher fees for them than Rome itself, but he was nowhere near as dependent on them for income as the curia was, and the fees were partly necessary to cover the administrative costs of issuing such graces.[117] And he had, of course, claimed that his aim in seeking legatine powers was not monetary gain but church reform. His reforming intent is best illustrated by his dispensations for religious (and his dealings with religious houses more generally).[118] In particular, he used such graces in conjunction with his suppression of houses, notably by issuing capacities to the last two priors of Poughley and a transfer to the last prior of Daventry in 1525, both of which priories Wolsey dissolved in order to convert their assets for the use of Cardinal College at Oxford. This redirection of ecclesiastical resources to a new religious purpose can be interpreted as reform. And his activity would set a precedent for the dissolution of all monasteries over ten years later. Not coincidentally, Thomas Cromwell who oversaw it was a former protégé of Wolsey, and his suppression of religious houses was also combined with the granting of capacities to their former brethren.[119] The latter were issued by the Faculty Office, which Henry VIII had established in 1534 to replace the curia as a source of graces within his

---

[116]John Dodington's letter of 28 June 1516 to Sir Robert Plumpton in *The Plumpton Letters and Papers*, ed. J. Kirby, Camden Society, 5th series, 8 (1996), no. 215: 'yt is sayd of certayne þat they comes a lyget [i.e. legate] from Rome to my lord Cartdenall' & shall bring to my lord Cardenall the paypis with <full> authryty & power of all maner of things <in> the reame of England'.

[117]*Letters and Papers*, IV, no. 4592, refers to John Hughes's payments to Robert Toneys, the scribe engrossing Wolsey's graces, out of the revenues these generated.

[118]Gwyn, *The King's Cardinal*, 316–337; Brown, 'Wolsey and the ecclesiastical order'. See Appendix 4. **19, 20,** and **22–3** on what follows.

[119]G. A. J. Hodgett, 'The unpensioned ex-religious in Tudor England', *Journal of Ecclesiastical History*, 13 (1962), 195–202; D. S. Chambers, *Faculty Office Registers, 1534–1549* (Oxford, 1966), xlii–lviii.

realm, and it was arguably here that Wolsey's dispensing activity led the way most of all for religious change.

First, Wolsey's legatine administration probably bequeathed the new office's name. The list of arrears compiled in late 1529 (Appendix 3) misleadingly referred to most of his graces as 'faculties' (properly speaking his powers to grant them rather than the graces themselves) and thus called their financial administration 'officium receptionis facultatum'. Wolsey's 'Faculty Office' effectively closed on his fall, and this list is part of a dossier of inventories recording his assets seized by the Crown. Doubtless, the list impressed on royal government how great the demand for and income from dispensations were, and influenced Henry VIII's decision to allow them to continue through a new 'Faculty Office' and to share in its revenue.[120] At least one former employee of Wolsey's 'Faculty Office', John Hughes, appears to have joined the new office, and his past experience potentially influenced it; (another, Edmund Bonner, also became a fellow traveller with the Henrician Reformation, rising to the episcopate by 1538). Above all, Wolsey's 'Faculty Office' had established a model for a local, national source of dispensations, preparing the way for a remarkable continuity within a reformed church and a radical change, as contact with Rome as a 'well of grace' became redundant.

A Note on Editorial Method

Appendices 1a, 1b, 2, and 3 comprise documents printed in full, while further documents are calendared in Appendix 4. The transcription of the (Latin) texts printed in full preserves the spelling and capitalization of the manuscripts, while the punctuation is editorial. Line breaks in these texts are indicated thus /, except in Appendix 1a as this contains a copy of an original text, while the texts in Appendices 1b, 2, and 3 are all original documents. Editorial comments (in italics) on these texts, foliation and words or letters supplied by the editor appear in square brackets; uncertain extensions of abbreviations in these texts appear in curved brackets, while [] refers to blank spaces where text has been left out and [. . .] where text has been lost. Words added on the writing line in these texts appear between these symbols \ /; words added in the margin appear between these \\ //. The numbering (in square brackets and bold) of the multiple entries in the texts in Appendices 2 and 3 is editorial. The calendared documents are also numbered (in square brackets and bold), and the English

---

[120] Chambers, *Faculty Office*, lxii; see *ibid.* xviii, xvii on what follows.

summary of these Latin texts seeks not only to convey their content but also to follow their formulaic wording as closely as possible. In these calendared documents Latin Christian names are given in their English equivalents, Latin forms of Welsh patronymics in their standard Welsh forms, and place names in their modern forms; surnames are given as they appear in the manuscripts, and any other original wording including place names appears in round brackets and italics. After the summary, the dating clause of the document is given with the date in the modern calendar form, followed by any annotations or endorsements to the document and its dimensions (if an original document, as opposed to a copy). Calendared documents end with their archival source (in italics) and, where applicable, folio numbers.

APPENDIX 1A:
ENREGISTERED COPY OF POPE LEO X'S
LETTER TO CARDINAL WOLSEY, 27 JUNE
1521 (ASV, REG. VAT. 1202, FOLS 109r–112v;
OLD FOLIATION: 110r–113v)

This letter is compared in the notes with Leo's letter to Wolsey of 1 April 1521 printed by Rymer in Foedera . . . , VI. 193–194 (XIII. 739–742), which it replicates in parts, especially before n. 40, and is here designated R.

Leo etc. [episcopus, servus servorum Dei], dilecto filio Thome tituli sancte Cecilie presbitero Cardinali in regno Anglie nostro et apostolice sedis legato salutem etc. [et apostolicam benedictionem]. Dudum postquam f̶e̶.̶ r̶e̶. circumspectionem tuam et dilectum filium nostrum Laurentium tituli sancte Anastasie tunc vero sancti Thome in Parione presbiterum cardinalem,[1] quem ad carissimum in Christo filium nostrum Henricum Anglie regem illustris[s]imum pro respublice [*recte* reipublice] Christiane arduis negociis nostrum et apostolice sedis legatum de fratrum nostrorum consilio per quasdam destinaveramus, in regno Anglie et aliis terris et locis eidem regi subiectis nostros et dicte sedis legatos de simili consilio per alias deputaveramus, necnon per reliquas circumspectioni vestre omnia et singula monasteria et loca virorum et mulierum ordinum quorumcunque in regno et locis predictis consistentia, exempta et non exempta, eorumque presidentes et alias personas tam in capite quam in membris, de spiritualibus et temporalibus quotiens opportunum foret, coniunctim per vos vel alios ydoneos quos ad id duceretis [*recte,* duxeritis] deputandos auctoritate nostra visitandi et reformandi, et de eorum vita inquirendi et castigandi et puniendi, et alia tunc expressa faciendi et exequendi concesseramus. Et cum ex certis aliis causis eundem Laurentium cardinalem et legatum ex regno et legatione predictis ad nos advocare intenderemus, per alias eidem circumspectioni tue omnes et singulas facultates in ipsis litteris expressas et concessas

---

[1]Lorenzo Campeggio was promoted by Pope Leo X as cardinal priest on 15 January and assigned the new title church of S. Tommaso in Parione on 24 January 1518, then translated to Sta Anastasia in 1519 after his return to the curia from England on 28 November (Eubel, *Hierarchia catholica*, III. 17).

motu proprio et ex certa scientia nostra[2] ac de apostolice potestatis plenitudine, intercessione etiam prefati Henrici regis, dederamus et concesseramus,[3] ac licentiam desuper in omnibus et per omnia elargiti fueramus[4] perinde ac si dicte littere et facultates a principio tibi soli directe et concesse fuissent, Tibique etiam seculares ecclesiasticas personas ac clerum regni et provinciarum huiusmodi cuiuscunque preeminentie existentes[5] [ad] honestiores vivendi mores in capite et in membris reformare [fol. 109v], et pro illorum reformatione huiusmodi facienda omnibus et singulis facultatibus predictis ut[i], et per penas et censuras per te vel alium seu alios super id a te deputandis [recte, deputandos] et alias contra eas et clerum ipsum procedere, corrigere, castigare et punire, et ad laudabiles mores reducere, et vices tuas, quotiens tibi videretur, committere et advocare posses, facultatem concesseramus,[6] Teque quoad premissa omnia de simili consilio nostrum et dicte sedis legatum de latere feceramus, constitueramus et deputaveramus,[7] ac legationem tuam huiusmodi per recessum dicti L. cardinalis a dicto regno non expirare sed ad annum a die recessus ipsius L. cardinalis computandum duntaxat quoad premissa durare decreveramus. Et deinde cum prefatus L. cardinalis ad nos rediisset et finis a die recessus sui ex regno huiusmodi instare nosceretur, Nos per reliquas motu,[8] scientia et potestatis plenitudine predictis, consideratione etiam prefati Henrici[9] regis, annum predictum, infra quem circumspectio tua[10] adhuc existebat, ac cum omnibus et singulis in eis contentis Clausulis singulas litteras predictas ad biennium a fine ipsius prioris anni computandum, quo durante eadem circumspectio tua omnibus et singulis facultatibus tibi per singulas litteras concessis huiusmodi[11] alias iuxta ipsarum continentiam et tenorem uti valeres, extenderamus et prorogaveramus,[12] Eidemque circumspectioni tue ut, etiam dicto prorogato biennio durante, quotiens in ecclesiis et regnis locis dicti regni in presentia ipsius regis et carissime in Christo filie nostre Catherine Anglie regine

[2]This standard formula 'de motu proprio et ex certa sciencia' implied that the pope had granted these faculties on his own initiative and incontestably.

[3]R: 'dedimus et concessimus'.

[4]R: 'fuimus'.

[5]R adds: ', vocatis tamen et in hoc Tibi assistentibus earum Ordinariis Episcopis et Praelatis, seu simul cum eisdem Ordinariis Episcopis et Praelatis,'.

[6]R: 'concessimus'.

[7]R: 'fecimus, constituimus et deputavimus'.

[8]R adds: 'proprio ac'.

[9]R lacks 'Henrici'.

[10]R adds 'tunc'.

[11]R lacks 'huiusmodi'.

[12]R: 'Extendimus et Prorogavimus'.

illustrissime[13] vel alterius eorum in pontificalibus missarum solemnia celebrares, omnibus et singulis utriusque sexus Christi fidelibus vere penitentibus et confessis [fol. 110r] seu confitendi propositum habentibus, et celebrationi alicuius missarum huiusmodi aut saltem benedictioni per te super populum inibi tunc interessentem largiende interessentibus, plenariam omnium peccatorum suorum remissionem concedendi[14] plenam et liberam facultatem etiam concesseramus.[15] Cum finis biennii prorogati huiusmodi instare etiam nosceretur, nos per alias[16] ex certis aliis causis animum nostrum moventibus, Motu sua et[17] potestate similibus, consideratione etiam prefati regis, biennium predictum[18] ac cum omnibus et singulis in eis contentis clausis singulas litteras predictas ad aliud biennium a fine ipsius prioris biennii computandum, quo durante eadem circumspectio tua omnibus et singulis facultatibus et plenaria remissione omnium peccatorum per prioris et posterioris litteras huiusmodi concessis predictis alias iuxta ipsarum priorum litterarum[19] continentiam et tenorem uti libere et licite valeres, auctoritate apostolica prefata nuper[20] extendimus et prorogavimus,[21] et nonnullas facultates, quibus erga familiares tuos et alios quoscunque infra limites tue legationis existentes uti posses, per reliquas nostras litteras tibi concessimus,[22] prout in singulis litteris predictis plenius continetur. Ut igitur ea que circumspectioni tue committenda duxerimus ardua negocia debite exequaris et ea plenarium consequantur effectum, motu et scientia ac potestatis plenitudine similibus, necnon consideratione prefati regis nobis super hoc humiliter supplicantis, ultimum prorogamus biennium huiusmodi ac cum omnibus et singulis facultatibus et clausis in eis contentis singulas litteras predictas ad quinquennium a fine ultimi prorogati biennii, et si illud nondum inceperit, computandum. Et deinde ad nostrum et sedis apostolice beneplacitum, quo toto legationis tue tempore durante, eadem circumspectio tua omnibus et singulis facultatibus ac etiam plenaria remissione omnium peccatorum per singulas priores et presentes litteras predictas tibi concessas et concedendas huiusmodi et alias iuxta ipsarum priorum litterarum continentiam et tenorem uti libere et licite valeas, auctoritate

---

[13]R: 'Illustris [sic]'.
[14]R: 'relaxandi'.
[15]R: 'concessimus. Et successive'.
[16]R adds: 'nostras litteras'.
[17]R lacks 'sua et'.
[18]R adds: 'infra quod adhuc existis'.
[19]R adds: 'hujusmodi'.
[20]R lacks 'nuper' (added here in reference to R).
[21]R: 'prorogamus'.
[22]R lacks 'et nonnullas facultates . . . tibi concessimus'.

apostolica tenore presentium extendimus et [fol. 110v] prorogamus, Et facultates tibi concessas huiusmodi illarum tenores [*recte* tenore] ac si de verbo ad verbum presentibus insererentur pro expressis habentes ad infradicendas facultates, Et quibus omnibus eadem circumspectio tua uti libere possit, ampliamus~~mus~~.[23] Et insuper cupientes tuam per amplius honorari personam et quod tu erga familiares tuos continuos commensales necnon personas in locis tue legationis residentes dicta durante legatione[24] te possis reddere gratiosiorum,[25] de qua in hii[s] et aliis specialem in domino fiduciam obtinemus,[26] quotcumque milites auratos et comites palatinos ac accolitos[27] capellanos creandi, ac etiam quotcumque[28] in nostros et dicte[29] sedis notarios auctoritate apostolica prefata[30] recipiendi, et aliorum nostrorum et eiusdem[31] sedis notariorum et accolitorum capellanorum ac aule nostre Lateranensis comitum palatinorum numero et consortio respective[32] aggregandi, ita quod omnibus et singulis privilegiis, prerogativis, honoribus, exemptionibus, graciis, libertatibus, immunitatibus et indultis gaudeant et utantur, quibus alii nostri et dicte sedis accoliti capellani et notarii[33] et[34] aule nostre Lateranensis comites palatini, etiam cum potestate creandi tabelliones et legitimandi bastardos in forma, utuntur potiuntur et gaudent, ac uti potiri et gaudere poterunt quomodolibet in futurum, exhibendique et exhiberi faciendi eis insignia notariatus huiusmodi, recepto tamen prius[35] ab eis solito iuramento; Ac quascumque personas, sufficientes tamen et ydoneas, volentes ad doctoratus seu licentiature aut baccalariatus in utroque vel alicio iurium et ad magistratus tam in

---

[23]R lacks the preceding text from 'Ut igitur'; however, see n. 24.

[24]This passage 'Et insuper cupientes . . . legatione' in R reads: 'Nos, cupientes tuam honorare personam, utque Negotia per Nos Tibi commissa plenum consequantur effectum, et ut erga personas in locis tuae Legationis residentes et Familiares tuos continuos commensales ac alios quoscunque infra Limites tue Legationis, durante hujusmodi Legatione,'. The phrase here 'utque . . . effectum' is echoed above in 'Ut igitur . . . effectum'.

[25]R adds: 'eidem Circumspectioni tue'.

[26]R adds: 'Officium Tabellionatus quibuscunque Personis ydoneis, recepto ab eis Juramento in forma solita, concedendi, illosque Tabelliones Creandi alias juxta formam in Quinterno Cancellariae Apostolicae descriptam'.

[27]This passage 'quotcumque . . . accolitos' in R reads: 'ac Milites Auratos Quinquaginta, et totidem Comites Palatinos, ac totidem Accolitos'.

[28]Instead of 'ac etiam quotcumque' R has: 'necnon quadraginta'.

[29]R: 'Apostolicae'.

[30]R lacks 'prefata'.

[31]R: 'dictae'.

[32]R adds 'favorabiliter'.

[33]This inverts the phrase in R: 'Notarii et Accoliti Capellani'.

[34]R: 'ac'.

[35]R: 'prius tamen'.

Theologia quam in artibus et medicina vel alios gradus promoveri, previo examine rigoroso et diligenti ac servatis constitutionibus Viennensis concilii[36] et aliis solemnitatibus in talibus adhiberi solitis, promovendi[37] seu promoveri faciendi, Eisque gradus huiusmodi et insignia solita et debita conferendi et exhibendi seu exhiberi et conferri faciendi, Quodque si[c] tunc promoti omnibus et singulis priuilegiis, libertatibus,[38] exemptionibus et indultis aliis ad huiusmodi gradus in universitatibus studiorum generalium promotis concessis et concedendis imposterum, etiam quoad [fol. 111r] assecutionem beneficiorum, prerogativas[39] ac si in studio generali ac alias iuxta constitutiones apostolicas promoti fuissent et requisita adimplevissent, uti potiri et gaudere libere et licite possint et debeant indulgendi; necnon cum[40] familiaribus tuis, tuis expensis viventibus, et aliis, nobilibus et graduatis, tria cum aliqua vero ut duo quecumque et si cum familiaribus tuis et nobilibus et graduatis ad tria dispensatum fuit quodcumque quartum curata seu alias invicem incompatibilia beneficia ecclesiastica, et si dignitates, personatus, administrationes vel officia in cathedralibus etiam metropolitanis vel collegiatis, et dignitates ipsi in cathedralibus et metropolitanis post pontificales maiores aut in collegiatis ecclesiis huiusmodi principales, seu duo ex eis pro qualibet persona parrochialis ecclesie vel earum perpetue vicarie fuerint, et ad dignitates, personatus, administrationes vel officia huiusmodi consueverunt qui [*recte* que consueverunt] per electionem assumi eisque cura immineat animarum; Necnon cum etatis in xviii. anno defectum patientibus et religiosis ordinum quorumcumque, non tamen mendicantium, quibuscumque, ut quodcumque beneficium ecclesiasticum curatum per clericos seculares teneri solitum, etiam si parrochialis ecclesia vel eius perpetua vicaria fuit, si eis alias canonice conferantur aut ipsi eligantur, presententur vel alias assumantur ad illa et instituantur in eis, recipere et insimul quoad vixerint retinere illaque simul vel successive simpliciter vel ex causa permutationis, quotiens eis placuit, dimittere et loco dimissi vel dimissorum aliud vel alia simile vel dissimile aut similia vel dissimilia beneficium seu beneficia ecclesiasticum vel ecclesiastica, quoad familiares et alios nobiles et graduatos tria et quoad alios duo incompatibilia, quo vero ad illos cum quibus ad tria dispensatum fuit quattuor, Et

---

[36]Constitutions of the Council of Vienne (1311–1312) appear in the canonical collection *Clementinae*, printed in *Corpus iuris canonici*, ed. E. Friedberg (Leipzig, 1879), II. 1128–1200.
[37]R: 'promovere'.
[38]R adds 'Immunitatibus,'.
[39]R: 'Praerogativis'.
[40]From here down to 'elargiendi ac indulgendi' on fol. 112r the text diverges totally from R, which continues: '(cum) quibusvis Personis super quibusvis Natalium Defectibus et Irregularitatibus . . . dicere et recitare valeant, Concedendi'.

quoad episcopatum defectum etatis in dicto xviii° anno, necnon
religiosos unum curatum seculare simililes [*recte* similes] recipere et,
dummodo inter illa omnia plura quam quattuor incompatibilia et
inter illas plures quam due parrochiales ecclesie vel earum perpetue
vicarie non existant, insimul quoad vixerint, ut prefertur, retinere,
necnon cum quibusvis personis secularibus et religiosis ad sacros
ordines promoveri volentibus secularibus, videlicet in xvii° \\ad
subdiaconatus, et in xviii° ad diaconatus, et in xxiii° ad presbiteratus ~~ordines et extra tempora a iure statuta aliquibus tribus diebus
dominicis vel festivis~~, religiosis vero cuiuscunque etiam mendicantium
ordinis ad subdiaconatus in xvi°, et ad diaconatus in xvii°//,[41]
et in xxii° suarum etatum annis ad presbiteratus ordines, etiam
extra tempora a iure statuta, aliquibus tribus diebus dominicis et
festivis, et duo ex ordinibus per dictos unica die, et a quocumque
maluerint catholico antistite graciam et communionem dicte sedis
habente alias tamen rite promoveri libere et licite possint; Et quod
obtinentes beneficia ecclesiastica curata seu alias sacros ordines
requirentia, Quod ratione beneficiorum predictorum, et si ex
statuto vel consuetudine aut fundatione seu de iure, sacros et
presbiteratus ordines huiusmodi requirant, usque ad septennium a
fine anni a iure prefixi computandum, dummodo infra primum
biennium dicti septenii subdiaconi fiant, ad alios sacros [fol. 111v]
etiam presbiteratus ordines se promoveri facere non teneantur,
nec ad id a quoquam quauis auctoritate inviti valeant coarctari,
dispensandi, Et taliter dispensatus [*recte?* dispensatis] septennium
huiusmodi et iteratis viebus(?) [*recte?* diebus] prorogandi; et cum
quibusvis personis tertio seu tertio et quarto mixtim consanguinitatis
et affinitatis gradibus invicem coniunctis seu se attinentibus aut
cognatione spirituali, dummodo non inter lerantem(?) et leratum(?),[42]
coniunctis et quocumque impedimento publice honestatis iusticie
impeditis, ut inuicem matrimonialiter copulari et in contractis
per eos etiam scienter matrimoniis remanere possint, prolem
exinde susceptam et suscipendam legitimam decernendo, ac eos ab
huiusmodi excessu absoluendo; necnon etiam quoscumque religiosos
ordinum quorumcunque, etiam mendicantium, qui ob sue habitus
non dilationem aut alias reatum apostasie incurrissent, ab illa
ac etiam excommunicationis alii[s]que sententiis, censuris et penis
ecclesiasticis, quas propterea iuxta instituta sacrorum canonum et

---

[41]Marginal addition and deletion signed 'Hip.'; this corrector's full name appears at the
end of the document.

[42]This presumably refers to the levirate, marriage to a dead brother's wife, which the
Old Testament prohibited (Leviticus 18:16 and 20:21), except where the brother had died
childless (Deuteronomy 20:5).

suorum ordinum regulas incurrissent, absolventes; Et cum hiis qui
ad laxiorem ordinem de facto translati fuerint ut ibi remanere
possint, et si de mendicantium ordinibus ad non mendicantium
ordines transiverint; Et super quacumque irregularitate per eos
contracta ac etiam ad [s]acros ordines, etiam in altaris ministerio,
dispensandi omnemque inhabilitatis et infamie maculam sive notam
inde contractam penitus abolendi; Et quorumcumque familiarum
tuorum ecclesias parrochiales aut alia beneficia aliis parrochialibus
ecclesiis et beneficiis per eos obtenta invicem seu una altera, ita
quod ipsi dictorum beneficiorum possessiones continuare seu illa
se de novo apprehendere et retinere ac in suos usus et utilitatem
convertere pos[s]int, diocesanorum locorum vel quorumvis aliorum
licencia super hoc minime requisita, ad vitam eorundem beneficiarum
huiusmodi obtinentium aut aliud tempus de quo tibi videbitur,
constitutionibus nostris de unionibus committendis ad plures et
exprimendis fructibus etiam beneficii cui aliud unire pelitittur [*recte*,
petitur] derogando, uniendi, annectendi et incorporandi; Necnon
tempus existentibus ultimarum voluntatum ad illas exequendum
prefixum semel vel pluries prorogandi easque in alios pios usus
convertendi et commutandi; ac quibusvis secularibus et ecclesiasticis,
ut confessorem ydoneum secularem vel cuiusuis ordinis regularem
in eorum possint eligere confessorem, qui eorum confessionibus
diligenter auditis eos in omnibus preterquam dicte sedi reservatis
casibus absoluere et semel in vita et in mortis articulo plenariam
indulgentiam elargiri, Necnon vota quecumque per eos emissa
ultramarin' liminum beatorum apostolorum Petri et Pauli ac sancti
Iacobi in Compostella, Necnon [*sic*] [fol. 112r] castitatis et religionis
votis dumtaxat exceptis, in alia pietatis opera com[m]utare Ac
iuramenta quecumque sine iuris alieni preiudicio relaxare possit;
ac nobilibus et presbiteris aut graduatis, ut liceat eis habere altare
portatile cum debitis reverencia et honore, super quo in locis
ad hoc congruentibus et honestis etiam non sacris etiam prefata
ordinaria auctoritate interdictis et sine iuris alieni preiudicio ac iure
parrochialis ecclesie et cuiuslibet alterius semper salvo, Et cum qualitas
negociorum id exigerit etiam antequam eviescat [*recte*, illucescat]
dies circa tamen diurnam lucem, per se ipsos qui presbiteri fuerint
aut proprium vel alium sacerdotem ydoneum in sua et familiarium
suorum domesticorum presentia missas et alia divina officia celebrare
et celebrari facere possint, dummodo causam non dederint interdicto
et id eis specialiter interdictum non fuerit, et alias iuxta formam
quinterni cancellarie apostolice; ac eis et quibuscumque aliis personis
ut, quadragesimalibus et aliis anni diebus et temporibus quibus
carnium, ovorum et lacticiniorum esus est prohibitus, ovis, butiro,
caseo et aliis lacticiniis totiens quotiens, carnibus vero de utriusque

medici consilio, absque conscientie scrupulo uti, vesci et frui; Necnon
matrimonium facie ecclesie, nullis bannis seu proclamationibus
precedentibus, etiam dictis quadragesimalibus et aliis a iure prohibitis
temporibus solemnizare possint; ac indulgencias X annorum et
totidem XL^{arum}, in quibusvis festivitatibus et diebus, quibuscumque
ecclesiasticis locis et personis perpetuo vel ad tempus prout tibi
videbitur concedendi et elargiendi ac indulgendi; Ac easdem personas
et familiares, quibus aliquas facultates predictarum concesseris,[43]
a quibusvis excommunicationis, suspensionis et interdicti aliisque
ecclesiasticis sententiis, censuris et penis a iure vel ab homine quavis
occasione vel causa latis, si quibus quomodolibet innodati fuerint,[44] ad
suarum graciarum et facultatum duntaxat consequendum effectum
absolvendi et absolutos fore decernendi;[45] Necnon quibuscumque
facul[ta]tibus legatis de latere a iure concessis et quibus te uti posse
alias forsan prohibuimus decetero in locis predicte tue legationis
libere, ac si illis utendi interdictum et prohibitum sibi [*recte*, tibi]
non fuisset, utendi plenam et liberam auctoritate apostolica tenore
presentium licentiam concedimus et facultatem;[46] Non obstantibus
defectibus et aliis premissis, Ac quibusvis cancellarie apostolice regulis,
necnon [fol. 112v] generalis Lateranensis[47] et Pictavensis conciliorum
et aliis apostolicis necnon bone memorie Ottonis et Ottoboni olim
in dicto regno Anglie dicte sedis legatorum[48] ac in provincialibus et
sinodalibus conciliis editis generalibus et specialibus constitutionibus
et ordinationibus, ac ecclesiarum in quibus incompatibilia et
alia beneficia huiusmodi forsan fuerint iuramento etc. roboratis
statutis et consuetudinibus, privilegiis quoque et indultis ac litteris
apostolicis eisdem ecclesiis locis ac Cisterciensi et Cluniacensi necnon
Premonstratensi et aliis ordinibus et eorum religiosis, monasteriis et
personis per quoscumque romanos pontifices predecessores nostros

---

[43]This passage 'Ac easdem . . . concesseris,' in R reads: 'Ac omnes et singulos, quibus
Gratias et Indulta hujusmodi, juxta Facultatem, quam ipsi in Litteris per Te expediendis
inseri facere non teneantur, tibi concessam, concesseris seu erga quos hujusmodi Facultatibus
uteris,'. The text then follows R, except where indicated below.

[44]R: 'erunt'.

[45]This passage 'ad suarum . . . decernendi;' in R reads: 'etiamsi forsan ultra Annum
insorduerunt aut pro Re Judicata Excommunicati fuerunt, ad effectum Gratiarum per
eandem Circumspectionem tuam concedendarum dumtaxat, Absolvendi et absolutos fore
Nunciandi,'.

[46]R lacks this passage 'Necnon quibuscumque . . . et facultatem'; the nearest equivalent
in R, after (not before as here) the *non obstante* clause, reads: 'Auctoritate Apostolica Tenore
Praesentium Facultatem Concedimus, Tibique pariter Indulgemus.'

[47]The four Lateran councils: I (1123); II (1139); III (1179); IV (1215).

[48]Cardinal Otto de Monteferrato, *Constitutiones* (1237): F. M. Powicke and C. R. Cheney,
Councils & Synods, with other documents relating to the English Church *2*: 1205–1313, 2
vols (Oxford, 1964), I. 245–259. Ottobuono Fieschi, *Constitutiones* (1268): *ibid.* II. 747–792.

ac nos et sedem eandem concessis, confirmatis et innovatis, quibus, et si ad illorum derogationem de illis eorumque totis tenoribus specialis [*recte?* specialibus] specifica, expressa et individua, et de verbo ad verbum non autem per clausas generales, Idem importantis inc(usa)tio(?) seu quauis alia expressio aut aliqua alia exquisita forma seruanda esset, illorum tenores presentibus pro sufficienter expressis habetis, illis alias in suo robore permansuris, hac vice duntaxat harum serie specialiter et expresse derogamus; Necnon omnibus illis que in singulis nostris litteris predictis volumus non obstare ceterisque contrariis quibuscumque, Proviso quod incompatibilia et alia beneficia huiusmodi debitis propterea non fraudentur obsequiis et animarum cura in eis quibus illa immineat nullatenus negligatur, sed illorum [*recte,* illarum] congrue supportentur onera consueta.[49] Dat' Rome etc. [sanctum Petrum] Anno etc. [incarnationis dominice] millesimo quingentesimo vigesimo primo, Quinto kal. Iulii, [pontificatus nostri] Anno Nono.

I. de Comutibus[50]
Collat' Hip. de Cesis.

[49] A far more elaborate *non obstante* clause than in R ('Praemissis ac quibusvis Constitutionibus . . . nequaquam obstantibus'). Before the dating clause (obviously different again in R), R adds the formula 'Nulli ergo omnino Hominum liceat hanc Paginam nostrae concessionis et Indulti infringere, etc.'
[50] Presumably the scribe who engrossed the original letter. The person named below was the *magister registri* who collated and corrected this copy of the letter (see n. 41).

APPENDIX 1B:
PURPORTED *BREVE* OF POPE CLEMENT VII TO CARDINAL WOLSEY, *c*.1527 (BL, COTTON MS VITELLIUS B.IX, FOLS 232r–237v; OLD FOLIATION: 218r–223v)

[*In an early 16th-c. humanist hand; centred heading:*] Clemens PP. vii / Dilecti fili &c. [salutem et apostolicam benedictionem]. Magnus ille / pietatis respectus, quem in christi-/anorum gregem cure sollicitudinique / nostre concreditum iam olim a / suscepto primum munere pastorali, / quo dei beneficio fungimur, in / terris animo impresum retinemus, / illas nobis cogitaciones etiam / in mediis malorum fluctibus, quibus / ingrato nimis et impio scelere / quorundam contumeliose iactati / ad miserum captivitatis scopulum / allidimur, et gravissimo naufragio [fol. 232v] laboramus, suggerere non desinit / et inculcare, ut congrue nihilominus / orbis tutele prospicere et precavere / itaque providere studeamus, ut / durissimi casus sevicia qui nos / patrem invasit a filiis quoad / fieri potest longissime arceatur, / nec sublato quotidianarum necessitatum / salubri remedio communem nobiscum / senciant captivitatem. Animadvertentes / itaque per captivitatis miseriam, / qua nunc turpissime detinemur, / nonmodo persone nostre copiam, [fol. 233r] quam omnibus eo loco expositam / esse convenit, quo veluti ad communem / parentem, tum liberrimus, tum tutissimus, / ultro citroque pateat accessus, coar-/tatam fore, Verum etiam propter deti-/nencium vim atque auctoritatem / animi indiciique nostri prout res / incidet prestandi et exequendi / libertatem non nihil impeditum / et diminutum iri, Ac volentes / proinde vices auctoritatemque / nostram aliis demandare, qui / ad sublevandas homini necessitates / cum omni nostre potestatis plenitudine [fol. 233v] presentes facili [*recte,* facile] tutoque adiri ac / libero aiiimi¹ [*recte,* animi] indicio in cohibendis, / refrenandis et relaxandis commisse / sibi auctoritatis habenis uti / possint et valeant, Te quem / pro tuis in sedem apostolicam / meritis unice² charum habemus / ac pro egregiis illis quibus prepolles / virtutibus longe dignissimum / iudicamus, qui partes nostras / tractes et vices absentis posses [*recte,* possis] / supplere, Ad exercendum, exequendum / et expediendum omnia ea et singula / que nos

---

¹The first minim is dotted but the second not.
²Corrected from 'unicum'.

de postestate vel ordinaria [fol. 234r] vel absoluta in remittendis, relax-/andis, limitandis aut derogandis / canonibus facere possemus, absque / aliqua restrictione, etiam si ad / divine legis relaxacionem, / limitacionem aut moderacionem / casus pertineat fueritque eiusmodi / in quo sedes apostolica non con-/sueverat dispensare; et necnon / gracias, privilegia, indulta et / indulgencias ex mero motu / vel ad postulacionem supplicantium / concedendum, concessa autem per / nos aut predecessores nostros declarandum, [fol. 234v] interpretandum et eadem ex viciis / surreptionis aut oblig obreptionis / aliisve causis que apparuerint cassandum, / irritandum et annullandum; Archiepiscopis, / episcopis et abbatibus per electionem, / postulacionem aut alias assumptis / sacras benedictionis manus imponendum, / ac illis ordinis et iurisdictionis sue / executionem conferendum; necnon de / Archiepiscopatibus, episcopatibus et / abbaciis ac aliis que consistorialia / dici solent providendum; Et generaliter / absque aliqua potestatis limitacione / omnia ea et singula faciendum, [fol. 235r] concedendum, indulgendum, committendum, / remittendum, relaxandum, astringendum, / firmandum, exequendum et mandandum, / quatenus nostra auctoritas a / domino deo nobis sine exceptione / commissa sese porrigat atque extendat, / ut in omnibus et per omnia nostre / vocis organum censearis, nec tanquam / alius a nobis aut delegatus sed / veluti nostro ore ac spiritu omnia / proferens ac faciens, citra omnem / iurisdictionis gradum et vllam ad / nos appellacionis interpositionem, [fol. 235v] quecunque homini [*recte*, hominis] necessitas efflagita-/verit, vicarium nostrum, ita tamen ut / per nominis huius appellacionem ex / legum interpretacione aut illius vocabuli / vi minus tibi commissum non intelligatur / quam quicquid nostre persone cohereat / auctoritatis, sed ut in inaudito casus / eventu insolitam potestatem per / delegacionem exerceas, et que a / nobis et pectoris nostri fonte per / te semper manare intelligatur, / facimus, constituimus et ordinamus, / omnem potestatis et ordinarie et [fol. 236r] extraordinarie plenitudinem conferentes, / ut illam vbique infra terminos / legationis tue libere exerceas et / exequaris. Et quicquid per circum-/spectio tua³ durante captivitate / nostra predicta per cognitionem / iudiciariam, solemnem, summariam / aut extraiudiciariam processus quoscunque / faciendo, decreta et sentencias ferendo, / pronunciando aut promulgando, easdemve / executioni mandando, dispensaciones / quascunque aut gracias \in premissis/⁴ concedendo / et faciendo,

---

³Erroneously corrected from 'circumspectionem tuam'.
⁴Added in another(?) hand above the line.

~~divinas humanasve / leges~~ remittendo, relaxando, limitando[5] [fol.
236v] ~~aut moderando~~, et generaliter in / aliquibus predictorum
potestatem / nostram vel ordinariam vel absolutam / exercendo, ut
prefertur, actum, / gestum, decretum dispensatum, / pronunciatum,
mandatum aut executum / fuerit, id omne et totum, quum primum
/ pristine libertati restituti fuerimus, / ratum, gratum et firmum
habentes, in / validissima et efficacissima forma / confirmabimus,
nec eorum aliqua / unquam infirmabimus aut infringemus, / aut
eorum alicui contraveniemus, / nec interim ante adeptam plenam [fol.
237r] et pristinam libertatem presentem / concessionem revocabimus,
declarantes / etiam et protestantes per presentes nostre / intencionis
esse, ut presens commissio / sive delegacio auctoritatis nostre /
tam diu suis viribus duret et / consistat, quam diu permanserit
captivitas / nostra et quoadusque fuerimus pristine / libertati restituti;
Non obstantibus / quibuscunque decretis, sentenciis, mandatis, /
rescriptis, litteris aut brevibus in contrarium [fol. 237v] deinceps
per nos tanquam irritatoriis, derogatoriis aut / revocatoriis presentis
concessionis nostre emittendis, / destinandis aut promulgandis, quibus
omnibus / expresse per presentes derogantes et illa omnia / pro nullis,
cassis, irritis et inanibus reputantes, / ac talia esse et haberi istisque
omnino anteriora / iudicari presentia, vero semper posteriora / et
post illa repetita, emissa et destinata / censeri, ac tanquam ultima
et posteriora / contrariis sic deinceps emittendis derogare / debere
pronunciamus, decernimus et / declaramus, et ceteris contrariis non
obstantibus / quibuscumque. Dat' &c.

---

[5] These three redundant verbs should have been crossed through with the surrounding
text.

APPENDIX 2:
LIST OF WOLSEY'S GRACES ISSUED BETWEEN 10 JULY 1525 AND 4 JULY 1526 (TNA, SP1/39, pp. 18–23)

p. 18]

[**1**] Licencia Richardi Waye Exoniensis diocesis diaconi ad recipiendum ordinem presbiteratus / in xxiii^{mo} anno. Dat' x^{mo} Iulii anno domini Millesimo ccccc xxv^{to} ___ xvi^s viii^d

[**2**] Pluralitas Thome Topclyff rectoris de Hogham[1] Lincolniensis diocesis absque clausula / non residendi.[2] Dat' xvi^{to} Iulii anno supradicto _____ vi^{li}

[**3**] Licencia Iohannis Phelipp et Matildis verch Water' Herefordensis diocesis ad remanendum / in matrimonio ignoranter contracto in tercio et iiii^{to} affinitatis. Dat' xv^{mo} / Iulii anno domini supradicto _____ xxiii^s iiii^d

[**4**] Pluralitas Nicholai Walweyn' rectoris de Craneh(a)m'[3] Londoniensis diocesis absque clausula / non residendi. Dat' xxviii^{mo} Iulii anno supradicto _____ vi^{li}

[**5**] Licencia Ed(ward)i Marshall' alias Burye Wigorniensis diocesis clerici ad obtinendum beneficium / in xvi^{to} sue etatis anno. Dat' ultimo Iulii anno supradicto _____ iii^{li}

[**6**] Licencia Thome Pratte et Margarete Presten' ad contrahendum in iiii^{to} / ~~affini~~ consanguinitatis. Dat' iiii^{to} Augusti anno supradicto _____ xxiii^s iiii^d

[**7**] Licencia Laurentii Hawth' et Christibelle Whalley Co<n>ventrensis et Lichfeldensis diocesis / ad contrahendum in iii^{to} et iiii^{to} consanguinitatis. Dat' xvi^{mo} Iulii anno supradicto _____ xxvi^s viii^d

[**8**] Licencia Iohannis Clifton' iunioris et Dienisie Polpera Exoniensis diocesis ad contrahendum / non obstante quod mater dicti Iohannis ipsam Dienisiam de sacro fonte levavit. Dat' / xvi^{mo} Iulii anno domini supradicto _____ xxvi^s vii^d

---

[1] Hougham (Lincs.).

[2] Doubtless the Thomas Topliff, Lincoln dioc., who obtained a papal dispensation in 7 Julius II (1509–1510) permitting his ordination despite a defect of his left eye; CPL, XIX, no. 2067 (rubricella of lost letter).

[3] Cranham (Essex).

[9] Licencia Walteri Will(el)mi' Landavensis diocesis ad recipiendum ordinem presbiteratus / in xxiii^{tio} anno. Dat' xiiii^{mo} Augusti anno supradicto[4] _____ xvi^s viii^d

[10] Licencia Iohannis Taleor[5] et Iohanne Fissh' Co[n]ventrensis et Lichfeldensis diocesis ad contrahendum / in iiii^{to} consanguinitatis. Dat' xxiii^{tio} Augusti anno supradicto __ xxvi^s iiii^d

[11] Licencia Ed(ward)i Blades et Catherine Alen' Eboracensis diocesis ad contrahendum in iiii^{to} / consanguinitatis. Dat' xxiii^{tio} Augusti anno supradicto _____ xxiii^s iiii^d

[12] Licencia Laurentii Abbot et Elene Petkill' Co[n]ventrensis et Lichfeldensis diocesis ad contrahendum / in iiii^{to} consanguinitatis. Dat' xxiii^{tio} Augusti anno supradicto ____ xxiii^s iiii^d

[13] Licencia Willelmi W̶i̶l̶l̶(̶e̶l̶)̶m̶i̶' Willan'[6] et Alicie Hoggerson' Eboracensis diocesis ad / contrahendum in iiii^{to} affinitatis ac iii^{tio} et iiii^{to} consanguinitatis. Dat' xxiii^{tio} Augusti anno predicto _____ xxx^s

[14] Licencia Willelmi Morgan' Landavensis diocesis diaconi ad recipiendum ordinem / presbiteratus in xxiii^{tio} anno. Dat' xiiii^{mo} Augusti anno supradicto[7] _____ xvi^s viii^d

[15] Licencia Iohannis Harrye alias ap Harrye Herefordensis diocesis diaconi ad recipiendum / ordinem presbiteratus in xxiii^{tio} anno.[8] Dat' xvi^{mo} Augusti anno supradicto _____ xvi^s viii^d

[16] Capacitas Ricardi Knevett canonici regularis de s [sic] Missenden'[9] Lincolniensis diocesis / cum clausa deferendi habitum sub chlamyde secularis presbiteri. Dat' xxvi^{to} Augusti anno predicto _____ vi^{li}

[17] Licencia Hugonis Lewys et Anne Gruffeth' Bangorensis diocesis ad contrahendum / in iiii^{to} consanguinitatis. Dat' xxiii^{tio} Augusti anno domini supradicto _____ xxiii^s iiii^d

[18] Licencia Iohannis ap Iohn' Landavensis diocesis diaconi ad recipiendum ordinem / presbiteratus in xxiii^{tio} anno. Dat' xxvi^{to} Augusti anno supradicto[10] _____ xvi^s viii^d

---

[4] = Appendix 4. **29**.

[5] Not the John Taylor, DCnL (of Oxford University), rector of Shottesbrook (Berks.) and of Bishop's Hatfield (Herts.) by 1504, and canon of Lichfield, commissioned as a papal judge delegate on 5 January 1512 and again on 30 April 1516: *CPL*, XVIII, no. 381; XIX, no. 856; XX, no. 745; (also *BRUO, 1501–1540*, 559–560).

[6] Probably not the William Williamson, BCnL (possibly of Cambridge University) and vicar of Cratfield (Suff.) by 1504, in *CPL*, XVIII, no. 305 (cf. *BRUC*, 641).

[7] = Appendix 4. **32**.

[8] Probably not the John Harrys, St David's dioc., who obtained a papal dispensation in 6 Julius II (1508–1509) to hold a plurality of incompatible benefices (*CPL*, XIX, no. 1819).

[9] Missenden Abbey (Bucks.), OSA.

[10] = Appendix 4. **33**.

[**19**] Licencia Ricardi Assby Wigorniensis diocesis diaconi ad recipiendum ordinem presbiteratus / in xxiiii^to anno. Dat' v^to Septembris anno supradicto _____ xiii^s iiii^d

[**20**] Licencia Thome Malett Bathonensis et Wellensis diocesis artium Baccalaurei ad / recipiendum ordinem presbiteratus et beneficium in xxiiii^to anno. Dat' ii^do Septembris anno predicto[11]

_____ xxx^s

p. 19]

[**21**] Licencia Iohannis Pety et Anne Turner Norwicensis diocesis ad solemnizandum matrimonium / absque bannis. Dat' vii^mo Septembris anno supradicto _____ xx^s

[**22**] Licencia Iohannis Kight' vicarii de Wenborough'[12] Sar' diocesis de non residendo / ex causa studii ad triennium. Dat' xvi^mo Maii anno predicto _____ xvi^s viii^d

[**23**] Capacitas Iohannis Killdermer canonici regularis de Ardebury[13] Co[n]ventrensis / et Lichfeldensis diocesis. Dat' xx^mo Iulii anno supradicto _____ v^li

[**24**] Licencia Iohannis ap Iohn' Menevensis diocesis[14] ad recipiendum omnes ordines non obstante / quod est de soluto genitus et soluta _____ xiii^s iiii^d

[**25**] Licencia Galfri(di) ap Iankyn' et Gwladesse verch Iankyn' Landavensis diocesis ad / contrahendum in iiii^to consanguinitatis et iii^tio et iiii^to affinitatis. Dat' penultimo Maii anno supradicto

_____ xxx^s

[**26**] Licencia Iohannis Sympson' Eboracensis diocesis accoliti ad recipiendum reliquos ordines / extra tempora [a iure statuta] et duos unico die.[15] Dat' xii^mo Iulii anno supradicto

_____ xvi^s viii^d

---

[11] = Appendix 4. **30**.

[12] Wanborough (Wilts.).

[13] Arbury Priory (Warwicks.), OSA.

[14] Perhaps the John ap [patronymic omitted], St David's dioc., who obtained a papal dispensation in 6 Julius II (1508–1509) to hold a plurality of incompatible benefices (*CPL*, XIX, no. 1820).

[15] Possibly the John Symson, cantarist at the altar of Holy Cross, St Anne, and St Anthony, York Minster, who obtained a papal dispensation on 18 April 1507 to hold three incompatible benefices; *CPL*, XVIII, no. 828.

[**27**] Licencia Iohannis Robynson' vicarii de Knavesburgh'[16] Eboracensis diocesis de non resi-/dendo ad triennium ex causa studii.[17] Dat' xx^{mo} Iulii anno supradicto _____ xvi^s viii^d

[**28**] Licencia Willelmi Hunte Landavensis diocesis diaconi ad recipiendum ordinem / presbiteratus in xxiii^{tio} anno. Dat' xxvii^{mo} Maii anno supradicto _____ xvi^s viii^d

[**29**] Unio ecclesie de Maekcresse[18] Landavensis diocesis valoris v marcharum facta / Thesaurarie Landavensis quamdiu Iohannes Ieuan Baccalaureus in decretis[19] / illam obtinuerit. Dat' xxvi^{to} Iunii anno supradicto
_____ iiii^{li}

p. 20]

[**30**] Licencia Ed(ward)i Waterton' Lincolniensis diocesis subdiaconi ad recipiendum ordines diaco-/natus et presbiteratus unico die a iure statuto. Dat' xvi^{to} Septembris 1525to _____ x^s

[**31**] Licencia Galfridi Lloyd Menevensis diocesis scholaris ad recipiendum omnes ordines / extra tempora a iure statuta. Dat' primo Octobris anno supradicto _____ xiii^s iii[. . .]^d

[**32**] Licencia Willelmi Whitebrooke Co[n]ventrensis et Lich-feldensis diocesis subdiaconi ad recipiendum / reliquos ordines extra tempora a iure statuta. Dat' xi^{mo} Octobris anno supradicto
_____ xiii^s [v?]i^d

[**33**] Licencia Roberti Stanley et Katherine Arden' Co[n]ventrensis et Lichfeldensis diocesis ad contra-/hendum in tertio et

---

[16]Knaresborough (W. Yorks.).

[17]Perhaps the John Robinson, BCnL, rector of Eastham (Worcs.), Hereford dioc., who had been granted a papal dispensation under Alexander VI (1492–1503) to hold an additional incompatible benefice, by virtue of which he obtained the vicarage of Overbury (Worcs.), Worcester dioc., and was granted a further papal dispensation on 19 November 1508 to hold a third incompatible benefice (*CPL*, XIX, no. 121). Possibly the same John Robynson, Durham dioc., who was fellow of Balliol College, Oxford, in 1497, and still in 1511; BA of Oxford University in 1497 and BCL by 1504; and ordained as priest on 25 March 1497 (*BRUO*, III. 1581).

[18]Marcross (Glamorg.).

[19]Doubtless the John ap Ieuan, BCnL, Llandaff dioc., perpetual vicar of St Mary's par. ch., Cardiff (*Cardmia*), Llandaff dioc., who obtained a papal dispensation on 10 December 1511 to receive an additional incompatible benefice and be absent from any of his benefices while resident in another or the Roman curia or studying at a university; *CPL*, XIX, no. 662. Perhaps the John ap Ieuan, Llandaff dioc., who obtained a papal dispensation in 5 Leo X (1517–1518) to hold a plurality of incompatible benefices, and received a papal commission in 8 Leo X (1520–1521) by virtue of an appeal to Rome; *CPL*, XX, nos 1139, 1424 (rubricelle of lost letters). A John Johnson was BCnL of Cambridge University by 1510–1511 and DCnL by 1513–1514 (Venn, II. 478). Not the John Jevan, St David's dioc., who was BCn & CL of Oxford University by 1476 and held a canonry of Abergwili (Carmarth.) from 1480 (*BRUO*, II. 1016).

iiii^{to} consanguinitatis. Dat' xi^{mo} Octobris anno supradicto
_____ xxvi^s viii^d

[**34**] Licencia Roberti Hobley et Margarete Ogle Eboracensis diocesis ad contrahendum / in iiii^{to} affinitatis. Dat' xi^{mo} Octobris anno supradicto _____ xxvi^s viii^d

[**35**] Licencia Iohannis Stavert vicarii de Langstoke²⁰ Wintoniensis diocesis de non / residendo ex causa studii. Dat' xv^{to} Octobris anno supradicto²¹ _____ xxvi^s viii^d

[**36**] Licencia Ricardi Carter canonici regularis de gestando habitum sub chlamyde / presbiteri secularis.²² Dat' xv^{to} Octobris anno supradicto _____ xxx^s

[**37**] Toleracio Thome Hay[ne]s vicarii de Layston'²³ Londoniensis diocesis de / absentando se ad triennium. Dat' xx^{mo} Octobris anno supradicto _____ xx[. . .]

[**38**] Commissio doctoris Snede²⁴ ad promovendum Ricardum Foxford²⁵ in doctorem / iuris canonici et civilis. Dat' ultimo Septembris anno supradicto _____ nihil

[**39**] Licencia Iacobi Thomson' Carleolensis diocesis et Alicie Weyrhorne Eboracensis diocesis / ad contrahendum in tertio et iiii^{to} consanguinitatis. Dat' xvi^{to} Octobris anno supradicto
_____ xxvi^s viii^d

[**40**] Licencia Thome Gilbert Assavensis diocesis ad celebrandum duas missas / singulis diebus dominicis ex causis con^t(?) in eadem. Dat' xxiiii^{to} Octobris anno supradicto _____ x^s

---

²⁰Longstock (Hants.).

²¹= Appendix 4. **37**.

²²Probably not the Richard Carter, BCnL, rector of Rodney Stoke (Somerset), Bath and Wells dioc., who obtained a papal dispensation on 3 June 1511 to hold an additional incompatible benefice; nor Richard Carter, Coventry and Lichfield dioc., who obtained a papal dispensation in 3 Leo X (1515–1516) to hold a plurality of incompatible benefices: *CPL*, XIX, no. 483; XX, no. 975 (rubricella of lost letter).

²³Layston (Herts.).

²⁴Doubtless Ralph Sneyd, son of William, of Bradwell Hall (Staffs.), who was BCL of Cambridge University by 1504–1505 and DCL by 1511–1512; Advocate of Doctors' Commons from 1 December 1514; rector of Tatenhill (Staffs.) in 1528; admitted as canon of Lichfield and prebendary of Bobenhull (Warwicks.) on 28 January 1529, till death; rector of Higham (Leics.), 1535–1553(?); and died before 8 October 1549 according to *Fasti*, but not before 1553 according to Venn (Venn, IV. 118; *Fasti*, X. 24).

²⁵Richard Foxford was admitted as BCL of Oxford University in 1514, incepted as DCL on 2 July 1526, and was DCn & CL by 1531; was collated as canon of St Paul's, London, on 23 December 1530 and admitted as rector of Harlington (Middlesex) on 5 January 1532, both till death; served as proctor in the Chancellor's Court, Oxford, in 1514 and was admitted to the College of Advocates, London, on 29 October 1526; was chancellor and vicar general of John Stokesley, bishop of London, in 1531; and was dead by August 1533 (*BRUO, 1501–1540*, 214).

[**41**] Licencia Iohannis Momford et Katherine Southurst Co[n]ventrensis et Lichfeldensis diocesis / ad contrahendum in iiii^{to} consanguinitatis. [Dat'] xxvi^{to} Octobris anno supradicto _____ xxiii^s ii(?)^d

[**42**] Licencia Willelmi Roper Eboracensis diocesis scholaris ad recipiendum omnes ordines / extra tempora a iure statuta. Dat' xxviii^o Octobris anno supradicto _____ xv[..]^s [..]i^d

[**43**] Licencia Willelmi Underhill et Agnetis Molls Co[n]ventrensis et Lichfeldensis diocesis ad / contrahendum in iiii^{to} consanguinitatis. Dat' ultimo Octobris anno supradicto _ xxiii^s iiii^d

[**44**] Licencia Thome Wescott et Alicie Colombe Exoniensis diocesis ad solennizandum [*sic*] / matrimonium absque bannis. Dat' secundo Novembris anno supradicto _____ xx^s

[**45**] Licencia Willelmi Lawrence et Edithe Baker Bathoniensis et Wellensis diocesis ad / contrahendum non obstante quod pater ipsius Willelmi ipsam Editham de sacro / fonte levavit. Dat' iiii^{to} Novembris anno domini supradicto _____ xxvi^s viii^d

[**46**] Licencia Ricardi Fowler'^{26} et Agnetis Amyse Co[n]ventrensis et Lichfeldensis diocesis ad contra-/hendum non obstante quod pater dicte Agnetis ipsum Ricardum in sacra confirmacione tenuit. Dat' iiii^{to} Novembris anno domini supradicto _____ xxiii^s [. . .]^d

[**47**] Licencia Thome Frenche et Agnetis Smyth' Bathoniensis et Wellensis diocesis ad / contrahendum in ii^{do} et iiii^{to} affinitatis. Dat' iiii^{to} Novembris anno supradicto _ x[xii]i(?)^s viii^d

[**48**] Licencia Iohannis Iayrver et Elizabeth Foxcrotte ad contrahendum in tertio / et iiii^{to} affinitatis Eboracensis diocesis. Dat' penultimo Augusti anno supradicto ___ [x]x[v]i(?)^s viii^d

[**49**] Pluralitas Thome Mede vicarii de Meyhymigot^{27} in Cornubia / Exoniensis diocesis magistri in artibus.^{28} Dat' xx^{mo} Augusti anno supradicto _____ vi^{li} xiii^s iiii^d

[**50**] Licencia Ricardi Aleynton' et Alicie Hawkyns de Evesham^{29} Wigorniensis diocesis / ad contrahendum non obstante quod dicta Alicia prolem ipsius Ricardi de sacro

---

^{26}Presumably not the Richard Fowler, Lincoln dioc., who obtained a papal dispensation in 1 Leo X (1513–1514) to hold a plurality of incompatible benefices; *CPL*, XX, no. 781 (rubricella of lost letter).

^{27}Menheniot (Cornw.).

^{28}Thomas Mede incepted as MA of Oxford University on 2 July 1509; was fellow from 1503 and rector from 1514 of Exeter College, Oxford, resigning both positions in 1518; was admitted as vicar of Menheniot (Cornw.), presented by Exeter College, on 3 November 1517 and rector of Dolton (Devon) on 19 October 1525, both till death; and was dead by February 1530 (*BRUO, 1501–1540*, 393). He doubtless obtained his second benefice (Dolton) by virtue of the dispensation above.

^{29}Evesham (Worcs.).

fonte / levavit. Dat' xii^{mo} Novembris anno supradicto

_____ v^{li}

[51] Licencia Edmundi Corwyn' et Iohanne Corwyn' alias Mosgrayff Eboracensis / et Carleolensis respective dioc' ad contrahendum in iiii^{to} consanguinitatis. Dat' ix^{o} Novembris anno supradicto

_____ xxiii^{s} iiii^{d}

[52] Licencia Roberti Monsy et Marione Brome Carleolensis diocesis ad contrahendum / in tertio consanguinitatis. Dat' ultimo Iulii anno supradicto _____ [. . .]^{li}

[53] Licencia Iohannis Norman' et Isabelle Hicke Landavensis diocesis ad contrahendum / in iiii^{to} consanguinitatis. Dat' xxii^{do} Novembris anno supradicto _____ xxiii^{s} iiii^{d}

p. 21]

[54] Trialitas Iohannis Stephyns rectoris de Drustenton'[30] Exoniensis diocesis / artium magistri.[31] Dat' xvi^{to} Novembris anno domini supradicto _____ viii^{li} vi^{s} viii^{d}

[55] Licencia Iohannis Gunner et Anne Kytmer' Wintoniensis diocesis ad contrahendum / non obstante quod pater dicte Anne ipsum Iohannem de sacro fonte levavit. Dat' / xvi^{to} Novembris anno domini supradicto _____ xxiii^{s} iiii^{d}

[56] Unio ecclesie de Folketon'[32] Eboracensis diocesis valoris .v. librarum ad ecclesiam / de Weme'[33] Co[n]ventrensis et Lichfeldensis diocesis quamdiu Iohannes Dakre baccalaureus in / decretis[34] et de nobili sanguine cretus illam obtinuerit. Dat' xx^{mo} Iulii

_____ [. . .]

[57] Licencia Ricardi Browne Exoniensis diocesis diaconi ad recipiendum ordinem presbiteratus / in xxiiii^{to} non completo sue etatis anno. Dat' x^{mo} Decembris anno supradicto

_____ [. . .]^{s} viii^{d}

---

[30] Drewsteignton (Devon).

[31] John Stevyns, Exeter dioc., incepted as MA of Oxford University on 9 February 1512, supplicating for BTh and DTh on 5 February 1532; was fellow of Oriel College, Oxford, 1509–1521; was ordained as priest on 12 April 1513; held various ecclesiastical benefices, including an Exeter canonry by 1531, and was still rector of Drewsteignton in 1535; and died on 21 March 1560 (*BRUO, 1501–1540*, 540).

[32] Folkton (E. Yorks.).

[33] Wem (Salop.).

[34] M. John Dacre, here designated BCnL, was probably a graduate of Oxford University; was still rector of both Folkton and Wem as well as master and rector of Greystoke College (Cumbd.) in 1535, the latter till death; was ordained as priest on 8 March 1533 and admitted as rector of Morpeth (Northd.) in 1532, till death; and was dead by May 1567 (*BRUO, 1501–1540*, 673). Probably the John Dacre, Carlisle dioc., who obtained a papal dispensation from defect of age in 8 Leo X (1520–1521), amplifying upon an earlier one, to hold a plurality of incompatible benefices; *CPL*, XX, no. 1528 (rubricella of lost letter).

[58] Licencia Galfridi Wallwyn' et Iosie Smyth' Co[n]ventrensis et Lichfeldensis diocesis ad / contrahendum in iiii^{to} affinitatis. Dat' viii° Octobris anno supradicto ____ xxiii^s iiii^d

[59] Capacitas Thome Augustine canonici regularis domus sive prioratus / de Maritona^{35} Wintoniensis diocesis ordini sancti Augustini. Dat' xiiii° Decembris anno supradicto ____ v^{li}

[60] Licencia Willelmi Lewys Wigorniensis diocesis accoliti ad recipiendum reliquos / ordines extra tempora [a iure statuta]. Dat' xviii° Decembris anno domini supradicto _____ xiii^s iiii^d

[61] Licencia Roberti Garett Lincolniensis diocesis accoliti ad recipiendum reliquos / ordines extra tempora [a iure statuta]. Dat' xviii(?)° Decembris anno domini supradicto^{36} ___ x^s [. . .]^d

[62] Licentia Thome Hunter Dunelmensis diocesis accoliti ad recipiendum reliquos / ordines in xxiiii^{to} non completo [sue etatis anno] etiam extra tempora [a iure statuta].^{37} Dat' xxii^{do} Decembris anno supradicto _____ [. . .]

[63] Licencia Willelmi Iohnson^{38} et Elizabeth' Willson' Co[n]ventrensis et Lichfeldensis diocesis ad / contrahendum in tertio affinitatis. Dat' xiiii^{to} Decembris anno supradicto __ [. . .]

[64] Licencia Iohannis Moryce^{39} et Elizabeth Powle Herefordensis diocesis ad / contrahendum in tertio affinitatis. Dat' xiiii^{mo} Decembris anno supradicto _____ [. . .]

[65] Licencia magistri fraternitatis sanctorum Christoferi et Georgii Eboracensis civitatis / ad colligendum eleemosynas pro uno anno cum Indulgencia centum dierum.^{40} Dat' / vicesimo secundo Decembris anno domini supradicto _____ [. . .]

---

^{35}Merton Priory (Surrey), OSA.

^{36}= Appendix 4. **38** (where this is dated 12 December 1525).

^{37}Not the Thomas Hunter, canon of Dunkeld, commissioned as papal judge delegate before February 1506; *CPL*, XVIII, nos 548, 885.

^{38}Probably not the William Johnson, Lincoln dioc., who obtained a dispensation in 5 Julius II (1507–1508) to hold a plurality of incompatible benefices; *CPL*, XIX, no. 1735 (rubricella of lost letter).

^{39}Probably not the John Morris, vicar of Castle Cary (Somerset) in 1516 (*CPL*, XX, no. 636).

^{40}The master and confraternity of SS. Christopher and George, York, obtained a papal grant on 1 October 1512 at the request of Christopher Bainbridge, Archbishop of York and cardinal priest of Santa Prassede, which amplified on previous papal grants to have a portable altar by licensing them to have masses celebrated at it before day-break and granted the confraternity's members who visited the chapels of SS. Christopher and George in York or three altars in churches outside York on the feasts and octaves of those saints, the BVM, Easter and Pentecost the same indulgence that they would have gained by visiting Rome (*CPL*, XIX, no. 714).

[**66**] Licencia magistri hospitalis sancti Anthonii Londoniensis[41] ad colligendum elee-/mosynas fidelium pro uno anno. Dat' xxiii[tio] Decembris anno supradicto _____ [. . .]

[**67**] Commissio magistrorum Bysse[42] et Borreman'[43] obtenta per par[r]ochianos / ecclesie de Trulle[44] Bathoniensis et Wellensis diocesis. Dat' ultimo Decembris anno supradicto __ [. . .]

[**68**] Unio ~~ecclesie~~ vicarie de Colmesolton[45] Wigorniensis diocesis valoris v marcharum / ad ecclesiam de Monkehelight'[46] Norwicensis diocesis quamdiu Thomas / Moscroffe doctor in medicinis illam obtinuerit.[47] Dat' v[to] Ianuarii anno supradicto _____ [. . .]

[**69**] Capacitas Roberti Abell' alias Mailand monachi monasterii de Colne[48] / Londoniensis diocesis ordinis sancti Benedicti.[49] Dat' iiii[to] Ianuarii anno supradicto _____ [. . .]

[41]John Chambre occurs as Master of St Anthony's Hospital, London, in 1521–1522, and Anthony Baker in 1541. The hospital was founded in 1254 by brothers of St Anthony of Vienne to care for twelve poor men and the sick; *VCH (London)*, 581–584.

[42]See also **88** below and Appendix 4. **44**.

[43]William Bowerman, clerk of Exeter dioc., was BCL of Oxford University by 1511; was ordained as priest on 20 December 1511; held numerous ecclesiastical benefices, including a Wells canonry by March 1523 and sub-deanery of Wells by March 1534, still in April 1554; was a notary public and appointed as registrar of Bath and Wells dioc. on 20 April 1515, still in January 1522; he also served as deputy of the vicar-general of Bath and Wells dioc. (along with Robert Bysse above) in April 1528, still in April 1529, and commissary of the same in December 1533; and was dead by February 1572 (*BRUO, 1501–1540*, 63–4; *Reg. Clerke ed.*, nos 2, 4, 46, 103, 139, 307, 334, 353, 389, 425, 470, 665). Probably the William Bowerman, Bath and Wells dioc., who secured a papal dispensation in 7 Julius II (1509–1510) to hold a plurality of incompatible benefices; *CPL*, XIX, no. 2239 (rubricella of lost letter).

[44]Trull (Somerset).

[45]Coln St Aldwyn (Gloucs.).

[46]Monks Eleigh (Suff.).

[47]Thomas Mosgroff, Coventry and Lichfield dioc., was fellow, 1511–1524, and sub-warden in 1521, still in 1524, of Merton College, Oxford; incepted as MA of Oxford University on 20 February 1514 and was admitted as DM on 23 March 1523 and BTh on 4 August 1524; was lecturer in astronomy at Merton College in February 1517 and Cardinal Wolsey reader in medicine at Corpus Christi College, Oxford, in 1523 and 1524, attending as physician on Edward Stafford, duke of Buckingham, in 1519; was admitted as rector of Monks Eleigh on 23 August 1524, vicar of Coln St Aldwyn on 12 July 1524, rector of Stisted (Essex) on 6 January 1526, and vicar of Braintree (Essex) on 19 January 1527, holding the latter three benefices till death; and was dead by September 1527 (*BRUO, 1501–1540*, 406–407). He perhaps obtained Stisted by virtue of this union.

[48]Earl's Colne Priory (Essex), OSB.

[49]Despite this grant Robert Abell was Prior of Earl's Colne from June 1526 till its dissolution in June 1536 (*Heads of Religious Houses*, III. 107).

[**70**] Licencia Iohannis Smyth[50] et Matildis Elys Eboracensis diocesis ad contrahendum / in iiii^{to} affinitatis. Dat' vi^{to} Ianuarii anno domini supradicto _____ xxiii^s iiii$^{[d]}$

[**71**] Licencia Hugonis Poole et Margarete Barseley Londoniensis diocesis / ad solemnizandum matrimonium absque bannis. Dat' ix^o Ianuarii anno supradicto _____ xx^s

[**72**] Licencia Iohannis Colyn' et Emme Sturgeon' Londoniensis diocesis ad remanendum / in matrimonio per eos ignoranter contracto postquam mater dicte Emme prefatum Iohannem / de sacro fonte levavit. Dat' xxii^{do} Ianuarii anno supradicto _____ xx^s

p. 22]

[**73**] Licentia Hugonis Halmarke et Iohanne Toste Co<n>ventrensis et Lichfeldensis diocesis ad [contrahendum] / in iiii^{to} consanguinitatis. Dat' xvi^o Ianuarii anno domini millesimo D. vicesimo [quinto(?) . . .]

[**74**] Licencia Christoferi Basset et Margarete [verch] Iohn' Richard Landavensis diocesis ad contrah[endum] / in iiii^{to} consanguinitatis. Dat' xvii^{mo} Ianuarii anno domini supradicto __ [. . .]

[**75**] Licencia Iohannis Willelmi et Marceline Lewys Landavensis diocesis ad contrahendum in̶ in quarto / affinitatis. Dat' xvii^{mo} Ianuarii anno suprascripto _____ xxiii^s iiii^d

[**76**] Licencia Thome Philipp Herberd et Elizabeth verch Roger Hergest Landavensis diocesis ad / contrahendum in tertio et iiii^{to} consanguinitatis. Dat' xvi^{mo} Ianuarii anno supradicto _____ xxvi^s viii^d

[**77**] Licencia Iohannis Dybyn' et Edithe Meter Sar' diocesis ad contrahendum in tertio et quarto / affinitatis. Dat' xviii^{vo} Ianuarii anno domini supradicto _____ xxvi^s viii^d

[**78**] Licencia Thome Long[51] et Elinore Foster Wintoniensis diocesis ad contrahendum in quarto / consanguinitatis. Dat' decimo octavo Ianuarii anno supradicto _____ xxiii^s iiii^d

[50] Perhaps the John Smyth, clerk or layman, possibly of Canterbury dioc., whom Joan Gere, laywoman, possibly also of Canterbury dioc., claimed as her husband in litigation before various auditors of causes of the archbishop of Canterbury, one of whom tried to enforce the supposed marriage; John appealed against his judgement to the papal curia, which commissioned papal judges delegate on 11 July 1509 to decide the case; CPL, XIX, no. 251.

[51] Probably not Thomas Longe, Salisbury dioc., rector of Malmesbury (Wilts.) by 1504–1505 and perpetual vicar of an unspecified parish by 1507–8, who obtained various papal dispensations under Julius II (1503–1512); CPL, XIX, nos 1136,1598, 1860 (rubricelle of lost letters).

[**79**] Licentia Morgani ap Dd' et Matildis verch Willelmi Landavensis diocesis ad [contrahendum] / in quarto affinitatis. Dat' xviii^{vo} Ianuarii anno supradicto _____ xx^s

[**80**] Licencia Thome Heylet' et Elizabeth' Wynfelde Co[n]ventrensis et Lichfeldensis diocesis ad contrahend[um non obstante] / quod mater dicti Thome prefatam Elizabeth[am] de sacro fonte levavit. Dat' xix$^{[o]}$ [Ianuar]ii / anno domini Millesimo quingentesimo vicesimo quinto _____ xxvi^s viii^d

[**81**] Licencia Thome Payne^{52} et Anne Hygche' Eliensis diocesis ad contrahendum in quarto consan/guinitatis. Dat' undevicesimo [*recte*?, vicesimo primo] Ianuarii anno domini predicto _____ xxiii^s iiii^d

[**82**] Licentia Willelmi Thomas Landavensis diocesis diaconi ad recipiendum ordinem presbiteratus in / xxiii^{tio} sue etatis anno a quocumque catholico antistite. Dat' xxiii^{tio} Februarii anno eodem _____ xiii^s iiii^d

[**83**] Pluralitas Henrici Horneby clerici cum clausula non residendi.^{53} Dat' xxiiii^{to} Ianuarii / anno domini Millesimo Quingentesimo vicesimo quinto _____ vi^{li} xiii^s iiii^d

[**84**] Toleracio Willelmi Ashpull' ad absentandum se a Cantaria sua per septennium. Dat' / xii^{mo} Iulii anno domini suprascripto _____ xxiii^s iiii^d

[**85**] Toleracio Willelmi Ashpull' ad absentandum se a Cantaria sua per biennium. Dat' / xii^{mo} Octobris anno supradicto _____ x[. . .]^s [. . .^{d}]

[**86**] Unio ecclesie par[r]ochialis de Mabilthorpe Marie^{54} Lincolniensis diocesis cuius [fructus] / viginti unius marcharum valorem annuum non excedit ecclesie par[r]ochiali de Setr[. . .]^{55} / Eboracensis diocesis quamdiu Radulphus Bulmer' no[ta]rius(?) illam obtinuerit.^{56} Dat' xxvii^o Ian[uarii] / anno domini Millesimo Quingentesimo vicesimo quinto _____ [. . .]

---

^{52}Probably not the Thomas Payn, Canterbury dioc., who obtained a papal dispensation to hold a plurality of incompatible benefices in 1 Leo X (1513–14); *CPL*, XX, no. 861.

^{53}Not the Henry Horneby, clerk, DTh of Cambridge University; master of Peterhouse, Cambridge; secretary of Lady Margaret Beaufort and one of her executors who petitioned for papal approval to refound St John's Hospital as St John's College, Cambridge, granted on 24 June 1510; and who died in 1518 (*CPL*, XVIII, nos 55, 63; *BRUC*, 313–314).

^{54}Mablethorpe (Lincs.).

^{55}Settrington (E. Yorks.).

^{56}M. Ralph Bulmer was rector of Settrington in 1525–1526, still in 1535, and probably a graduate of Oxford University (*BRUO, 1501–1540*, 666).

[**87**] Unio ecclesie par[r]ochialis sancti Abell' de Machayn'[57] Landavensis diocesis cuius fructus / iiii^{or} librarum valorem annuum non excedit prebende de Warthacum'[58] in ecclesia cathedrali / Landavensi. Dat' xii^{mo} Ianuarii anno predicto
_____ iiii^{li}

[**88**] Pluralitas magistri Roberti Bysse rectoris ecclesie par[r]ochialis de Badcombe[59] Bathoniensis et / Wellensis diocesis legum doctoris cum clausula non residendi. Dat' xxi^{mo} Februarii anno supradicto[60]
_____ vi^{li} xiii^s iiii^d

[**89**] Licentia Roberti Prediaux accoliti rectoris ecclesie par[r]ochialis de Esse Raffe[61] Exoniensis / diocesis de non promovendi ad sacros ordines ratione ecclesie sue predicte ad triennium dummodo / infra primum biennium triennii huiusmodi subdiaconus fiat. Dat' x[. . .] anno predicto
_____ xiii^s iiii^d

[**90**] Pluralitas Iohannis Thewe rectoris ecclesie par[r]ochialis de Eyot Petri[62] Lincolniensis diocesis / cum clausula non residendi. Dat' xvi^o Martii anno supradicto _____ v^{li}

[**91**] Licencia Patricii Barre Eboracensis diocesis accoliti ad recipiendum ordines extra tempora [a iure statuta]. [Dat'] / quarto decimo Martii anno sepedicto _____ [. . .]

[**92**] Licencia Roberti Schary Lincolniensis diocesis accoliti ad recipiendum omnes ordines extra [tempora a iure statuta] / et duos unico die. Dat' vi^{to} Aprilis anno domini Millesimo Quingentesimo vicesimosexto [. . .]

[**93**] Licencia Willemi Botolf Norwicensis diocesis accoliti ad recipiendum omnes reliquos ordines [extra] / tempora [a iure statuta] et duos unico die. Dat' xxvii^{mo} Aprilis anno domini Millesimo D. xxvi^{to}
_____ xvi(?)^s viii$^{[d]}$

[**94**] Licencia Iohannis Opynshay et El[en]e Wood Co[n]ventrensis et Lichfeldensis diocesis ad contrahendum in tertio / et iiii^{to} consanguinitatis. Dat' xxvi^{to} Aprilis anno supradicto
_____ xxvi^s viii^d

---

[57] St Abel the Martyr par. ch., Machen (Monmouth.).

[58] On 10 September 1505 a bull of Julius II similarly authorized Thomas Warner, BCL, to unite his prebend of Warthacwm (Monmouth.), Llandaff dioc., with his parish church of Wytham (Berks.), Salisbury dioc. (*CPL*, XVIII, no. 512). Roger Gruffudd was prebendary of Warthacwm and canon of Llandaff by 1535 (*Fasti*, XI. 30). Probably the Roger ap Gryffyth, rector of Machen, Llandaff dioc., who obtained a papal dispensation on 25 June 1511 to hold an additional incompatible benefice (*CPL*, XIX, no. 570), and hence likely to be the beneficiary of the union authorized by Cardinal Wolsey above.

[59] Batcombe (Somerset).

[60] = Appendix 4. **44**. See also **67** above.

[61] Possibly Rose Ash or Ashreigney (both Devon).

[62] Ayot St Peter (Herts.).

[**95**] Licencia Roberti Fawcet et Iohanne Wadesan' Eboracensis diocesis ad contrahendum in iiii^{to} consanguinitatis. / Dat' iiii^{to} Martii anno domini Millesimo Quingentesimo vicesimo sexto _____ xxiii^s iiii^d

[**96**] Pluralitas Rogeri Dyngley vicarii ecclesie par[r]ochialis de Banbury^{63} Lincolniensis diocesis cum clausula / non residendi. Dat' xii^{mo} Aprilis anno supradicto _____ vi^{li}

p. 23]

[**97**] Licentia Iohannis Holborough' et Agnetis Ingham Londoniensis diocesis ad contrahendum [non] / obstante quod uxor dicti [Iohannis] prolem prefate Agnetis de sacro fonte levavit. Dat' [. . .] / Maii anno domini Millesimo Quingentesimo vicesimo sexto ___ [. . .]

[**98**] Licencia Willelmi ap Ieuan et Iohannis Morgan Menevensis diocesis diaconi ad re[liquum] / presbiteratus ordinem in xxiiii^{to} anno non completo. Dat' iiii^{to} Maii anno suprascripto _____ [. . .]

[**99**] Licencia Iohannis Sargeant et Elene Legh' Co[n]ventrensis et Lichfeldensis diocesis ad contrahendum in iiii^{to} con/sanguinitatis. Dat' iiii^{to} Maii anno suprascripto _____ xxiii^s iiii^d

[**100**] Licentia Roberti Godhelpe et Iohanne Botte Co[n]ventrensis et Lichfeldensis diocesis ad contrahendum in / iiii^{to} consanguinitatis. Dat' viii^o Martii anno predicto _____ xxiii^s iiii^d

[**101**] Licencia Ricardi Plommer et Alicie To(ur)ner Wigorniensis diocesis ad contrahendum non obstante quod / prefatus Ricardus prolem antedicte Alicie [de] sacro fonte levavit. Dat' xvi^o Iunii anno predicto _____ iiii^{li}

[**102**] Licencia Iohannis Agille et Iohanne Horner Eboracensis diocesis [ad contrah]endum in iiii^{to} affinitatis. / Dat' xxii^{do} Iunii anno supradicto _____ xxiii^s iiii^d

[**103**] Non residentia Thome Elynon' vicarii perpetui ecclesie par[r]ochialis de Lo[n]gowesby^{64} Lincol[niensis] / diocesis causa studii vel quoad vixerit in servicio Regis etc. Dat' xii^{mo} Maii anno supra[dicto(?) . . .]

[**104**] Licencia Iacobi Lome Bathoniensis et Wellensis diocesis ut in xxiiii^{tio} anno ad omnes [ordines] / promoveri valeret. Dat' xii^{mo} Calen' Iul[ii] anno domini Millesimo D. vicesimo [sexto . . .]^{65}

---

^{63}Banbury (Oxon.).
^{64}Probably Lowesby (Leics.).
^{65}Possibly the same as James Smythe *alias* Lyne in Appendix 4. **41**.

[**105**] Licencia Thome Ockley et Agnetis Bedle Wintoniensis diocesis ad contrahendum non obstante [quod . . .] / dicte Agnetis prefatum Thomam antistiti se confirmanti tenuit. Dat' ultimo Iuni [. . .]

[**106**] Licencia Thome Chorlton' et Agnetis Baynley Co[n]ventrensis et Lichfeldensis diocesis ad contrahendum in te[rtio et] / iiii^{to} consanguinitatis. Dat' penultimo Iunii anno supradicto _____ xx[v]i^s [. . .]i$^{[d]}$

[**107**] Licencia Willelmi Lonyes et To[. . .]ee Countres Norwicensis diocesis ad contrahendum in iiii^{to} / affinitatis. Dat' xxvii^{mo} [. . . anno] supradicto _____ xxiii^s iiii^d

[**108**] Licencia Roberti Bolton' et [. . . . . .]thington' Co[n]ventrensis et Lichfeldensis diocesis ad contrahendum / in iiii^{to} consanguinitatis. D[at' . . .] anno domini suprascripto ___ xxiii^s iiii^d

[**109**] Licencia Henrici Ogden' et Ele[ne . . .]awson Co[n]ventrensis et Lichfeldensis diocesis ad contrahendum in tertio / et quarto consanguinitatis. Dat' iiii^{to} Iulii anno [. . .] ___ xxvi^s viii^d

[**110**] Item ~~pl~~ Capacitas cuiusdam monachi de Lewys[66] / cuius nomen remanet in registro magistri Toneys ___

Summa totalis _____ ~~ccix^{li} xiii^s iiii^d~~
Summa(?) inde ut patet _____ clx^{li}
per billas / preter a[. . .] allocationes _____ [. . .]
Summa remanens _____ ~~xliv^{li} viii^s iiii^d~~
Quedam [. . .] sunt expedita sed nondum extracta / [. . . p]reter computata et non extracta / [. . .] Registro vestro ad [D]ei solicitacionem / [. . .] eid[em] pro eisdem Docto inde / [. . .] Iohannis Ingham et Gracie Hancoke / [. . .]ave.

---

[66]Lewes Priory (E. Sussex), OSB (Cluniac).

APPENDIX 3:
LIST OF WOLSEY'S GRACES ISSUED IN THE THREE YEARS PRECEDING 23 OCTOBER 1529 AND IN ARREARS (TNA, E36/171, FOLS 44r–53r)

fol. 44r]
in left margin:] Officium / Receptionis / facultatum
Arreragia debita domino Cardinali per diversas personas ratione / facultatum predictarum expeditarum pro tribus annis finitis xxiii^{cio} / die Octobris Anno xxi^o Regis Henrici Octavi

[1] De Thoma Yegge pro pluralitate sua / de arreragiis suis aretro} vi^{li} x^s

[2] De Thoma Hale^1 pro unione sua de / arreragiis suis aretro} cv^s iiii^d

[3] De Thoma Wodmansey pro plurali-/tate sua de arreragiis suis aretro} vi^{li} ix^s viii^d

[4] De Alano Percie^2 pro unione sua / de arreragiis suis aretro} ix^{li}

[5] De Ed(ward)o Sponer pro pluralitate sua / de arreragiis suis aretro} ~~viii^{li} x^s~~ vi^{li}

[6] De Iohanne Swale pro pluralitate sua / de arreragiis suis aretro} vi^{li}

[7] De Willelmo Webster pro unione sua / de arreragiis suis aretro} viii^{li} x^s

---

^{1}A Thomas Hale, York dioc., was granted a papal dispensation in 4 Leo X (1516–1517) to hold a plurality of incompatible benefices; *CPL*, XX, no. 1063 (rubricella of lost letter). A Thomas Halle, rector of Suckley (Worcs.), Worcester dioc., secured a papal dispensation on 18 January 1512 to hold an additional incompatible benefice and be non-resident, and obtained a papal letter on 30 January 1516 authorizing his rectory's union with the par. ch. of St Michael the Archangel on the Hill, Bristol, Worcester dioc.; the same man as perpetual vicar of Elberton(?) (Glos.), Worcester dioc., had obtained a papal letter on 29 December 1515 authorizing his vicarage's union with the same par. ch.: *CPL*, XIX, no. 793; XX, nos 428, 565. Another Thomas Halle, rector of Stockton (Wilts.), Salisbury dioc., was granted a papal dispensation on 4 August 1511 to hold an additional incompatible benefice; *CPL*, XIX, no. 489.
^{2}Probably the Alan Percy, York dioc., who was granted a papal dispensation in 1 Julius II (1503–1504) to hold two benefices with cure of souls on reaching his twenty-third year and a third on reaching the legitimate age (twenty-five); another papal dispensation in 2 Julius II (1504–1505) to hold a plurality of incompatible benefices; and a papal letter in 5 Julius II (1507–1508) authorizing the union of a vicarage to a par. ch. for life: *CPL*, XIX, nos 963, 1305, 1688 (rubricelle of lost letters).

[**8**] De Thoma Thornton pro trialitate / sua de arreragiis suis aretro} vi^{li} xv^s viii^d

[**9**] De Thoma Benet^3 pro unione sua / de arreragiis suis aretro} xiii^{li} vi^s viii^d

[**10**] De Roberto Philippes^4 pro pluralitate / sua de arreragiis suis aretro} c^s

[**11**] De Ricardo Baldewar' pro pluralitate / sua de arreragiis suis aretro} vi^{li}

fol. 44v]

in left margin:] Arreragia debita per diversas / personas pro diversis / dispensationibus eis factis / que adhuc re-/manent in manibus / supradicti computantis

[**12**] De Thoma Aglionby pro capacitate / sua de arreragiis suis aretro} iiii^{li}

[**13**] De Iohanne Chambyr^5 pro dispensacione sua / de arreragiis suis aretro} lxvi^s viii^d

[**14**] De Mauricio Deonyse pro dispensacione sua / de arreragiis suis aretro} iiii^{li}

[**15**] De Iohanne More^6 et Elizabeth Har-/well pro dispensacione sua de arreragiis suis aretro} lxii^s viii^d

---

^{3}Perhaps the Thomas Bennet, Bath and Wells dioc., who obtained two papal dispensations to hold a plurality of incompatible benefices in 5 Leo X (1517–1518) and 9 Leo X (1521) respectively; *CPL*, XX, nos 1214, 1530 (rubricelle of lost letters).

^{4}A Robert Philipson, rector of South Kelsey (Lincs.), Lincoln dioc., secured a papal dispensation on 30 August 1505 to hold an additional incompatible benefice; a Robert Philipson, London dioc., obtained a papal licence in 2 Leo X (1514–1515) authorizing his non-residence by reason of study: *CPL*, XVIII, no. 492; XX, no. 885 (rubricella of lost letter).

^{5}Perhaps the John Chamber, MA, MD, physician to Henry VIII, who claimed to hold the treasurership of Wells cathedral and parish churches of Thornton Dale (N. Yorks.), York dioc., and Great Bowden (Leics.), Lincoln dioc., by virtue of a papal dispensation to hold three incompatible benefices, and obtained a further papal dispensation on 30 January 1512 to hold a fourth incompatible benefice; *CPL*, XVIII, no. 149. The same man, originally from Northumberland, was fellow of Merton College, Oxford, 1495–1508, and warden from 30 August 1525 to 1544; incepted as MA of Oxford University on 30 June 1495, was admitted as MD at Padua in 1505 and incorporated at Oxford on 16 November 1531; was admitted as treasurer of Wells on 18 February 1511, till May 1543, and as rector of Great Bowden and of Thornton Dale on 9 April and 4 May 1508 respectively, still holding the former in 1526 and retaining the latter till death; held numerous other ecclesiastical benefices, including canonries at Lincoln, Wells, Salisbury and St George's Chapel, Windsor; archdeaconries at Meath and Bedford; and another canonry then deanery of St Stephen's Chapel, Westminster; was appointed as physician to Henry VII in *c*.1506 and to Henry VIII, 1509–1546; was first President of the Barber-Surgeons' Guild of London in 1541; and died in 1549 (*BRUO*, I. 385–386).

^{6}Probably not the John Moor', perpetual vicar of Burlescombe (Devon), Exeter dioc., who obtained Leo X's confirmation on 19 March 1513 of a papal dispensation to hold an

[**16**] De Ricardo Putrell et Elizabeth Bruce / pro dispensacione sua de arreragiis suis aretro} c^s

[**17**] De Iohanne Denham[7] pro dispensacione sua de / arreragiis suis aretro} xxv^s

[**18**] De Thoma Snedall et Iohanna / Mursyng pro dispensacione sua de arreragiis suis aretro} xxii^s iiii^d

[**19**] De Roberto Morton pro dispensacione sua / de arreragiis suis aretro} xxx^s

[**20**] De Gilberto Hill et Elizabeth Wal-/ker pro dispensacione sua de arreragiis suis aretro} vi^{li}

[**21**] De Dionisio Morison pro dispensacione sua de / arreragiis suis aretro} xix^s

[**22**] De Iacobo Robyns et Iohanna Bete / pro dispensacione sua de arreragiis suis aretro} xxvi^s viii^d

[**23**] De Ricardo ap Dd[8] et Iuliana verch Thomas / pro dispensacione sua de arreragiis suis aretro} c^s

fol. 45r]
[**24**] De Olivero Ullake et Iohanna Gibson / pro dispensacione sua de arreragiis suis aretro} xx^s viii^d

[**25**] De Georgio Smyth et aliis pro / dispensacione sua de arreragiis suis aretro} l^s

[**26**] De Thoma Conye pro dispensacione sua / de arreragiis suis aretro} vii^s viii^d

[**27**] De Iohanne Gruffith'[9] pro commiss(ione) sua / de arreragiis suis aretro} xx^{li}

additional incompatible benefice, dated 26 December 1511 but never issued under Julius II; *CPL*, XX, no. 179.

[7] Perhaps the John Denham, BTh, rector of North Kilworth (Leics.), Lincoln dioc., who was granted a papal letter on 12 October 1514 authorizing his rectory's union with Tinwell par. ch. (Rut.), Lincoln dioc.; *CPL*, XX, no. 290. The same man, from Durham dioc., incepted as MA of Oxford University in 1488 and was BTh by 1500; was fellow of Lincoln College, Oxford, from 1487 until he became Ingledew fellow of Magdalen College, Oxford, in *c.*1496, still in 1499; was admitted as rector of North Kilworth and of Tinwell on 1 January 1500 and 30 January 1515 respectively; held several other ecclesiastical benefices, including a Lincoln canonry; and died in 1533 (*BRUO*, I. 569–570).

[8] Probably not the Richard ap David, St David's dioc., who obtained a papal dispensation in 2 Julius II (1504–1505) to wear his monastic habit under any dark-coloured clerical garb; *CPL*, XIX, no. 1091 (rubricella of lost letter).

[9] Probably not the John Griffith', BCnL, treasurer of St David's cathedral, who was granted a papal dispensation in 5 Julius II (1507–1508) to hold an additional incompatible benefice, by virtue of which he obtained Burton Ferry par. ch. (co. Pembroke), St David's dioc., then secured a further papal dispensation on 14 March 1516 to hold a third incompatible benefice: *CPL*, XIX, no. 1816 (rubricella of lost letter); XX, no. 539. The latter was probably an Oxford University graduate, was a canon of St David's in 1504 and its treasurer till death, and was dead by May 1523 (*BRUO, 1501–1540*, 247).

[28] De Iohanne Barbo(ur) pro capicitate / sua de arreragiis suis aretro} vi^{li}

[29] De Ricardo Tottynham pro capellanat(u) / honoris de arreragiis suis aretro} xl^s

[30] De Roberto Ionson pro capacitate sua / de arreragiis suis aretro[10]} vi^{li}

[31] De Thoma Lidgold pro capacitate / sua de arreragiis suis aretro} vi^{li} xii^s iiii^d

[32] De Ricardo Howley alias Morton pro ca-/pacitate sua de arreragiis suis aretro} vi^{li} xix^s

[33] De Baldewino Gilbert et Nicholao / Skynner pro dispensacione de arreragiis suis aretro} xii^s

[34] De Elia Smarte et Iohanna Humfrey / pro dispensacione sua de arreragiis suis aretro} xix^s

[35] De Iohanne Lucas pro dispensacione sua de arreragiis suis / aretro} xii^s iiii^d

fol. 45v]
[36] De Thoma Iohannis[11] et Elizabeth / verch Thomas pro dispensacione sua de arreragiis suis / aretro} xix^s

[37] De Waltero Wodward [et] Iohanna Tailo(ur) / pro dispensacione sua de arreragiis suis aretro} xxv^s viii^d

[38] De Iohanne Popley pro dispensacione sua / de arreragiis suis aretro} xxvi^s viii^d

[39] De Ricardo Bonde pro dispensacione sua de / arreragiis suis aretro} xi^s viii^d

[40] De Iohanne Symonds[12] pro dispensacione sua / de arreragiis suis aretro} iii^s iiii^d

---

[10] Possibly the Robert Johnson who occurs as prior of the Gilbertine Priory of St Katharine, Lincoln, on 1 May 1509 (*Heads of Religious Houses*, III. 599). Probably not the Robert Johnson, BCnL, vicar of St Michael's par. ch., Derby, Coventry and Lichfield dioc., who was granted a papal dispensation on 19 August 1510 to hold an additional incompatible benefice and be non-resident; nor the Robert Johnson *alias* Waynslete, priest, Salisbury dioc., who secured a papal dispensation on 2 June 1512 to hold two incompatible benefices and be non-resident: *CPL*, XIX, nos 367, 623. The former was BCnL probably of Oxford University; admitted as rector of Glatton (Hunts.) on 25 July 1510, still in 1526, and as vicar of St Michael's, Derby, on 19 December 1510, till death; and was dead by February 1530 (*BRUO, 1501–1540*, 685; cf. *ibid.* 321–322).

[11] Perhaps the Thomas John, layman, St David's dioc., who was granted on 7 August 1505 a papal licence to choose a personal confessor; *CPL*, XVIII, no. 496.

[12] Perhaps the John Symondi *alias* Tayllones, London dioc., who obtained a papal dispensation in 1 Julius II (1503–1504) to hold any benefice and was doubtless the John Symonidi, London(?) dioc., granted a papal dispensation in 2 Julius II (1504–1505) to hold a plurality of incompatible benefices; *CPL*, XIX, nos 1029, 1339.

[**41**] De Ricardo ap Iohn' et Iohanna Fle-/myng pro dispensacione sua de arreragiis suis aretro} xxiii^s iiii^d

[**42**] De Iacobo Ayray pro dispensacione sua / de arreragiis suis aretro} vii^s viii^d

[**43**] De Georgio Marvyn' pro dispensacione sua / de arreragiis suis aretro} vi^s viii^d

[**44**] De Thoma Dykyns pro dispensacione sua / de arreragiis suis aretro} iii^s iiii^d

[**45**] De Roberto Thomson[13] pro dispensacione sua / de arreragiis suis aretro} xv^s viii^d

[**46**] De Thoma Harper et Alicia Broke[14] / pro dispensacione sua de arreragiis suis aretro} x^s

[**47**] De Thoma Fowle pro dispensacione sua / de arreragiis suis aretro} xv^s viii^d

fol. 46r]

in left margin:] Adhuc arreragia debita / per diversas personas / pro diversis dispensationibus / eis factis que remanent / in manibus / supradicti computantis

[**48**] De Iohanne Topping pro dispensacione sua de arreragiis / suis aretro} vi^s viii^d

[**49**] De Roderico ap Ieuan et Agnet(e) verch Dd / pro dispensacione sua de arreragiis suis aretro} xii^s iiii^d

[**50**] De Willelmo Mychell pro dispensacione sua de / arreragiis suis aretro} iiii^s vi^d

[**51**] De Ed(ward)o Blongate pro dispensacione sua de arreragiis / suis aretro} xii^s iiii^d

---

[13]Perhaps the Robert Thomson, BTh, rector of Corringham (Essex), London dioc., who obtained a papal dispensation on 10 November 1515 to hold an additional incompatible benefice; *CPL*, XX, no. 512. The latter was of Durham dioc. and fellow of Queens' College, Cambridge, 1498–1499; incepted as MA of Cambridge University in 1499, was admitted as BTh in 1509–1510 and as DTh in 1516–1517; ordained as priest on 2 April 1496; admitted as rector of Corringham on 12 May 1506 and as vicar of Alconbury (Hunts.) on 21 January 1515, both till death; and was dead by October 1533 (*BRUC*, 582). Probably not the Robert Tomson, clerk, St Andrews dioc., who was granted a papal letter on 6 September 1509 awarding him a pension from Minto par. ch., Glasgow dioc.; nor the Robert Thomson, Whithorn dioc., who obtained a papal letter in 6 Julius II (1507–1508) also granting him a pension: *CPL*, XIX, nos 864, 1656.

[14]Perhaps the Alice Broke, laywoman of Wells, defamed of practizing sorcery and poisons, who appealed to the provincial court of Canterbury against the inquiry concerning these charges conducted by the vicar general of Hadrian de Castello, bishop of Bath and Wells and cardinal priest of S. Crisogono; the vicar general counter-appealed with his bishop's support to Rome obtaining a papal commission to judges delegate on 1 December 1511: *CPL*, XIX, no. 751.

[52] De Willelmo Gibbes pro dispensacione sua / de arreragiis suis aretro} x^s

[53] De Willelmo Pike pro dispensacione sua de / arreragiis suis aretro} viii^s

[54] De Henrico Kenworth pro dispensacione / sua de arreragiis suis aretro} vii^s viii^d

[55] De Christofero Mychell pro dispensacione sua de / arreragiis suis aretro} vi^s

[56] De Iohanne Whitwell pro dispensacione sua de / arreragiis suis aretro} ix^s

[57] De Iohanne Holland pro dispensacione sua / de arreragiis suis aretro} iiii^s vi^d

[58] De Iohanne Stanley pro dispensacione sua de / arreragiis suis aretro} x^s

[59] De Roberto Hood[15] pro dispensacione sua de / arreragiis suis aretro} iii^s

fol. 46v]

[60] De Collector(ibus?) denar(iorum?) indulgenc(ie) / concess(e) fraternitati sancti Cornelii West(monasterii) / de arreragiis suis aretro} iii^s v^s viii^d

[61] De Willelmo Creting pro facultate / sua de arreragiis suis aretro} iiii^{li}

[62] De Henrico Ioye pro facultate sua de / arreragiis suis aretro} xl^s

[63] De ~~Henr~~ Laurentio Spencer et / Alicia Swallow pro facultate sua / de arreragiis suis aretro} xxii^s iiii^d

[64] De Willelmo Hamond pro facultate / sua de arreragiis suis aretro} xv^s viii^d

[65] De Iohanne Chubnall et Agnet(e) Batt / pro facultate sua de arreragiis suis aretro} v^s viii^d

[66] De Hugone Louther et Dorathea / Clifford pro facultate sua de arreragiis suis aretro} iiii^{li} xv^s

[67] De Andreo Wodmytte pro facultate / sua de arreragiis suis aretro} vi^{li}

[68] De Willelmo Cha(m)berlayn pro / facultate de arreragiis suis aretro} c^s

[69] De Willelmo Conway pro fa-/cultate sua de arreragiis suis aretro} vi^{li}

---

[15] Perhaps the Robert Hood', rector of Acton Burnell (Salop.), Coventry and Lichfield dioc., who secured a papal dispensation on 24 April 1511 to hold an extra incompatible benefice and be non-resident; *CPL*, XIX, no. 427.

[70] De Nicholao Brocket pro facultate / sua de arreragiis suis aretro} xx^s

fol. 47r]

in left margin:] Adhuc arreragia debita / per diversas personas / pro diversis dispensationibus / eis factis que / adhuc remanent / in manibus supra-/dicti computantis

[71] De Thoma White et Elizabeth Cocks / pro facultate sua de arreragiis suis aretro} xl^s

[72] De Willelmo Grace pro facultate sua de / arreragiis suis aretro} xii^s ii^d

[73] De Willelmo Gray[16] pro facultate sua de / arreragiis suis aretro} vi^{li}

[74] De Iohanne Harrys[17] pro facultate sua de / arreragiis suis aretro} vii^{li} xv^s viii^d

[75] De Ed(ward)o Halyman pro facultate sua / de arreragiis suis aretro} vi^{li}

[76] De Iohanne Langford[18] pro facultate sua / de arreragiis suis aretro} vi^{li}

[77] De Thoma Balam pro facultate / sua de arreragiis suis aretro} vi^{li}

[78] De Iohanne Kyngston' pro facultate / sua de arreragiis suis aretro} vi^{li}

[79] De Iohanne Watwod' pro facultate sua / de arreragiis suis aretro} vii^{li} xv^s viii^d

[80] De Roberto Wittney pro facultate / sua de arreragiis suis aretro} xlv^s viii^d

[81] De Thoma Raynolds et aliis / pro facultate sua de arreragiis suis aretro} xx^s

fol. 47v]

[82] De Iacobo Middelmore pro facultate / sua de arreragiis suis aretro} lx^s

[83] De Ricardo Heyton' pro facultate sua de / arreragiis suis aretro} lx^s

---

[16] Perhaps the William Grey, rector of All Saints' par. ch., Woolfardisworthy (Devon), Exeter dioc., who gained a papal dispensation on 1 December 1505 to hold an additional incompatible benefice and be non-resident; *CPL*, XVIII, no. 590.

[17] Perhaps the John Harrys, St David's dioc., who obtained a papal dispensation in 6 Julius II (1508–1509) to hold a plurality of incompatible benefices; *CPL*, XIX, no. 1819 (rubricella of lost letter).

[18] Perhaps the John Langford, Worcester dioc., who obtained a papal dispensation in 2 Leo X (1514–1515) to hold a plurality of incompatible benefices; *CPL*, XX, no. 926 (rubricella of lost letter).

[**84**] De Thoma Smyth[19] et Ieneta Pitt / pro facultate sua de arreragiis suis aretro} xxv^s vi^d

[**85**] De Morgano Dd pro facultate sua de / arreragiis suis aretro} vi^{li}

[**86**] De Iohanne Lancaster alias Turno(ur) pro fa(culta)te / sua de arreragiis suis aretro} xv^s vi^d

[**87**] De Humfrido Key pro facultate sua de / arreragiis suis aretro} xv^s viii^d

[**88**] De Ricardo Hynton pro facultate / sua de arreragiis suis aretro} xx^s

[**89**] De Henrico Wellwright' et Iohanna / Wellwright' pro facultate sua de arreragiis / suis aretro} xx^s

[**90**] De Roberto Chambir et Agnet(e) / Wasshington' pro facultate sua de arreragiis suis aretro} xx^s

[**91**] De Iohanne Wodward pro facul-/tate sua de arreragiis suis aretro} iiii^{li} xiii^s iiii^d

fol. 48r]

in left margin:] Adhuc arreragia debita / per diversas personas / pro diversis dispensationibus / eis factis que / adhuc remanent / in manibus supra-/dicti computantis

[**92**] De Ada More pro facultate sua de arreragiis / suis aretro} vi^{li}

[**93**] De Ricardo Hill'[20] pro facultate sua de / arreragiis suis aretro} vi^{li}

[**94**] De Willelmo Mooke pro facultate sua de / arreragiis suis aretro} c^s

[**95**] De Iohanne Stapleton pro facultate sua de / arreragiis suis aretro} vi^{li}

[**96**] De Willelmo Pare pro facultate sua de / arreragiis suis aretro} vi^{li}

[**97**] De Galfrido ap Thomas pro facultate sua de / arreragiis suis aretro} xii^s iiii^d

---

[19] Probably not the Thomas Smith, rector of Calstone Wellington (Wilts.), Salisbury dioc., who was granted a papal dispensation on 20 August 1512 to hold an additional incompatible benefice and be non-resident; nor the Thomas Smith, Lincoln dioc., who secured two papal dispensations to hold a plurality of incompatible benefices in 2 Leo X (1514–1515) and 7 Leo X (1519–1520) respectively: *CPL*, XIX, no. 728; XX, nos 881, 1369 (rubricelle of lost letters). Even less likely to be Thomas Smyth', canon of Maxstoke Priory (Warwicks.), OSA, Coventry and Lichfield dioc., who gained a papal dispensation on 10 February 1506 to hold any benefice as if a secular priest; *CPL*, XVIII, no. 655.

[20] Perhaps the Richard Hill, layman, Worcester or another dioc., an executor of the will of Alice Berriman, parishioner of Stow-on-the-Wold (Glos.), who appealled to Rome against the alleged impeding of the will's execution by the bishop of Worcester's commissary general and obtained a papal letter on 13 September 1514 commissioning papal judges delegate to settle this dispute; *CPL*, XX, no. 279.

[98] De Georgio Barne et Alicia Relf pro ~~falt~~ / facultate sua de arreragiis suis aretro} v^s vi^d

[99] De procuratoribus gilde sancti Cornelii pro facultate / sua de arreragiis suis aretro} v^s vi^d

[100] De Philippo Yorke et Elizabeth Stenyns pro / facultate sua de arreragiis suis aretro} v^s viii^d

[101] De Iohanne Combe[21] pro facultate sua de / arreragiis suis aretro} viii^s

[102] De Bartholomeo Cowde pro facultate / sua de arreragiis suis aretro} [ ]

fol. 48v]

[103] De Willelmo Motershed pro facultate / sua de arreragiis suis aretro} xv^s viii^d

[104] De Ricardo Harper pro facultate sua de / arreragiis suis aretro} vi^{li}

[105] De Iacobo Rogers pro facultate sua de / arreragiis suis aretro} xl^s

[106] De Iohanne Glenisford pro facultate sua / de arreragiis suis aretro} iiii^{li} xv^s vi^d

[107] De Nicholao Lee pro facultate sua de / arreragiis suis aretro} vi^{li}

[108] De Iohanne Holden' pro facultate sua de / arreragiis suis aretro} vi^{li}

[109] De Willelmo Harper pro facultate sua / de arreragiis suis aretro} xx^s

[110] De Waltero Sem(er) pro facultate sua / de arreragiis suis aretro} xv^s viii^d

[111] De Iohanne Payne[22] pro facultate sua de / arreragiis suis aretro} xii^s

[112] De Roberto Shold et Io[h]anna / Schoke pro facultate sua de arreragiis suis aretro} xii^s ii^d

---

[21] Perhaps the John Cogyn' *alias* Combe, monk of the Cluniac priory of Montacute (Somerset), Bath and Wells dioc., who obtained a papal dispensation on 29 May 1511 to hold any benefice as if a secular priest; *CPL*, XIX, no. 487.

[22] Not the John Payne, OP, DTh of Cambridge University by 1472–1473, Dominican prior provincial in England from 1474 until his provision as bishop of Meath in Ireland on 17 March 1483, till his death on 6 March 1507; an appeal from whose episcopal judgement to Rome resulted in a papal letter of 3 October 1506 commissioning papal judges delegate: *BRUC*, 445–456; *CPL*, XVIII, no. 692.

[**113**] De Willelmo Clerke[23] pro facultate sua / de arreragiis suis aretro} x^s

fol. 49r]

in left margin:] Adhuc arreragia debita / per diversas personas pro / diversis dispensationibus eis / factis que adhuc / remanent in ma-/nibus supradicti computantis

[**114**] De Willelmo Popley et Gracia Rodney pro / facultate sua de arreragiis suis aretro} xx^s

[**115**] De Roberto Franklen' pro facultate sua de / arreragiis suis aretro} v^s iiii^d

[**116**] De Edwardo Torrell pro facultate sua de / arreragiis suis aretro} vii^s viii^d

[**117**] De Iohanne Kirkebie pro facultate sua de arreragiis / suis aretro} viii^s

[**118**] De Iohanne Polken' pro facultate sua de / arreragiis suis aretro} ix^s

[**119**] De Willelmo Russell pro facultate sua de / arreragiis suis aretro} xx^s

[**120**] De Iohanne Mooreton' et Iohanna Ellys / pro facultate sua de arreragiis suis aretro} iii^s

[**121**] De Willelmo Westwray pro facultate sua de / arreragiis suis aretro} vii^s viii^d

---

[23]A William Clerk, rector of Ufford par. ch. (Northants.), Lincoln dioc., obtained a papal dispensation in 2 Julius II (1504–1505) to hold an additional incompatible benefice; a William Clerk, rector of Springfield par. ch. (Essex), London dioc., and a William Clerk, rector of Welbourn par. ch. (Lincs.), Lincoln dioc.,obtained like dispensations in 3 Julius II (1505–1506); *CPL*, XIX, nos 1069, 1072, 1073 (rubricelle of lost letters); cf. *ibid*. 1511, 1528. William Clerk, rector of Welbourn, was the same as William Clerk, MA, perpetual chaplain in Towcester par. ch. (Northants.), Lincoln dioc., who was granted a papal dispensation on 18 December 1513 to hold an additional incompatible benefice and be non-resident; probably the same William Clerk, Norwich dioc., who obtained a papal letter in 5 Leo X (1517–1518) authorizing the union of his par. ch. to another: *CPL*, XX, nos 9, 1176 (rubricella of lost letter). William Clerk, MA, was MA of Cambridge University by 1500, admitted as rector of Welbourn on 25 January 1506 and still in 1520, collated as warden of the Sponne chantry in Towcester ch. on 26 September 1508, and held various other ecclesiastical benefices including a canonry at St Mary's, Warwick (*BRUC*, 140); not the same as William Clarke who was admitted as MA of Cambridge University in 1510–1511, incorporated at Oxford in 1516, fellow of King's College Cambridge, 1507–1524, and rector of Little Kemble (Bucks.), 1524–1531 (*BRUO, 1501–1540*, 120).

[**122**] De dompno Thoma Rouland abbate de / Abyndon'[24] pro facultate sua de arreragiis suis aretro} xxv^s viii^d

[**123**] De Willelmo Persey pro facultate sua de arreragiis / suis aretro} l^s

[**124**] De Radulpho Kempe pro facultate sua de / arreragiis suis aretro} vi^{li}

fol. 49v]

[**125**] De Ricardo Heys[25] pro facultate sua de arreragiis / suis aretro} vi^{li}

[**126**] De Benedicto Mulsho pro facultate sua / de arreragiis suis aretro} vi^{li}

[**127**] De Iohanne Fissher[26] pro facultate sua de / arreragiis suis aretro} lx^s

[**128**] De Willelmo Baker[27] pro facultate sua de / arreragiis suis aretro} iiii^{li}

[**129**] De Iohanne Hurte pro facultate sua de / arreragiis suis aretro} vi^{li}

[24] Thomas Rowland *alias* Penthecoste was a monk of Abingdon Abbey (Berks.), OSB, by 1504 and his election as abbot in 1511 received the royal assent on 23 February 1512; he remained abbot till the abbey's dissolution on 9 February 1538. He supplicated for BTh at Oxford University on 17 May 1514 and was granted a papal dispensation for study on 3 February 1521. He was ordained as priest on 21 September 1504 and dispensed by the Faculty Office on 12 February 1538 to hold a benefice with change of habit; he was dead by 1540 (*BRUO, 1501–1540*, 493; *Heads of Religious Houses*, III. 13).

[25] Perhaps the Richard Haws, London(?) dioc., who was granted a papal dispensation in 3 July II (1505–1506); *CPL*, XIX, no. 1516 (rubricella of lost letter).

[26] Perhaps John Fisher, born at Beverley (E. Yorks.) in 1469, fellow of Michaelhouse from c.1491 and master from 1496 to 1498; MA and DTh of Cambridge University by 1510; Vice-Chancellor of Cambridge University from 15 July 1501, its Chancellor from October 1514 till death, and first Lady Margaret reader in divinity from 8 September 1502. As chaplain of Henry VIII, he was provided as bishop of Rochester under papal letters of 14–15 October 1504, and as former chaplain and confessor to Lady Margaret Beaufort he was co-petitioner for the papal licence of 24 June 1510 authorizing her plans to refound St John's Hospital as St John's College, Cambridge; an author of sermons and other theological works, he wrote treatises against Henry VIII's divorce from Catherine of Aragon in 1527–1532 and was executed on 22 June 1535 for refusing to swear the oath required by the Act of Succession: *BRUC*, 229–230; *CPL*, XVIII, nos 55, 63, 197–199. Or John Fisher, plaintiff in a case before the consistory court of York, from which the defendants appealed to Rome resulting in a papal letter of 8 July 1514 commissioning papal judges delegate to settle the case; *CPL*, XX, no. 271.

[27] Perhaps the William Baker, rector of Costock par. ch. (Notts.), York dioc., who obtained a papal dispensation on 10 June 1508 to hold an additional incompatible benefice and be non-resident; or the William Marshall' *alias* Baker, scholar, Coventry and Lichfield dioc., who secured a papal dispensation from defect of age on 9 January 1516 so that on becoming a clerk and reaching his nineteenth year he might hold a benefice, and on reaching his twentieth year he might hold an extra incompatible benefice and be non-resident: *CPL*, XIX, no. 30; XX, no. 550; cf. Appendix 4. **17**.

[130] De Iacobo Penglas pro facultate sua / de arreragiis suis aretro} lx^s

[131] De Roberto Blackebourne pro facultate sua / de arreragiis suis aretro} lx^s

[132] De Waltero Sydenham pro facultate sua / de arreragiis suis aretro^{28}} xii^s

[133] De Iohanne Neiler pro facultate sua de / arreragiis suis aretro} xx^s

[134] De Ricardo Philpote^{29} pro facultate sua / de arreragiis suis aretro} xxv^s vi^d

[135] De Iohanne Maymnam pro facultate sua / de arreragiis suis aretro} vi^{li}

fol. 50r]
in left margin:] Adhuc arreragia debita / per diversas personas / pro diversis dispensationibus / eis factis que / adhuc remanent / in manibus supra-/dicti computantis

[136] De Capella in ponte Cothie pro facultate / sua de arreragiis suis aretro} xxv^s vi^d

[137] De Willelmo Smyth'^{30} pro facultate sua de / arreragiis suis aretro} vi^{li}

---

^{28}? = Appendix 4. **3**.

^{29}Perhaps the Rigaud Philpot, clerk, Winchester dioc., allegedly of noble birth, who gained a papal dispensation on 14 July 1505 from defect of birth, then being in his tenth year or thereabouts, to hold any cathedral canonries and prebends, *CPL*, XVIII, no. 109

^{30}A William Smith was archdeacon of Lincoln in December 1511, when he was commissioned as a papal judge delegate, and in July 1513, when an appeal to Rome from his court resulted in a papal commission of papal judges delegate: *CPL*, XIX, no. 752; XX, no. 218. He was BCL of Cambridge University by 1500, DCnL of Ferrara by 1506 (incorporated at Cambridge in 1505–1506), and collated as archdeacon of Northants. on 4 January 1500, resigning on his admission as archdeacon of Lincoln on 21 August 1506, till death (*BRUC*, 538). A William Smyth, York dioc., was MA of Cambridge University, fellow of Pembroke Hall, Cambridge, from *c*.1486 to 1501, and vicar of Overton Watervile par. ch. (Hunts.), Lincoln dioc., from 5 November 1500 till his death in 1532; as vicar of Overton Watervile he obtained a papal dispensation in 2 Julius II (1504–1505) to hold an additional incompatible benefice: *BRUC*, 537; *CPL*, XIX, no. 1056; cf. *ibid*. 1520 (rubricelle of lost letters). A William Smyth, rector of St Lawrence's par. ch., Oxhill (Warwicks.), Worcester dioc., and another William Smyth, rector of Great Catworth par. ch. (Hunts.), Lincoln dioc., secured like dispensations on 23 June and 24 July 1507 respectively; *CPL*, XVIII, nos 791, 843. Another William Smyth, vicar of Colwich par. ch. (Staffs.), Coventry and Lichfield dioc., secured a like dispensation in 1 Julius II (1503–1504); probably the same William Smyth, Coventry and Lichfield dioc., who was granted a papal dispensation in 2 Julius II (1504–1505) to hold a plurality of incompatible benefices: *CPL*, XIX, nos 932, 1336 (rubricelle of lost letters). A William Smith, Chichester dioc., gained a similar dispensation in 1 Leo X (1513–1514); and another William Smith and Mary Harris, Coventry and Lichfield dioc., obtained a marriage dispensation in 5 Leo X (1517–1518): *CPL*, XX, nos 756, 1234 (rubricelle of lost letters).

[**138**] De Willelmo Paynet pro facultate sua de / arreragiis suis aretro} xl^s

[**139**] De Iohanne Stratton' pro facultate sua de arreragiis / suis aretro} vi^s viii^d

[**140**] De Georgio Poole pro facultate sua de / arreragiis suis aretro} v^s vi^d

[**141**] De Ricardo Crispyn' pro facultate sua de / arreragiis suis aretro} v^s vi^d

[**142**] De Henrico Herttley pro facultate sua de arreragiis / suis aretro} xx^s

[**143**] De Henrico Perpoynt pro facultate sua de / arreragiis suis aretro} ii^s

[**144**] De Iohanne Mabbes pro facultate sua de arreragiis / suis aretro^{31}} viii^s x^d

[**145**] De Willelmo Tenn(ur)le(?) pro facultate sua de / arreragiis suis aretro} iii^s

[**146**] De Iohanne Rampoley pro facultate sua de / arreragiis suis aretro} vi^s viii^d

fol. 50v]
in left margin:] Adhuc arreragia debita / per diversas personas pro / diversis dispensationibus / eis factis que / adhuc remanent / in manibus supradicti / computantis

[**147**] De Willelmo Bucleberd et Io[h]anna Tann(er) / pro facultate sua de arreragiis suis aretro} xxii^s ii^d

[**148**] De Georgio Knottell et Agnet(e) Rutter / pro facultate sua de arreragiis suis aretro} xx^s

[**149**] De Thoma Mydleton' et Alicia Wen-/scerley pro facultate sua de arreragiis suis aretro} xxvii^s x^d

[**150**] De Gilberto Grerson et Elizabeth Dale-/rumpell pro facultate sua de arreragiis suis aretro} xl^s

[**151**] De Roberto Bigge pro facultate sua de / arreragiis suis aretro} xvi^s vi^d

[**152**] De Willelmo Smyth^{32} pro facultate sua de / arreragiis suis aretro} xvi^s viii^d

[**153**] De Ricardo Pescod de [*sic*] pro facultate sua de / arreragiis suis aretro^{33}} lxxv^s

[**154**] De Ionet Linch' et Mar(gare)t(a) Skirret pro / facultate sua de arreragiis suis aretro} lxv^s

---

^{31}? = Appendix 4. **91**.
^{32}Cf. **137** above.
^{33}? = Appendix 4. **65**.

[**155**] De Thoma Inrie [*or* Iurie?] pro facultate sua de arreragiis / suis aretro} x^s

[**156**] De Hugone ap Richard pro facultate sua de / arreragiis suis aretro} vi^s

[**157**] De Willelmo Thurgood et Io[h]anna / Crabbe pro facultate sua de / arreragiis suis aretro} xxxv^s

fol. 51r]

[**158**] De Iohanne Bere pro facultate sua de arreragiis suis aretro _ c^s

[**159**] De Griffino Dd Duye[34] pro facultate sua de arreragiis / suis aretro} iiii^{li}

[**160**] De Thoma Lloid'[35] pro facultate sua de arreragiis / suis aretro} iiii^{li}

De diversis personis pro denariis per ipsos / debitis per obligaciones et billas videlicet … [*various individuals are specified with their debts, not in separate entries but in a block of continuous text; only those said to owe taxes for dispensations are noted below:*] …

[fol. 52r]
in left margin:] Arreragia debita per / diversas personas pro / quibus tenentur / per obligaciones et billas
in right margin:]} ccclxxv^{li} xviii^s vi^d

… [**161**] Doctore Clai-/burghe' pro capacitate mon' de vale crucis / lxxv^s viii^d [**162**] eodem Doctore Clai-/burgh pro dispensacione Roberti Salisburne / abbatis de vale crucis[36] vi^{li} [**163**] eodem / Doctore

---

[34]Doubtless the Griffin [ap] Davydd Duy, rector of St Giles the Abbot par.ch., Wendlebury (Oxon.), Lincoln dioc., who was granted a papal letter on 8 July 1513 authorizing his rectory's union with the perpetual vicarage of St Miliceus par. ch., Llanarth (Cardigans.), St David's dioc.; *CPL*, XX, no. 25. A Griffin ap David, perpetual vicar of Ystrad(?) par. ch. (Cardigans.), St David's dioc., claimed to have received a papal dispensation from defect of birth, being born of a married man and an unmarried woman, to be promoted to all, even holy, orders and hold two benefices, even one with cure of souls, and secured a further dispensation on 26 November 1503 to hold an additional incompatible benefice and be non-resident; *CPL*, XVIII, no. 233. A Griffin ap David, rector of Aberporth (Cardigans.), St David's dioc., similarly claimed to have secured as a clerk a papal dispensation from defect of birth, being born of unmarried parents, to be promoted to all holy, even priest's, orders and hold a benefice even with cure of souls, and obtained a further dispensation on 15 May 1512 to hold an additional incompatible benefice and be non-resident; *CPL*, XIX, no. 297.

[35]A Thomas Lloyd, Exeter dioc., was granted a papal dispensation in 2 Leo X (1514–1515) to hold a plurality of incompatible benefices; a Thomas Lloyd, St David's dioc., secured a similar dispensation in 8 Leo X (1520–1521): *CPL*, XX, nos 906, 1419 (rubricelle of lost letters).

[36]Robert Salisbury was abbot of Valle Crucis Abbey (Denbigh), OCist, by 1 April 1528, and arrested for robbery and forgery in 1534, the abbey's administration being committed

Claiburgh pro indulgencia domini / in temporalibus de Lawar' viii^s / [**164**] dicto Doctore Claiburg' pro facultate / Chidley iiii^{li} ... [**165**] Willelmo Gascoign' / milite pro dispensacione Thome Crue xvi^s / viii^d ... [**166**] Doctore Lee / pro Whithede[37] xls Eodem Doctore / Lee pro unione sua c^s [**167**] Iohanne Wodward / pro pluralitate sua iiii^{li} xiii^s iiii^d / [**168**] Mauricio Wogan pro dispensacione / sua xii^s ii^d [**169**] Iohanne Gostwike pro / pluralitate consanguinei sui c^s / [**170**] Thoma Benet Doctore[38] pro unione / sua xv^{li} ... [fol. 52v] ... [**171**] Iohanne Senclem vice-/camerario debit(a?) pro residuo taxe unio-/nis Roberti Clerke alias Fabian'[39] / lvii^s x^d ... [**172**] Doctore Claiburgh' pro taxa gracie facte / Iohanni Stephyns cappellano marchionis / Exonie[40] quam recepit ab illo xxxiii^s / iiii^d [**173**] Eodem Doctore Claiburgh' pro / taxa unionis Iohannis Egerton[41] quam [fol. 53r] recepit ix^{li}. [**174**] Eodem Doctore Claiburgh / pro taxa dispensacionis Willelmi Nu'gent(?) quam / recepit iiii^{li} iiii^s vi^d ... In toto prout per diversas / obligaciones et billas penes magistrum Iohannem / Hughes nuper receptor facultatum domini / Cardinalis remanen(tes?) apparet.

De magistro Iohanne Hughes Receptore facultatum / predictarum de arreragiis suis aretro} lx^s vii^d quarta.

Summa totalis omnium / arreragium predictarum} dcccxxii^{li} vii^s v^d quarta.

to the prior and four others on 4 August 1534. He was imprisoned in the Tower of London by 6 July 1535, and commissioners informed Thomas Cromwell on 1 September 1535 of their intention to deprive Salisbury of office on 4 or 5 September; he occurs as a clerk in 1542 (*Heads of Religious Houses*, III. 344–345).

[37] ? = Appendix 4. **83**.

[38] Possibly Thomas Benett, DCL (of Oxford University) by 1512, who held numerous ecclesiastical benefices, including canonries at St Paul's London and Salisbury; was appointed as the bishop of Salisbury's vicar general in 1524, still in September 1533; and died in 1558 (*BRUO, 1501–1540*, 42–43). Probably the same as Thomas Bennet, Bath and Wells dioc., who secured two papal dispensations to hold a plurality of incompatible benefices in 5 Leo X (1517–1518) and 9 Leo X (1521) respectively; *CPL*, XX, nos 1214, 1530 (rubricelle of lost letters).

[39] Doubtless the Robert Clerk *alias* Fabyan', MA, rector of St George's par. ch., Toddington (Beds.), Lincoln dioc., who was granted a papal dispensation on 9 April 1507 to hold an additional incompatible benefice and be non-resident; a Robert Clarke *alias* Fabyan whom Emden identifies as rector of Toddington in 1518 (till death) incepted as MA (of Oxford University) on 14 March 1524, held several other benefices including canonries at Stoke by Clare (Suff.) and Chulmleigh (Devon), was steward of the countess of Oxford's household, and was dead by February 1534: *CPL*, XVIII, no. 724; *BRUO, 1501–1540*, 119. Probably not Robert Clerk, Winchester dioc., who obtained a papal dispensation in 4 Julius II (1506–1507); *CPL*, XIX, no. 1630 (rubricella of lost letter).

[40] Henry Courtenay, marquess of Exeter (d. 1538); see *Oxford DNB*, XIII. 678–681.

[41] Perhaps the John Egerton, Lincoln dioc., who was granted a papal dispensation in 1 Leo X (1513–1514) to hold a plurality of incompatible benefices; *CPL*, XX, no. 834 (rubricella of lost letter).

APPENDIX 4:
CALENDAR OF LETTERS OF
DISPENSATION OF CARDINAL WOLSEY

[1] Letter of Cardinal Wolsey as legate *a latere* of Leo X to Henry VIII and his realm dispensing Thomas Stafford, brother of the Hospital of St John the Baptist, OSA, Northampton,[1] Lincoln dioc., under a papal faculty, to receive and retain a benefice with cure of souls as if a secular clerk. Dated at our residence near Westminster, 12 August 1521. *Reg. Longland*, fol. 70v.

[2] Letter of Cardinal Wolsey as legate *a latere* of Leo X to Henry VIII and his realm dispensing Giles Dawbeny, priest, rector of South Perrott (*Southeperoll'*) par. ch., Salisbury dioc., under a papal faculty, to receive and retain an additional incompatible benefice. Dated at our residence near Westminster, 17 August 1521. *Reg. Nykke, 4*, fols 126r–7r.

[3] Letter of Cardinal Wolsey as legate *a latere* of Pope Leo X to Henry VIII and his realm dispensing Walter Sidenham, perpetual vicar of Shorwell (*Sharwell*), Winchester dioc., under a papal faculty, to receive and retain an additional incompatible benefice and to be absent from any of his benefices while resident in another or studying at a university. Dated at our residence near Westminster, 24 Dec. 1521.[2] *Reg. Fox, 5*, fols 53v–4r.

[4] An entry dated 14 April 1522 records that Robert Tregunwell, MA,[3] vicar of St Austell (*Austoli*) par. ch., Cornwall, swore before

---

[1] The Hospital of SS John the Baptist and John the Evangelist, Northampton (Knowles & Hadcock, 328, 380).

[2] This letter follows in *Reg. Fox, 5*, fol. 53r–v, a bull of Leo X dispensing Sidenham to retain Shorwell vicarage or receive and retain any other incompatible benefice as if he were promoted to priest's orders, to be absent from any of his benefices while resident in another or the Roman curia, and not to be promoted to holy, even priest's, orders by reason of any of his benefices for seven years provided that he became subdeacon within the first two of these years; dated at Santa Severa, Porto dioc., 22 November 1520. Both these letters follow at fol. 52v Bishop Richard Fox of Winchester's citation of Sidenham dated 31 October 1523 to explain why the fruits of his vicarage ought not to be sequestrated because of his non-residence.

[3] Robert Tregonwell was fellow of Corpus Christi College, Oxford (1517–1522), and incepted as MA of Oxford University in June 1518; took deacon's orders on 17 December 1519; was vicar of St Austell (Cornw.) till death and held various other ecclesiastical benefices, including a canonry of Exeter by 1537 and the chancellorship of Wells by 1542; was chaplain to Henry VIII in 1540 and was dead by January 1543 (*BRUO, 1501–1540*, 576).

M. Richard Tollet, DCL, the bishop of Exeter's vicar-general-in-spirituals, on his institution to that vicarage to reside there in person unless otherwise dispensed and then exhibited certain letters of Cardinal Thomas [Wolsey] sealed with his great seal (*videlicet cera rubea caps(ula?) canapi circumdata cum cordulis canapis pendentibus*), lacking any suspect features, in which it was provided that he might be absent from any of his benefices while resident in another or at a university for the sake of study for up to seven years and which were dated at the cardinal's residence, 9 January 1521/2.[4] In margin: 'Exhibicio littere dispensacionis'. *Reg. Veysey, 2*, fol. 13r.

[5] Letter of Cardinal Wolsey as legate *a latere* of the late Leo X to Henry VIII and his realm notifying John [Longland], bishop of Lincoln, that under a faculty of Leo X to license certain persons within his legation to eat meat, eggs, and dairy produce in Lent and other fasting periods he licenses all inhabitants of the English realm to eat eggs, cheese, butter and other dairy produce during Lent and other fasting periods and this is to be publicised every Sunday in all churches of the realm by their clergy. Dated under our seal at our residence near Westminster, 24 February 1521/2. *Reg. Longland*, fols 96v–7r.

[6] Letter of Cardinal Wolsey as legate *a latere* of Leo X, to Henry VIII and his realm dispensing John Hunte, priest, perpetual vicar of St Winnow(?) (*Wynnoti*) par. ch., Exeter dioc., under a faculty of Leo X, to receive and retain an additional incompatible benefice and be absent from any of his benefices while resident in another or in a university for the sake of study for up to seven years. Dated at our residence near Westminster, 5 March 1521/2.[5] In margin: 'Bulla pluralitatis domini Iohannis Hunte' capellani'. *Reg. Veysey, 2*, fols 39v–40r.

---

[4]Doubtless there was only one letter, it further dispensed Tregunwell to receive and retain an additional incompatible benefice (as **6** below), and Wolsey's residence was that near Westminster usually specified in the dating clause of his letters. The same vicar general admitted Tregunwell as vicar of St Austell (*de sancto Austolo*), Exeter dioc., on 14 April 1522, the same date as above (*Reg. Veysey, 1*, fol. 11v).

[5]Preceding the letter it is recorded that on 10 July 1524 John Hunte, chaplain, exhibited before M. Richard Tollet, DCL, the bishop of Exeter's vicar-general-in-spirituals, this letter described as 'certain letters' of Cardinal Thomas [Wolsey] sealed with his great seal (*videlicet cera rubia caps(ula?) canapi circumdata cum cordulis canapis pendentibus*) and lacking any suspect features; the same vicar general admitted dom. John Hunte, chaplain, as perpetual vicar of Modbury (*Modbery*), Exeter dioc., on the same date (*Reg. Veysey, 1*, fol. 21r). Following this letter in *Reg. Veysey, 2*, fols 40v–41r, another entry records that Hunte exhibited before Tollet 'certain apostolic letters' with bull attached and lacking any suspect features, and recites a letter of Clement VII authorizing John Hunte, rector of Zeal Monachorum (*Zele Monachorum*) par. ch., Exeter dioc., to unite with that church Cadeleigh (*Cadelegh*) par. ch., Exeter dioc., without diocesan licence, dated at St Peter's, Rome, 13 April 1524 (in margin: 'Alia bulla dispensacionis eiusdem domini Iohannis Hunte').

[7] Letter of Cardinal Wolsey as legate *a latere* of Leo X to Henry VIII and his realm dispensing Alexander Boston, MA,[6] perpetual vicar of Broad Chalke (*Burchalke*) par. ch., Salisbury dioc., under a faculty of Leo X, to receive and retain an additional incompatible benefice and be absent from any of his benefices while resident in another or studying for up to seven years. Dated at our residence near Westminster, 14 May 1522. Signed under plica on right: 'Toneys' [with scribal sign]. Endorsed: 'Card. Wolsey (Leg. a Latere)'s Faculty to A.B. for plurality & Non-residence'; 'Card. Wolsey'; 'Exhibitum per Alexandrum Boston iiii Maii A° 1537'; 'Exemplatum per mess. r.'; 'Boston' Sar.' 36.8 × 22.1 cm. Plica: 4.3 cm. Slits for seal strings. *LPL, Papal Document 131* (original).

[8] Letter of Cardinal Wolsey as legate *a latere* of Leo X to Henry VIII and his realm dispensing Robert Waterhouse and Sybil Sayvell, York dioc., under a faculty of Leo X to dispense men and women in his legation to *marry* in either the third, third and fourth or fourth and fourth degrees of consanguinity and affinity or to remain married if they contracted and consummated marriage unaware of their kinship in the same degrees, so that they may marry in the third and third degrees of consanguinity with legitimation of future issue. Dated at our residence near Westminster, 14 May 1522: Below on right: 'R. Toneys' (with scribal sign). *Reg. Wolsey (York)*, fol. 109r–v.

[9] Letter of Cardinal Wolsey as legate *a latere* licensing Richard Egerton,[7] rector of Stoke and Edenfield(?) (*Endefylde*) parish churches and vicar of Frodsham (*Frodysham*), Coventry and Lichfield dioc., to hold Grendon par. ch., co. Warwicks., Coventry and Lichfield dioc. in *commendam*. Dated at our residence near Westminster, 4 July 1522. *Reg. Blythe*, fol. 105v.

[10] Letter of Cardinal Wolsey as legate *a latere* of the late Leo X to Henry VIII and his realm dispensing Francis Pollard, BA,[8] perpetual vicar of St Peter the Apostle's par. ch., Chalfont (*Chalfonte*), Lincoln dioc., under a faculty of Leo X, to receive and retain an additional incompatible benefice with cure of souls and be absent from any of his benefices while resident in another or studying at a university.

---

[6]As a scholar from Eton, aged 17, Boston was admitted on 4 April 1506 to King's College, Cambridge, where he was fellow 1509–1521; he was MA of Cambridge University by 1514; was ordained as priest on 18 September 1518; vicar of Broad Chalke (Wilts.), his home village, by 1521; and died *c*.1558–1559 (Venn, I. 184).

[7]Probably the same Richard Egerton, Coventry and Lichfield dioc., who obtained a papal letter authorizing the union of two of his parochial benefices for life in 2 Leo X (1514–1515); *CPL*, XX, no. 915 (rubricella of lost letter).

[8]Perhaps the Francis Pollarde, BA of Oxford University by 1512; fellow of Magdalen College, Oxford, from 1507 and still in 1512–1513; and cantarist of the first chantry, called Kalendars, in All Saints', Bristol, from 27 April 1528 (*BRUO, 1501–1540*, 455).

Dated at our residence near Westminster, 7 July 1522. *Reg. Longland*, fols 118v–19v.

[**11**] Letter of Cardinal Wolsey as legate *a latere* of the late Leo X to Henry VIII and his realm dispensing Maurice Brythinsha, BCL,[9] rector of Snargate (*Snergat*) par. ch., Canterbury dioc., under a faculty of Leo X, to receive and retain an additional incompatible benefice with cure of souls and be absent from any of his benefices for seven years while resident in another or studying at a university. Dated at our residence near Westminster, 9 October 1522. *Reg. Longland*, fols 155v–6r.

[**12**] An entry records that on 16 March 1526/7 M. John London,[10] proctor of M. Richard Pate,[11] exhibited to Bishop Richard Fox of Winchester letters of Cardinal Wolsey as legate *a latere* dispensing Pate to receive a benefice in his nineteenth year and not be bound thereby to be promoted to the priesthood for seven years provided that he becomes a subdeacon within two years, dated 28 December 1522.[12] *Reg. Fox, 5* fol. 123v.

[**13**] Letter of Cardinal Wolsey as legate *a latere* of the late Leo X and now Adrian VI to Henry VIII and his realm authorizing M. Maurice Brythinsha, BCL, our familiar chaplain, (who had been dispensed[13]

---

[9]Not otherwise known as a graduate of Cambridge or Oxford universities since neither Venn; *BRUC*; *BRUO*; nor *BRUO, 1501–1540* list him.

[10]Probably the John London, scholar of Winchester College from 1497; scholar (from 1503), fellow (1505–1518), and warden (1526–1542) of New College, Oxford; DCL of Oxford University, having incepted on 28 February 1519; a member of the College of Advocates, London, from 1519; bishop of Lincoln's commissary in Oxford archdeaconry by 1521; ordained as priest on 14 June 1522; notary public by 1533; the King's visitor in Lincoln diocese, 1537–1518; and holder of numerous ecclesiastical benefices, including canonries at York, Lincoln, Chichester, Salisbury, and St George's Chapel, Windsor, the mastership of St John's Hospital, Wallingford, and deanship of Oseney, Oxford (*BRUO, 1501–1540*, 359–360).

[11]Richard Pates was nephew of John Longland, bishop of Lincoln; admitted to Corpus Christi College, Oxford, aged 18, on 1 June 1522; determined as BA of Oxford University in 1524, supplicating for BTh there in 1536; holder of numerous ecclesiastical benefices, including canonries at Lincoln, St Paul's London, and Wells, and the bishopric of Worcester (1541–1559); Henry VIII's ambassador to the court of Emperor Charles V, 1533–1537 and again in 1540; and died on 5 October 1565 (*BRUO, 1501–1540*, 435–436).

[12]This entry adds that the proctor also exhibited a papal letter, dated 13 April 1526, authorizing Pate to unite Great Haseley (*Hasley*) par. ch. with his canonry and prebend of Cropredy, and another dated 1523 dispensing Pate to retain three incompatible benefices provided that two were parish churches. Another entry also dated 16 March 1526/7 follows in *Reg. Fox, 5*, fols 123v–125v, recording Pate's resignation of his Lincoln canonry and Cropredy prebend in exchange for Winchester archdeaconry. He was collated as canon of Lincoln on 4 June 1524 and to the Lincoln prebend of Cropredy on 25 September 1525, exchanging the latter for Sanctae Crucis prebend in March 1527, when he was also admitted as archdeacon of Winchester; he was admitted as rector of Great Haseley (Oxon.) on 18 Sepember 1525 (*BRUO, 1501–1540*, 435).

[13]See **11** above.

to receive and retain two incompatible benefices with cure of souls and thereby obtained the canonry and prebend of Easton in Gordano (*Eston in Gordano*) in Wells cathedral[14] and Weston par. ch., Coventry and Lichfield dioc.), under a faculty of Leo X including the uniting of benefices and confirmed by Adrian VI, to unite Berrynarbor (*Bery Narber*) par. ch., Exeter dioc., to his canonry and prebend so that he may possess that church and use the fruits of both. Dated at our residence near Westminster, 8 April 1523. *Reg. Longland*, fols 156r–7v.

[**14**] Letter of Cardinal Wolsey as legate *a latere* of the late Leo X and now Adrian VI to Henry VIII and his realm dispensing John Malory, knight, and Anne Yorke, York dioc., under a faculty of Leo X confirmed by Adrian VI to dispense men and women in his legation to marry in the third or third and fourth degrees of consanguinity and affinity or to remain married if they contracted and consummated marriage unaware of these degrees or even contracted marriage aware of them, so that they may remain married, having contracted and consummated marriage formerly unaware of their kinship in the third and fourth degrees of affinity, only later becoming aware of this, with legitimation of existing and future issue. Dated at our residence near Westminster, 4 September 1523. *Reg. Wolsey (York)*, fol. 130v.

[**15**] A bull of Clement VII authorizing William Bettis, BCL,[15] rector of Grasmere (*Gresmere*) par. ch. in Richmond archdeaconry, York dioc., to receive and retain the rectories of Harlington (*Hardelyngton*), London dioc., and Coulsdon (*Cullesdon*), Winchester dioc., in union with Grasmere, notes that Cardinal Wolsey as legate *a latere* had under a papal faculty dispensed Bettis to receive and retain two incompatible benefices and be absent from these benefices for seven years while at university for the sake of study or at the Roman curia. Dated at St Peter's, Rome, 26 November 1523.[16] *Reg. Fox, 5*, fols 63r–4r.

[**16**] Letter of Cardinal Wolsey as legate *a latere* of Clement VII to Henry VIII and his realm dispensing Richard Clerk[17] and Cecily Reynold', Coventry and Lichfield dioc., under a faculty of Leo X confirmed by Clement VII to dispense by apostolic authority men and women of that realm to marry in the third or third and fourth degrees of consanguinity and affinity or to remain married if they contracted and consummated marriage unaware of their relationship in those degrees or even knowing of this, so that they might marry

---

[14]M. Maurice Brekynshall (Birckinshawe) still held this prebend in March 1524 and in 1535 (*Fasti*, VIII. 47).

[15]Probably not the William Bettes noted in *BRUO, 1501–1540*, 47, and Venn, I. 146; or William Walsingham *alias* Bett, Norwich dioc., in *CPL*, XX, no. 1418.

[16]An entry preceding this bull in *Reg. Fox, 5*, fol. 63r, records his collation as rector of Cullesdon on 2 February 1523/4.

[17]Probably not the Richard Clerk, Lincoln dioc., recorded in *CPL*, XIX, nos 1246, 1550.

in the third degree of consanguinity with legitimation of future issue. Dated in our residence near Westminster, 13 June 1524. *Reg. Blythe*, fol. 14r.[18]

[**17**] Letter of Cardinal Wolsey as legate *a latere* of Clement VII to Henry VIII and his realm dispensing William Marschall,[19] rector of Harpsden (*Haspiden*) par. ch., Lincoln dioc., under a faculty of Leo X confirmed by Clement VII, to receive and retain an additional incompatible benefice and be absent from any of his benefices while resident in another or studying at a university. Dated at our residence near Westminster, 2 January 1524/5. *Reg. Longland*, fol. 84r–v.

[**18**] Letter of Cardinal Wolsey as legate *a latere* of Clement VII to Henry VIII and his realm dispensing Thomas Molence, rector of Blackland (*Blakland*) par. ch. or free chapel, Salisbury dioc., to receive and retain an additional incompatible benefice with cure of souls and be absent from any of his benefices while resident in another or studying at a university. Dated at our residence near Westminster, 1 February 1524/5.[20] Below: 'R. Toneys' (right); note authenticating Wolsey's seal. *Reg. Campeggio*, fol. 78v.

[**19**] Letter of Cardinal Wolsey as legate *a latere* of Clement VII to Henry VIII and his realm dispensing John (D)evenyshe, formerly prior of Poughley (*Poghley*) Priory,[21] OSA, Salisbury dioc., professed in Bradenstoke (*Bradnestoke*) Priory, OSA, Salisbury dioc., and ordained as a priest, to receive and retain an incompatible benefice with or without cure of souls, wear his habit under secular priest's garb and be absent from his benefice. Dated at our residence near Westminster, 12 February 1524/5. *Reg. Campeggio*, fol. 73r.

[**20**] Letter of Cardinal Wolsey as legate *a latere* of Clement VII to Henry VIII and his realm dispensing John Som(er), canon of

---

[18] Recorded in the section of the register concerning Coventry archdeaconry.

[19] Possibly the William Marshall' *alias* Baker, Coventry and Lichfield dioc., who obtained a papal dispensation on 9 January 1516 to receive a benefice on reaching his nineteenth year and becoming a clerk, and an additional incompatible benefice on reaching his twentieth year, and to be absent from any of his benefices while resident in another, the Roman curia or a university (*CPL*, XX, no. 550); cf. Appendix 3. **128**. A William Marschall, rector of Todwick par. ch. (W. Yorks.), York dioc., was granted a papal dispensation on 16 April 1507 to hold an additional incompatible benefice (*CPL*, XVIII, no. 720).

[20] The same letter occurs without these subscriptions in *Reg. Ghinucci*, 2, pp. 176–177, where the supplicant's surname is spelled 'Molente' and Blackland, 'Blackeland'.

[21] Poughley Priory (Berks.) was suppressed by Wolsey in 1525 for its assets to be converted to the use of the Cardinal's College at Oxford (Knowles & Hadcock, 143, 171); cf. **22**n John Devynyshe had been a canon of Bradenstoke Priory (Wilts.) before his election as prior of Poughley in 1521 (*Heads of Religious Houses*, III. 507); by 1525 John Somers appears to have succeeded him as prior (see **20**n).

Bradenstoke (*Bradenestok*) Priory, OSA, Salisbury dioc.,[22] who was professed and became a priest in that priory, to receive and retain a benefice with cure of souls as if a secular clerk, wear his habit under secular priest's garb and be absent from his benefice while studying at a university. Dated at our residence near Westminster, 12 February 1524/5. Below: 'R. Toneys' (right); note signed 'T. Candell' (with notarial sign) authenticating Wolsey's seal. *Reg. Campeggio*, fol. 83r.

[21] Letter of Cardinal Wolsey as legate *a latere* dispensing Thomas Thebolde, scholar, Rochester dioc., so that on becoming a clerk he might receive and retain any incompatible benefice with or without cure and be absent from it while attending a university, despite his defect of age, he being in his seventeenth year. Dated at our residence near Westminster, 16 February 1524/5.[23] *Reg. Fisher*, fol. 124r.

[22] Letter of Cardinal Wolsey as legate *a latere* of Clement VII to Henry VIII and his realm dispensing Alexander Colyns, recently prior of the house or priory of Daventry (*Daventre*),[24] OSB, Lincoln dioc., dispensing him by papal authority to wear his regular habit under secular priest's garb. Dated at our residence near Westminster, 7 March 1524/5. *Reg. Tunstall*, fols 85v–6r.

[23] Letter of Cardinal Wolsey as legate *a latere* dispensing Alexander Colyns, recently prior of the house or monastery of Daventry (*Daventre*), OSB, Lincoln dioc., who had been professed in OSB at the monastery of BVM, Glastonbury, Bath and Wells dioc.,[25] and then elected as prior of Daventry, which office he had resigned after holding it for some years, so that he might transfer from OSB to St Bartholomew's Hospital, OSA, West Smithfield, London dioc.

<hr>

[22] Probably John Somers, the last prior of Poughley Priory, who surrendered the priory at its dissolution on 14 February 1525, and presumably not the same person as John Devynyshe, also prior of Poughley, as Smith speculates (*Heads of Religious Houses*, III. 507; see **19** above).

[23] Following this letter in *Reg. Fisher*, fols 124r–125r, is a notarial procuratorium of Thomas Thebalde constituting a proctor to receive a benefice on his behalf, dated at St John's College, Cambridge, 17 February 1524/5; and at fol. 125r an entry recording the institution of Thomas Thebot, scholar, as perpetual vicar of Kemsing (*Kempfynd*) par. ch. with the chapel of Seal (*Seale*), Rochester dioc., on 24 February 1524/5.

[24] Daventry Priory (Northants.) was a Cluniac house suppressed by Wolsey in 1525 for its assets to be converted to the use of the Cardinal's College at Oxford (Knowles & Hadcock, 96, 99); cf. **19**n. As its prior Colyns was elected in 1515, surrendered the priory on 16 February 1525 at its dissolution, and resigned four days later; he became master of St Bartholomew's Hospital, Smithfield, on 6 April 1525 (see **23**n below) and died on 25 June 1528 (*Heads of Religious Houses*, III. 235–236).

[25] As a monk of Glastonbury Abbey (Somerset) he was granted a papal dispensation on 20 August 1512 to hold a secular benefice with or without cure of souls, and obtained a papal indult on 4 April 1513 licensing him to be absent from any of his benefices while resident in another, or in his monastery, the Roman curia or a university (*CPL*, XIX, no. 866; XX, no. 40).

Dated at our residence near Westminster, 18 March 1524/5.²⁶ *Reg. Tunstall*, fol. 85r–v.

[**24**] Letter of Cardinal Wolsey as legate *a latere* dispensing Christopher Fowey, acolyte, Salisbury dioc., to be ordained to all holy, even priest's, orders by any Catholic bishop on any three Sundays or feasts even *extra tempora a iure statuta* and licensing any bishop to ordain him thus. Dated at our residence near Westminster, 28 March 1525. Below: 'R. Toneys' (right); note signed 'Tho. Candell' authenticating Wolsey's seal. *Reg. Campeggio*, fol. 77r.

[**25**] An entry in an ordination list dated 1 April 1525 recording the promotion as priest of Robert Danyell,²⁷ St David's dioc., to the title of Carmarthen Priory, [OSA], St David's dioc., notes that he was 'sufficienter dimissus' and had been legitimately dispensed by the lord Cardinal [Wolsey] as legate *a latere* from defect of age, being aged twenty-two. *Reg. Clerke*, fol. 114v.

[**26**] Letter of Cardinal Wolsey as legate *a latere* of Clement VII to Henry VIII and his realm absolving Robert Stoone, canon of Croxton monastery, OPrem, Lincoln dioc., under a papal faculty, from apostasy for not wearing his habit etc. and from excommunication, suspension, interdict and other ecclesiastical censures, and dispensing him to receive and retain an incompatible benefice, wear his habit under secular priest's garb and be absent from that benefice for the sake of university study. Dated at our residence near Westminster, 1 April 1525. Below: 'R. Tonys'. *Reg. Nykke, 4*, fols 197v–8r.

[**27**] Letter of Cardinal Wolsey as legate *a latere* of Clement VII to Henry VIII and his realm dispensing John de la Lynde, scholar, Salisbury dioc., from defect of age, he being in his sixteenth year, so that he may receive and retain a benefice with cure of souls after becoming a clerk. Dated at our residence near Westminster, 1 June 1525. Below: 'R. Toneys' (on right); note signed 'Tho. Candell' authenticating Wolsey's seal. *Reg. Campeggio*, fol. 74v.

[**28**] Letter of Cardinal Wolsey as legate *a latere* of Clement VII to Henry VIII and his realm dispensing William Willoughby, scholar, Salisbury dioc. (under a faculty of Leo X confirmed by Clement VII to dispense any in that realm from defect of birth so that they may be promoted to all holy, even priest's, orders and receive and retain two compatible benefices with or without cure of souls) from his defect

---

²⁶Following this letter in *Reg. Tunstall*, fol. 86r–v, are the sentence of Geoffrey Wharton, DCnL, vicar-general-in-spirituals of the bishop of London, confirming the election of Colyns as master or *custos* of St Bartholomew's Hospital, West Smithfield, London; Colyns's oath of obedience as confirmed master-elect to the bishop; *acta* for confirming his election and the vicar general's mandate for installing him as master-elect, dated 6 April 1525.

²⁷Probably not the Robert Danell, advocate of the Court of Arches in 1511 and DCn & CL by 1512 (*CPL*, XIX, nos 549, 870).

of birth, he being born of an unmarried man and an unmarried woman, so that he may be ordained to all holy, even priest's, orders and receive and retain two compatible benefices with or without cure of souls. Dated at our residence near Westminster, 4 July 1525. *Reg. Campeggio*, fol. 72v.

[**29**] Letter of Cardinal Wolsey as legate *a latere* dispensing Walter Gwilym, deacon, Llandaff dioc., from defect of age, he being in his twenty-third year, so that he may be ordained to the holy order of the priesthood by any Catholic bishop and minister in it. Dated at our residence near Westminster, 14 August 1525.[28] *Reg. Campeggio*, fol. 57r.

[**30**] Letter of Cardinal Wolsey as legate *a latere* dispensing Thomas Malett, BA,[29] Bath and Wells dioc., (whom Wolsey had dispensed so that he might be promoted to the holy order of the priesthood in his twenty-third year by any Catholic bishop and minister in it), now being in his twenty-fourth year and ordained as a priest, so that he may receive and retain an incompatible benefice with cure of souls. Dated at our residence near Westminster, 2 September 1525. Below: note signed 'Tho. Candell' authenticating Wolsey's seal. *Reg. Campeggio*, fol. 74r.

[**31**] Incomplete letter of Cardinal Wolsey as legate *a latere* for life [dispensing] William Cooke, clerk, Winchester dioc., under a faculty of Clement VII to dispense by apostolic authority any resident within his legation from defect of age so that on reaching the age of fifteen and while in their sixteenth year they may receive and retain any incompatible benefice with or without cure of souls;[30] (following an entry recording Cooke's admission as rector of Ashley (*Assheley*) par. ch., Winchester dioc., on 15 September 1525). *Reg. Fox, 5*, fol. 109v.

[**32**] An entry in an ordination list dated 23 September 1525 recording the promotion as priest of Gwilym Morgan, Llandaff dioc.,[31] to the title of Llantarnam (*Lanternam*) monastery, [OCist], Llandaff dioc., notes that he was 'sufficienter dimissus' and had been dispensed by the lord Cardinal [Wolsey] as legate *a latere*, being aged twenty-three.[32] *Reg. Clerke*, fol. 116v.

---

[28] = Appendix 2. **9**. This follows an entry in an ordination list recording Gwilym's promotion to the priesthood on 23 September 1525, under letters dimissory and this dispensation, to the title of St Mary's Priory, [OSB], Usk, Llandaff dioc.

[29] Presumably the Thomas Mallette who determined as BA of Oxford University in Lent 1524 and was admitted as rector of North Wraxall (Wilts.) on 22 November 1525 and rector of Charlynch (Somerset) on 4 November 1526 (*BRUO, 1501–1540*, 374, 689).

[30] The text ends reciting Cooke's petition seeking a benefice to support his study of letters.

[31] Probably not the same man as William Here *alias* Morgan, St David's dioc., recorded in *CPL*, XX, no. 1194.

[32] = Appendix 2. **14** (which dates Wolsey's letter dispensing him 14 August 1525).

[33] An entry in an ordination list dated 23 September 1525 recording the promotion as priest of Ieuan ap Ieuan (*John*), Llandaff dioc.,[33] to the title of Margam (*Morgan*) monastery, [OCist], Llandaff dioc., notes that he was 'sufficienter dimissus' and had been dispensed by the lord Cardinal [Wolsey] as legate *a latere* from defect [of age], having reached the age of twenty-two and a half that Michaelmas [29 September].[34] *Reg. Clerke*, fol. 116v.

[34] Letter of Cardinal Wolsey as legate *a latere* dispensing William Tisehurst, apostolic protonotary, rector of Coulsdon (*Cowllesdon*) par. ch., Winchester dioc., our chaplain and familiar, to unite that church with Horsmonden par. ch., Rochester dioc., to which Henry Percy, Earl of Northumberland, has recently presented him as rector. Dated at our manor of Hampton Court, 30 September 1525. *Reg. Fisher*, fols 131v–2v.

[35] Letter of Cardinal Wolsey as legate *a latere* dispensing Francis Yong, clerk, Salisbury dioc., from defect of age, he being in his twentieth year, so that he may receive and retain an incompatible benefice with cure of souls and that on reaching the age of twenty-three he may be ordained to all, even holy and priest's, orders by any Catholic bishop and minister in them. Dated at our residence at Hampton Court, 4 October 1525. *Reg. Campeggio*, fol. 73r.

[36] Letter of Cardinal Wolsey as legate *a latere* dispensing Thomas Silke, BA,[35] Worcester dioc., to be promoted by any Catholic bishop to all, even holy and priest's, orders, even two on the same day, on any Sundays or feasts *extra tempora a iure statuta* and conceding a licence and faculty to any Catholic bishop to promote him thus. Dated at our manor of Hampton Court, 9 October 1525.[36] *Reg. Clerke*, fol. 117r (= *Reg. Clerke ed.*, no. 480).

[37] Letter of Cardinal Wolsey as legate *a latere* dispensing John Stavarte, clerk, perpetual vicar of Longstock (*Langstok*) par. ch., Winchester dioc., to be absent from any of his benefices while resident in another, studying at university or serving the King or Queen of England or any duke or marquess and living at their expense, and

---

[33] Probably not the same man as John Ieuan, BCnL, in Appendix 2. **29**.

[34] = Appendix 2. **18** (which dates Wolsey's letter dispensing him 26 August 1525).

[35] Thomas Sylke determined as BA of Oxford University in 1523, incepting as MA on 2 July 1526, and was in priest's orders by January 1526. He held various ecclesiastical benefices between 1539 and 1574, including the provostship of Kalendars in All Saints', Bristol, and a canonry at Bristol (*BRUO, 1501–1540*, 552).

[36] A note preceding this entry in Clerke's register records that on 28 October 1525 Thomas Silke, BA, acolyte, Worcester dioc., 'sufficienter dimissus' by his bishop, sought promotion to subdeacon and deacon's orders to the title of the house of white nuns of 'Whitston' [Whistones Priory, OCist], Worcester dioc., by virtue of this letter of Cardinal Wolsey as legate *a latere*, and that he was promoted to these orders on Sunday, 29 October.

to receive the fruits of that vicarage and any other benefices held by him, and relaxing any oath of residence sworn by him. Dated at our residence near Westminster, 15 October 1525.[37] Hampshire Record Office (Winchester), 21M65/B1/3 (Visitation Book for Winchester dioc., 1527–8), p. 44.

[38] Letter of Cardinal Wolsey as legate *a latere* of Clement VII to Henry VIII and his realm dispensing Robert Garret, acolyte, Lincoln dioc., to be ordained to all holy, even priest's, orders *extra tempora a iure statuta*, even two on one day, by any Catholic bishop and minister in them and licensing any bishop to ordain him thus.[38] Dated at our residence near Westminster, 12 December 1525. *Reg. Campeggio*, fol. 58v.

[39] Letter of Cardinal Wolsey as legate *a latere* of Clement VII to Henry VIII and his realm dispensing Ralph Bollum, STP,[39] perpetual vicar of St John the Baptist's par. ch., Peterborough, Lincoln dioc., to receive and retain an additional incompatible benefice with cure of souls and be absent from any of his benefices while resident in another, studying at a university or serving the aforesaid king, Queen Katharine or any duke or marquess and living at their expense. Dated at our residence near Westminster, 12 January 1525/6. *Reg. Longland*, fols 152v–3r.

[40] Letter of Clement VII dispensing Henry Willoughby,[40] rector of Wylye (*Wylly*) par. ch., Salisbury dioc., (who claimed that Cardinal Wolsey as legate *a latere* had dispensed him from defect of birth, he being born of an unmarried man and an unmarried woman, so that he might be promoted to all, even holy and priest's, orders by any catholic bishop on any Sundays or feasts *extra tempora a iure statuta*, and receive and retain two compatible benefices with or without cure of souls, by virtue of which he was promoted to all holy orders *extra tempora*, ministered in them and obtained Chicklade (*Chekeland*) par. ch., Salisbury dioc., then exchanged it for Wylye, but now some doubt that Wolsey's faculty extended to illegitimate men being ordained

---

[37] = Appendix 2. **35**. Appended to the record of the visitation conducted on 9 September 1527 when presumably this dispensation was exhibited to justify Stavart's non-residence; noted by Houlbrooke, 185.

[38] = Appendix 2. **61**. This appears in an ordination list dated 24 February 1526.

[39] Probably the Ralph Bolland or Bollam who was MA of Cambridge University by 1507, DTh by 1520–1521 and University Preacher in 1510–1511, and who was possibly the 'Mr Dr Bowlam', rector of Yate (Gloucs.) before 1532 and non-resident at the episcopal visitation in 1551; he died c.1552 (Venn, I. 174).

[40] Henry Willoughby was admitted as BA of Oxford University on 15 July 1528; in priest's orders by December 1527; admitted as rector of All Saints', Cricklade (Wilts.), in 1525, ~aining so and rector of Wylye (Wilts.) till death; and died in 1581 (*BRUO, 1501–1540*, 631). ~itted to Wylye rectory before June 1515 when Thomas Martyn held it by L, XX, no. 486).

extra tempora, so he feared contracting *inhabilitas*), to minister in his orders, retain Wylye and receive and retain an additional incompatible benefice, and be absent from either of them, and clearing him of any *inhabilitas* and infamy. Dated at St Peter's, Rome, 13 January 1525. *Reg. Campeggio*, fol. 72r.

[**41**] Letter of Cardinal Wolsey as legate *a latere* dispensing James Smythe alias Lyne, scholar, Worcester dioc., from defect of birth, he being born of an unmarried man and an unmarried woman, so that he may be promoted to all holy orders by any Catholic bishop and minister in them and receive and retain any benefice even with cure of souls, and conceding licence for him to receive such orders and any bishop to confer them despite his originating in Worcester dioc. Dated in our residence near Westminster, 25 January 1525/6.[41] Copy headed 'Tenor dispensacionis ipsius Reverendi Patris in hiis quibus cum Iacobo Smythe subdiacono existit dispensatum sit sequitur'. In margin in a later hand: 'dispensatio facta Iohanni Smyth de soluto genito et soluta ut possit ad omnes sacros ordines admitti et promoveri non obstante defectu natalium'. *Reg. Clerke*, fol. 119r–v (= *Reg. Clerke ed.*, no. 480).

[**42**] Letter of Cardinal Wolsey as legate *a latere* dispensing Robert Duke, acolyte, Salisbury dioc., from defect of age, he being in his twenty-third year, so that he may be promoted to all holy, even priest's, orders by any Catholic bishop, even two on one day, and minister in them and licensing any bishop to ordain him thus. Dated at our residence near Westminster, 31 January 1525/6.[42] Below: 'R. Toneys' (on right); note signed 'Tho. Candell' authenticating Wolsey's seal. *Reg. Campeggio*, fol. 59r.

[**43**] Letter of Cardinal Wolsey as legate *a latere* licensing Thomas Holson, rector of St George's par. ch., Fovant (*Fovent*), Salisbury dioc., to be absent from that church and receive its fruits for five years. Dated at our residence near Westminster, 7 February 1525/6. Below: note signed 'Tho. Candell' (with notarial sign) authenticating Wolsey's seal. *Reg. Campeggio*, fol. 74v.

---

[41] An entry in an ordination list dated 17 March 1525/6 records that James Smythe, Worcester dioc., was promoted as subdeacon to the title of the house of St John, Wells, and had been dispensed from defect of birth and 'sufficienter dimissus' by the Reverend father Thomas, lord Cardinal of York, as legate *a latere* 'sub tenore infrascripto' (*Reg. Clerke*, fol. 118v). An entry in an ordination list dated 26 May 1526 records that he was promoted as priest to the title of St John's Hospital, Wells, 'dispensative dimissus ut patet in precedentibus' (*Reg. Clerke*, fol. 121r). Possibly the same man as James Lome in Appendix 2. **104**. Probably not the James Lyne, canon of Dunkeld by 1510, in *CPL*, XVIII, no. 61.

[42] This appears in an ordination list at fol. 59r–v including an entry recording Duke's promotion as subdeacon and deacon, both to the title of St Mary's Abbey, Vale Royal, OCist, Lincoln dioc., on 31 March 1526.

[**44**] Letter of Cardinal Wolsey as legate *a latere* dispensing Robert Bysse, DCL,[43] rector of Batcombe (*Badcombe*) par. ch., Bath and Wells dioc., to receive and retain an additional incompatible benefice and be absent from any of his benefices while resident in another or studying at university. Dated at our residence near Westminster, 21 February 1525/6. In margin: 'Copia pluralitatis magistri Roberti Bysse'. *Reg. Clerke*, fols 33v–34r (= *Reg. Clerke ed.*, no. 343).

[**45**] Letter of Cardinal Wolsey as legate *a latere* dispensing Anthony Skevington, BCnL,[44] rector of Lutterworth (*Lutterworthe*) par. ch., Lincoln dioc., to receive and retain an additional incompatible benefice with cure of souls and be absent from any of his benefices while resident in another, studying at a university or serving King Henry, Queen Katharine, or any duke or marquess and living at their expense. Dated at our residence near Westminster, 1 March 1525/6. *Reg. Longland*, fol. 125r–v.

[**46**] Letter of Cardinal Wolsey as legate *a latere* dispensing John Potte, acolyte, York dioc., to be promoted to all holy, even priest's, orders by any Catholic bishop *extra tempora a iure statuta*, even two on one day, and minister in them. Dated at our residence near Westminster, 5 March 1525/6.[45] Below: 'R. Toneys' (right); note signed 'T. Candell' (with notarial sign) authenticating Wolsey's seal. *Reg. Campeggio*, fol. 77r.

[**47**] Letter of Cardinal Wolsey as legate *a latere* dispensing Brian Carter, scholar, London dioc., from his defect of age, he being in his sixteenth year, so that after becoming a clerk he may receive and retain any incompatible benefice with or without cure of souls and be absent from it for seven years while studying at a university. Dated at our residence near Westminster, 26 March 1526. *Reg. Longland*, fol. 129v.

---

[43] = Appendix 2. **88**; see also **69** below. Robert Bysse, Bath and Wells dioc., was fellow of All Souls College, Oxford, from 1502, still in 1517. He supplicated for DCL at Oxford University on 10 December 1507; this doctorate was incorporated at the Roman Curia on 2 November 1513; and he supplicated for DCnL at Oxford University in 1518 and 1519 after thirteen years of study in canon law, being dispensed in 1532. He was ordained as priest on 6 June 1517 and held several ecclesiastical benefices, including Batcombe rectory (Somerset), from 5 September 1524 till death, and canonry at Wells by 1536. He was appointed as vicar general of John Clerk, bishop of Bath and Wells, on 4 June 1524, and was the vicar general's deputy in 1527. He was dead by April 1547 (*BRUO*, I. 335–336; *Reg. Clerke ed.*, p. x, nos 178, 184, 188, 255, 294, 322, 339–340, 343, 460, 575, 647, 939).

[44] He was BCL of Cambridge University by 1522–1523; he was perhaps second son of Sir William of Skevington (Leics.), Lord Deputy of Ireland, and possibly rector of Seaton (Rut.) and rector of Glaston Hill (Hants.?) till 1554, when he died (Venn, IV. 84).

[45] Following this entry in Campeggio's Register is a letter of Thomas [Vivian], bishop of *Megariensis* (Megara, Greece), stating that on 17 March 1525/6 he ordained Potte as priest under this dispensation in the conventual church of St Mary Overy, Southwark, Winchester dioc., with a note authenticating the letter's seal as that of Thomas [Vivian], Prior of Bodmin (on whom see *Heads of Religious Houses*, III. 383).

[48] Letter of Cardinal Wolsey as legate *a latere* dispensing Henry Marshall,[46] BA, rector of St Nicholas's par. ch., St Nicholas (*Seint colas*), Llandaff dioc., to receive and retain an additional incompatible benefice with cure of souls and be absent from any of his benefices while resident in another or studying at a university. Dated at our residence near Westminster, 20 April 1526. *Reg. Longland*, fols 128v–9r.

[49] Letter of Cardinal Wolsey as legate *a latere* dispensing Ninian Markenfeld, knight, and Eleanor Clifford, York dioc., under a faculty of Leo X confirmed by Clement VII to dispense men and women in his legation to marry in the third or third and fourth degrees of consanguinity and affinity or to remain married even if they contracted marriage aware of such impediments, with legitimation of existing and future issue, so that they may remain married, having contracted marriage while formerly unaware of their kinship in the third and third degrees of consanguinity [*in margin*: and affinity], with legitimation of existing and future issue. Dated at our residence near Westminster, 18 May 1526. Below: 'R. Toneis'. *Reg. Wolsey (York)*, fol. 130r.

[50] A list of papal 'privileges' and dispensations granted to M. John Alen, DCn & CL,[47] refers to a letter of Cardinal Wolsey as legate *a latere* authorizing the union of Little Wilbraham par. ch., Ely dioc., on Alen's admission as rector there, to Monks Risborough (*Monk Ryseborough*) par. ch. (subject to Canterbury), Lincoln dioc., dated under Wolsey's seal 3 June 1526.[48] *Reg. West*, fol. 36v.

---

[46] Perhaps the Henry Marshall admitted as BA of Oxford University on 11 July 1520; rector of Ickleford (Herts.) in 1526; and admitted as vicar of Pirton (Herts.) on 1 May 1526, vacating this post in April 1530 (*BRUO, 1501–1540*, 380).

[47] John Alen, London dioc., born in 1476, entered Peterhouse, Cambridge, in 1495, becoming fellow, 1496–1504; incepted as MA of Cambridge University in 1498; was DCn & CL of a foreign university by 1508 and obtained a grace to incorporate this doctorate at Cambridge University in 1522–1523. He was dispensed for ordination to the priesthood below the canonical age on 8 March 1499 (see n. 48 below) and ordained as priest on 25 May 1499. He held numerous ecclesiastical benefices including Chislet vicarage (Kent) from 1503; Sundridge vicarage (Kent), 1508–1528; the rural deanery of Monks Risborough (Bucks.), 1512–1528; South Ockendon rectory (Essex), 1516–1526; Calipolis archdeaconry from 1518; canonries at Lincoln (1503–1528), Westbury-on-Trym (from 1505, still in 1508), Southwell (1526–1528), St Paul's London (1527–1528), and Exeter (1528); and was provided as Archbishop of Dublin on 3 September 1529, till death. He was also chaplain of the English Hospice at Rome by 1502 and its acting warden, 1504–1511; legatine commissary of Cardinal Wolsey, 1523–1529; and Chancellor of Ireland, 1528–1532. He was an unpopular agent of Wolsey and fined £1466 13s 4d on the latter's fall in 1529 for offences against the statute of *praemunire*; he complained of his impoverishment to Thomas Cromwell in 1532, after being pardoned as Wolsey's commissary and chancellor of Ireland. He was murdered on 27 July 1534 by Irish rebels following Lord Thomas Fitzgerald (*BRUC*, 8–9, 669).

[48] This list, beginning in *Reg. West*, fol. 36r, also refers to the following items: (1) 'litteras propter defectum etatis' dated 8 March 1499/1500; (2) 'bullam apostolicam trialitatis' dated at St Peter's, Rome, 11 February 1503/4; (3) 'bullam unionis' of Chislet (*Chestlett*) vicarage,

[51] Letter of Cardinal Wolsey as legate *a latere* dispensing William Breton, MA,[49] rector of Stour Prevost (*Stowre prialaux*) par. ch., Salisbury dioc., to receive and retain an additional incompatible benefice and be absent from any of his benefices while resident in another, studying at university or serving King Henry, Queen Katharine, or any duke or marquess and living at their expense. Dated at our residence near Westminster, 10 June 1526. Signed under plica on right: 'Toneys' (with scribal sign). Endorsed: 'Dispensation for Non-residence granted to W. Breton, Anno 1526. by The Archbishop of York..'; 'Exhibitum per dominum Alex' Boston' procuratorem Willelmi breton' retronominati iiii Maii Anno 1537'; 'Exemplatum per mess.r.' ; 'Breton' Sar.' 43.4 × 26.2 cm. Plica: 4.3 cm. Slits for seal strings. *LPL, Papal Document 132* (original).

[52] Letter of Cardinal Wolsey as legate *a latere* dispensing John Loo, friar of the Carmelite house of Aylesford (*Aylefford*), co. Kent, Rochester dioc., to receive and retain any incompatible benefice with or without cure of souls, wear his habit under secular priest's garb and be absent from that benefice while attending a university. Dated at our residence near Westminster, 2 July 1526. *Reg. Fisher*, fol. 134r–v.

[53] Letter of Cardinal Wolsey as legate *a latere* for life dispensing Laurence Holande of London and Elizabeth Shakerley of Ditton (*Dytton*),[50] Rochester dioc., under a faculty of Leo X confirmed by Clement VII to dispense those resident within his legation to marry in the third or third and fourth degrees of consanguinity and affinity with legitimation of future issue, so that they might marry in second and third degrees of affinity with legitimation of future issue. Dated

Canterbury dioc., to canonry and prebend of (Leicester) St Margaret's in Lincoln cathedral, dated at Ostia (*Ostre*), 12 April 1505; (4) 'bullam unionis' of Sundridge (*Sindrig*) ch., Rochester dioc., to canonry and prebend of Westbury(-on-Trym), dated at St Peter's, Rome, 19 June 1508; (5) 'bullam apostolicam unionis' of South Ockendon (*Sowthwokyngton*) par. ch., London dioc., to canonry and prebend of Asgarby (*Askerbye*) in Lincoln cathedral, dated Florence 7 February 1515/16. The list follows a memorandum dated 8 June 1526 on fols 35v–6v that M. Anthony Husye appeared on behalf of Sir Richard Fowler, patron of Little Wilbraham par. ch., before Nicholas West, bishop of Ely, exhibiting these papal *privilegia* and dispensations as well as letters of presentation to that church in favour of Alen, and that West empowered his commissary general or official M. Robert Clyff to inspect the *privilegia* and dispensations. The union of Chislet with Leicester St Margaret's prebendary authorized by item 4 was not acted on since Alen was not admitted to the prebend (*BRUC*, 8). Item 3 (dispensing him to hold three incompatible benefices and be absent from any of them) was copied into the Vatican registers, where it is dated 13 (not 11) February 1504, and items 4 and 5 were copied into the Lateran registers (*CPL*, XVIII, no. 142; xix, no. 858; XX, nos 582, 621).

[49] Possibly the William Breton admitted to incept in Arts at Cambridge University in 1486–1487, becoming MA, who was chaplain to King Henry VII in 1485; master of St Katherine's College by the Tower of London from 1485; vicar of Dullingham (Cambs.), 1488–1534; and vicar of Bottisham (Cambs.), 1534–1535 (*BRUC*, 92).

[50] Her place of origin is named in the margin only.

at our residence near Westminster, 26 September 1526. *Reg. Fisher*, fol. 139r.

[54] Letter dimissory of Cardinal Wolsey as legate *a latere* dispensing John Parker, Rochester dioc., scholar, to be promoted to all holy, even priest's, orders by any Catholic bishop on any Sundays or feasts *extra tempora a iure statuta* and minister in the same. Dated at our residence near Westminster, 9 October 1526. *Reg. Blythe*, fol. 42v.[51]

[55] Letter of Cardinal Wolsey as legate *a latere* for life dispensing Thomas Waterman, BCnL,[52] rector of St Michael's par. ch., Geldeston (*Goldeston*), Norwich dioc., under a papal faculty, to receive and retain an additional incompatible benefice and be absent from any of his benefices while resident in another or studying at university. Dated at our residence near Westminster, 18 November 1526. Below: 'Iohannes Hughes / Actuarius et / Registrarius' (left); 'Willelmus Claiburn' (right). *Reg. Nykke, 4*, fols 108v–9v.

[56] Letter of Cardinal Wolsey as legate *a latere* for life authorizing Roger Stocley, MA,[53] canon of the nunnery of the BVM, Winchester, OSB, and prebendary of Itchen Abbas (*Ichen*) in the same nunnery, under a faculty of Clement VII to unite parish churches and other benefices of any resident within his legation, even if not his familiars, provided that they are nobles or graduates, to other benefices obtained by them, to unite Brightwell par. ch., Salisbury dioc., to his canonry and prebend. Dated at our residence near Westminster, 26 November 1526.[54] *Reg. Fox, 5*, fols 119v–20v.

[51] Recorded in the section of the register concerning Derby archdeaconry.

[52] Possibly Thomas Waterman, BCnL of Cambridge University by 1515–1516 (Venn, IV. 346).

[53] Roger Stockley, Coventry and Lichfield dioc., was fellow (1506–1520) and warden (1534–1536) of All Souls College, Oxford; incepted as MA of Oxford University on 2 July 1509; was ordained as priest on 21 May, 1513; held numerous ecclesiastical benefices, including the prebend of Itchen Abbas in St Mary's Abbey, Winchester, to which he was admitted on 30 October 1522, till death; and was dead by January 1558 (*BRUO, 1501–1540*, 541).

[54] This letter precedes in *Reg. Fox, 5*, fol. 118r–v, an entry recording the collation of Roger Stocley, MA, as rector of Alresford par. ch., Winchester dioc., subject to payment of an annual pension of £16 13s 4d to M. Ralph Lexton, the former rector, for life, on 29 December 1526; and a note on fol. 118v that on the same day Stocley exhibited to Bishop Richard Fox of Winchester two rescripts of Clement VII, the first for plurality and the second for the union of Warnford par. ch. to Itchen Abbas (*Ichyn*) prebend in the nunnery of the BVM, Winchester, and this letter of Cardinal Wolsey, legate *a latere*, for the union of Brightwell par. ch. to the same prebend. The two papal 'rescripts' are then recited: a bull of Clement VII (on fols 118v–119r) dispensing Roger Stocley, MA, rector of Warnford par. ch., Winchester dioc., to receive and retain an additional incompaible benefice and be absent from any of his benefices while resident in another or the Roman curia or studying at a university, dated at St Peter's, Rome, 27 November 1523; a bull of Clement VII (at fol. 119r–v) authorizing Roger Stokley, clerk, prebendary in the nunnery of the BVM, Winchester, OSB, to unite Warnford par. ch., Winchester dioc., to his prebend, dated at St Peters's,

[**57**] Letter of Cardinal Wolsey as legate *a latere* dispensing Brian Nasshe, cantarist of the perpetual chantry for the souls of Thomas Belcher and his wife Christiana in St Stephen's par. ch., Bristol, Worcester dioc., to receive and retain an additional incompatible benefice with cure of souls and be absent from any of his benefices while resident in another or studying at a university. Dated at our residence near Westminster, 15 December 1526. Below: 'Iohannes Hughes / actuarius et registrarius' (left); 'Willelmus Claiburgh / eiusdem reverendissimi patris datarius' (right); note signed 'Tho. Candell' authenticating Wolsey's seal. *Reg. Campeggio*, fol. 75r.

[**58**] Letter of Cardinal Wolsey as legate *a latere* dispensing Thomas Knyght, priest, rector of *Fissherton*[55] par. ch., Salisbury dioc., and perpetual vicar of Steeple Ashton (*Stipellaston*) par. ch., Salisbury dioc., to be absent from both churches and receive their fruits for two years. Dated at our residence near Westminster, 1 January 1526/7.[56] Below: 'Iohannes Hughes / actuarius et registrarius' (left); 'Willelmus Claiburgh / eiusdem reverendissimi / patris / datarius' (right); note signed 'Tho. Candell' authenticating Wolsey's seal. *Reg. Campeggio*, fol. 75v.

[**59**] Letter of Cardinal Wolsey as legate *a latere* dispensing Ralph Grene, rector of Church Lawton (*Church Laton*) par. ch., Coventry and Lichfield dioc., to receive and retain an additional incompatible benefice and be absent from any of his benefices while resident in another or attending a university. Dated at our residence near Westminster, 19 February 1526/7. Note signed Gregory Stonyng (with notarial sign) certifying this as a copy of the original. *Reg. Blythe*, fol. 47v.[57]

[**60**] Letter of Cardinal Wolsey as legate *a latere* dispensing Robert Josepp, BCnL,[58] rector of All Saints' par. ch., Kimcote (*Killmondecote*), Lincoln dioc., to receive and retain an additional incompatible benefice with cure of souls and be absent from any of his benefices while resident in another or studying at a university. Dated at our

Rome, 9 February 1523/4. Wolsey's letter above then follows. Roger Stockley was collated as rector of Warnford (Hants.) on 2 May 1523, till death, and admitted as rector of Brightwell (Berks.) on 20 April 1524, which he was still in 1553, and licensed to exchange one of his four incompatible benefices on 13 February 1540; he also held Alresford rectory (Hants.) till death (*BRUO, 1501–1540*, 541).

[55] Either Fisherton Anger or Fisherton Delamere (both Wilts.).

[56] See **62** below.

[57] Recorded in the section of the register concerning Salop archdeaconry.

[58] Robert Josopp was BA by 1515 and BCL by 1527, probably of Oxford University; was ordained as priest on 3 March 1515; was admitted as rector of Kimcote (Leics.) on 28 February 1516, rector of Ditchampton in Wilton (Wilts.) on 18 March 1527 (until 1530), and vicar of Tolpuddle (Dorset) on 14 June 1530, which he was still in 1535; and was also vicar of Glen Magna (Leics.) in 1544 (*BRUO, 1501–1540*, 685).

residence near Westminster, 11 March 1526/7. Below: 'Iohannes Hughes / actuarius et registrarius' (left); 'Willelmus Claiburgh / eiusdem reverendissimi / patris / datarius' (right); note signed 'Thomas Candell' authenticating Wolsey's seal. *Reg. Campeggio*, fol. 81r.

[**61**] Letter of Cardinal Wolsey as legate *a latere* dispensing John Clappe, clerk, Salisbury or another dioc. of the English realm, from defect of age, he being in his twenty-third year, so that he may be promoted to the priesthood by any Catholic bishop and licensing any bishop to ordain him thus. Dated at our residence near Westminster, 11 April 1527.[59] Below: 'Johannes Hughes / Actuarius et Registrarius' (on left); note signed 'Tho. Candell' authenticating Wolsey's seal. *Reg. Campeggio*, fol. 61r.

[**62**] Letter of Cardinal Wolsey as legate a latere dispensing Thomas Knyght, priest, vicar of Steeple Ashton (*Stiple Aston*) par. ch., Salisbury dioc., (who also held the rectory of *Fissherdon*,[60] Salisbury dioc., by papal dispensation but had not been resident in that vicarage for a year thereby incurring perjury, for breach of his oath to be perpetually resident, and perhaps *inhabilitas*), to hold those churches and minister in his orders, absolving him of that excess and other reserved sins, and clearing him of *inhabilitas* and infamy. Dated at our residence near Westminster, 12(?) April 1527.[61] Below: 'Iohannes Hughes / actuarius et registrarius' (left); note signed 'T. Candell' authenticating Wolsey's seal. *Reg. Campeggio*, fol. 75v.

[**63**] Letter of Cardinal Wolsey as legate *a latere* dispensing Geoffrey Watt', priest, Austin friar of the house of King's Lynn (*Lynne*), Norwich dioc., to receive and retain any incompatible benefice and be absent from it for the sake of study at a university. Dated under our seal at our residence near Westminster, 14 April 1527. Signed below plica on left: 'Iohannes Actuarius et / Hughes [*scribal sign*] Registrarius'. Endorsed: 'Introducta per Robert(um) Hatteley nomine Galfridi Watts iiii[to] Iulii anno 1537'; 'Exemplificatum per Christoforson Norwicen.'; 'Exhibitum in visitacione regia Cowper [*scribal sign*]'; 'Dispensation for Non-Residence granted to Galfrid Watts 152[.]' 38.1 × 20.8 cm. Plica: 3.8 cm. Slits in plica for seal strings. *LPL, Papal Document 133* (original).

[**64**] Letter of Cardinal Wolsey as legate *a latere* dispensing Walter Baron', Salisbury dioc., deacon, from defect of age, he being in his

---

[59] This follows an ordination list including an entry recording the promotion of Clappe, deacon, Bath and Wells dioc., as priest to the title of Abbey 'de bene dona' [probably Bindon Abbey, Dorset], OCist, on 20 April 1527.
[60] On the latter place-name see n. 55.
[61] See **58** above.

twenty-second year, so that he may be promoted to the holy order of the priesthood by any Catholic bishop on reaching the age of twenty-three and minister in it and conceding a licence and faculty to any bishop to ordain him thus. Dated at our residence near Westminster, 17 May 1527.[62] Below: 'Iohannes Hughes actuarius et registrarius' (left); 'W. Claiburgh datarius' (left); note signed 'Tho. Candell' authenticating Wolsey's seal. *Reg. Campeggio*, fol. 61v.

[**65**] Letter of Cardinal Wolsey as legate *a latere* dispensing Richard Pescod, fellow of the College of the BVM in the Soke (*Soca*), Winchester, to retain his fellowship together with Shaw (*Shawe*) par. ch., Salisbury dioc.[63] Dated at our residence near Westminster, 1 June 1527. *Reg. Fox, 5*, fol. 144r–v.

[**66**] Letter of Cardinal Wolsey as legate *a latere* dispensing George Planklnay, Lincoln dioc., MA, acolyte,[64] in his twenty-third year, to be promoted by any Catholic bishop to all, even holy and priest's, orders, even two on the same day, *extra tempora a iure statuta* on any Sundays or feasts, and granting licence and faculty to any bishop to promote him thus. Dated at our residence near Westminster, 6 July 1527. Notarial mark of Gregory Stonyng certifying this as a copy of the original. *Reg. Blythe*, fol. 114r.

[**67**] Letter of Cardinal Wolsey as legate *a latere* dispensing William Philipson, rector of St Wilfrid's par. ch., York, under a papal faculty, to receive and retain an additional incompatible benefice and be absent from any of his benefices while resident in another or studying at university. Dated at our residence near Westminster, 18 August 1527. Below: 'Io. Hughes' (left); 'Willelmus Claiburgh / Datarius' (right). *Reg. Nykke, 4*, fols 114v–15v.

---

[62] This follows an ordination list including an entry recording Baron's promotion as priest to the title of 'Myddelton' monastery [presumably Milton Abbey, OSB, Dorset], Salisbury dioc., under this dispensation on 15 June 1527.

[63] ? = Appendix 3. **153**. Richard Pescod of Newton Valence (Hants.) was admitted to Winchester College as scholar, aged 10, in 1494; to New College, Oxford, as scholar on 9 April 1502 and as fellow in 1504, resigning by August 1506; and to Winchester College as fellow in 1508, probably till death (certainly still in 1527, as above). He was rector of Shaw (Berks.) till death, dying by March 1533 (*BRUO 1501–1540*, 444). The validity of this dispensation was contested by the Winchester consistory court in June 1527; see p. 25.

[64] A false start for this entry breaking off at this point, after three lines, occurs in *Reg. Blythe*, fol. 47r (in the section of the register concerning Salop archdeaconry), naming the addressee as 'Planknay' and marked 'vacat' in the margin. George Plankney entered Merton College, Oxford, in April 1523, becoming fellow (1524–1527), and incepted as MA of Oxford University on 8 April 1527; was rector of St Mary Arches, Exeter, in 1535, till death; was collated as vicar of St Gwinear (Cornw.) on 19 July 1535 and canon and sacrist of Glasney (Cornw.) on 26 February 1537, vacating these posts in December 1535 and July 1537 respectively; and died in August 1537 (*BRUO, 1501–1540*, 451).

[**68**] Letter of Cardinal Wolsey as legate *a latere* dispensing James Robert, acolyte, Canterbury dioc., from defect of age, he being in his twenty-third year, so that he might be promoted to holy, even priest's, orders by any Catholic bishop on any Sundays or feasts *extra tempora statuta a iure*, even two on one day, and minister in them, and conceding a faculty and licence to any bishop to promote him thus. Dated at our residence near Westminster, 23 August 1527.[65] *Reg. Fisher*, fol. 141r.

[**69**] Letter of Cardinal Wolsey as legate *a latere* dispensing Humfrey Dad', perpetual vicar of Compton Chamberlain (*Compton Champrlayn*') par. ch., Salisbury dioc., to be absent from that vicarage and receive its fruits for two years, relaxing his oath of residence. Dated at our residence near Westminster, 6 November 1527. Below: 'Iohannes Hughes / actuarius et registrarius' (left); 'W. Claiburgh / datarius' (right); note signed 'Tho. Candell' authenticating Wolsey's seal. *Reg. Campeggio*, fol. 77v.

[**70**] Letter of Cardinal Wolsey as legate *a latere* licensing Thomas Lililow, BCnL,[66] rector of Matlock par. ch., Coventry and Lichfield dioc., to hold that church in union with Bonsall (*Bontishall*) par. ch., Coventry and Lichfield dioc. Dated at our residence near Westminster, 18 November 1527. *Reg. Blythe*, fol. 41r.[67]

[**71**] Letter of Cardinal Wolsey as legate *a latere* dispensing Richard Hamnair', Coventry and Lichfield dioc., scholar, from defect of age, being in his seventeenth year, so that as soon as he is made a clerk, he may receive and retain an incompatible benefice and be absent from that benefice while attending a university. Dated at our residence near Westminster, 23 December 1527. Below on left: 'Jo. Hughes'. Note signed by Gregory Stonyng (with notarial sign) certifying this as a copy of the original. *Reg. Blythe*, fol. 113v.

[**72**] Letter of Cardinal Wolsey as legate *a latere* dispensing John Alcoke, Coventry and Lichfield dioc., subdeacon, from defect of age, being in his twenty-fourth year, so that he may be promoted by any Catholic bishop to holy, deacon's and priest's orders even on any Sunday or feast *extra tempora a iure statuta* and minister in them, and granting a faculty and licence to any bishop to promote him thus.

---

[65] Following this letter in *Reg. Fisher*, fol. 141v, are James Robert's *littere ordinum* recording his promotion as subdeacon and deacon on 15 September and as priest on 21 September 1527 by virtue of this dispensation; he is said to be of 'Bremhley' (?Bromley, Kent) in the margin.

[66] He was BCnL probably of Oxford University and rector of both Matlock (Derbys.) and Bonsall (Derbys.) by 1535 till death; his other ecclesiastical benefices included a Lincoln canonry; and he died in 1545 (*BRUO, 1501–1540*, 687). Probably the Thomas Lyliwe, Lincoln dioc., who obtained a papal dispensation to hold a plurality of incompatible benefices in 8 Leo X (1520–1521); *CPL*, XX, no. 1380 (rubricella of lost letter).

[67] Recorded in the section of the register concerning Derby archdeaconry.

Dated at our residence near Westminster, 3 January 1527/8. *Reg. Blythe*, fol. 115r.

[**73**] Notarial summary of a letter of Cardinal Wolsey as legate *a latere* dispensing Richard Shepherd,[68] OFM of the house of Bridgnorth (*Brigenorth*), Coventry and Lichfield dioc., to obtain any benefice and wear his habit under secular priest's garb. Dated 6 February 1528 and said to bear Wolsey's seal 'cum subscriptione Datarii et Actuarii facultatum eiusdem [*i.e. John Hughes*]'. *Reg. Ghinucci*, *1*, p. 25.

[**74**] Letter of Cardinal Wolsey as legate *a latere* dispensing Anthony Sherington, acolyte, Coventry and Lichfield dioc., to be promoted by any Catholic bishop to all, even holy and priest's, orders on any Sundays and feasts *extra tempora a iure statuta*, even two orders on the same day. Dated at our residence near Westminster, 23 March 1527/8. *Reg. Blythe*, fol. 61r.[69]

[**75**] Letter of Cardinal Wolsey as legate *a latere* dispensing Thomas Kent, clerk, Winchester dioc., from defect of age, he being in his twenty-third year, so that he may receive and retain an incompatible benefice with cure of souls, be absent from it for seven years while studying at a university and, provided that he becomes a subdeacon in the first two years, not be obliged to be promoted to the other holy, even priest's, orders during those seven years. Dated at our residence near Westminster, 26 May 1528. *Reg. Longland*, fols 158v–9r.

[**76**] Letter of Cardinal Wolsey as legate *a latere* dispensing James Tailio(r), rector of Norton in Hales (*Norton in Hayles*) par. ch., Coventry and Lichfield dioc., to receive and retain an additional incompatible benefice and to absent himself from any of his benefices while resident in another or attending a university. Dated at our residence near Westminster, 1 June 1528. *Reg. Blythe*, fol. 64r.[70]

[**77**] Letter of Cardinal Wolsey as legate *a latere* dispensing Henry Sampson, priest, perpetual vicar of Wood Ditton (*Woddytton*) par. ch. with chapel of Newmarket, Norwich dioc., to receive and retain an additional incompatible benefice and be absent from them while studying at university. Dated at our residence near Westminster, 29 July 1528. Signed under plica: 'Io. Hughes' (left); 'W. Claiburgh datarius' (right, with scribal sign). Endorsed: 'Exhibit(a) per W. Damosell nomine Henrici Sampson 2 die Iunii a° 1537 script(a) per Frysh'; 'Sampson' Norwicen.'; 'Litera Thomae Archiep. Ebor. absolventes

---

[68] Probably not the Richard Cheppard [*sic*], perpetual vicar of Charing par. ch. (Kent), Canterbury dioc., who obtained a papal dispensation on 17 January 1516 to hold an additional incompatible benefice; *CPL*, XX, no. 553.

[69] Recorded in the section of the register concerning Chester archdeaconry.

[70] Recorded in the section of the register concerning Chester archdeaconry.

Henricum Sampson de Wooddytton 1528'. 37.6 × 22.1 cm. Plica: 4.1 cm. Slits for seal strings. *LPL, Papal Document 134* (original).

[**78**] Letter of Cardinal Wolsey as legate *a latere* dispensing William Reed, Norwich dioc.,[71] acolyte, under a papal faculty, from *corporis viciatus*, he having become lame (*clauditus*) in his left foot perhaps through contraction of the nerves or otherwise but by no fault of his own, and having been promoted to minor orders and desiring to serve God as a clerk in the ministry of the altar, so that he may be promoted by any Catholic bishop to all holy, even priest's, orders and minister in them. Dated at our residence near Westminster, 7 September 1528. Below right: 'Willemnus Claiburgh / Datarius'. *Reg. Nykke, 4*, fol. 118r.

[**79**] A letter of John [Howden], bishop of Sodor,[72] notified all that by virtue of a dispensation of Cardinal Wolsey he had ordained John Wilkoke, acolyte, York dioc.,[73] in St John the Evangelist's chapel in Rievaulx Abbey, OCist, York dioc., as subdeacon and deacon on the same day, 11 October 1528, to the title of St Mary Magdalene monastery, [OSB], Monk Bretton, York dioc. *Reg. Wolsey (York)*, fol. 132v.

[**80**] Letter of Cardinal Wolsey as legate *a latere* dispensing Nicholas Harres, BA,[74] Salisbury dioc., who is in minor orders, to be promoted to all, even holy and priest's, orders by any Catholic bishop *extra tempora a iure statuta*, even two on one day, and minister in them. Dated at our residence near Westminster, 4 November 1528. Below: note signed 'Tho. Candell' authenticating Wolsey's seal. *Reg. Campeggio*, fol. 81v.

[**81**] Letter of Cardinal Wolsey as legate *a latere* dispensing Francis Bigod, esq., and Catherine Conyers, *generosa*, York dioc., to contract marriage in the third and fourth degrees of consanguinity and have it solemnised in the church of their choice without banns, with legitimation of future issue. Dated at our residence near Westminster, 4 November 1528. *Reg. Wolsey (York)*, fol. 132v.

[**82**] Letter of Cardinal Wolsey as legate *a latere* dispensing Nicholas Holland, subdeacon, Salisbury dioc., from defect of age, he being in his twenty-third year, so that he may be promoted to the holy orders of the diaconate and priesthood by any Catholic bishop and minister

[71] Probably not the William Rede, Lincoln dioc., recorded in *CPL*, XIX, nos 1727, 1743.

[72] John Howden, OP, DTh of Oxford University, was appointed by papal provision as bishop of Sodor and Man in 1523 and vacated the see by February 1530 (*BRUO, 1501–1540*, 301; Eubel, *Hierarchia catholica*, III. 302).

[73] Probably not the John Wylcolck, York dioc., recorded in *CPL*, XIX, no. 1298. Not the John Wylcokk', MTh (of Cambridge University), in *CPL*, XX, no. 164, who had died by December 1514 (cf. *BRUC*, 639; *BRUO, 1501–1540*, 628).

[74] Probably the Nicholas Harris admitted as BA of Oxford University on 13 July 1528 (*BRUO, 1501–1540*, 270).

in them, and conceding a licence and faculty to any bishop to ordain him thus. Dated at our residence near Westminster, 18 November 1528.[75] Below: 'Jo. Hughes'; note signed 'Tho. Candell' authenticating Wolsey's seal. *Reg. Campeggio*, fol. 65r.

[**83**] Letter of Cardinal Wolsey as legate *a latere* dispensing Ralph Whitehed,[76] chancellor of Lichfield cathedral, to receive and retain a third incompatible benefice and be absent from any of these benefices while resident in another or attending a university. Dated at our residence near Westminster, 22 November 1528. Note signed by P. Wyrevyne (with notarial sign) confirming that this copy agrees with the original. *Reg. Blythe*, fol. 15r–v.[77]

[**84**] Letter of Cardinal Wolsey as legate *a latere* dispensing Thomas Williams, scholar, Winchester dioc., from defect of birth, he being born of a married man and unmarried woman, so that he may be promoted to all, even holy and priest's, orders by any Catholic bishop at *tempora a iure statuta* or other Sundays or feasts outside them, even two on one day, and minister in them, and then receive and retain two compatible benefices with or without cure of souls and be absent from either of them while resident in another or studying at a university. Dated at our residence near Westminster, 10 December 1528. Below: 'Io. Hughes' (left); 'W. Claiburgh / datarius' (right); note signed 'Tho. Candell' authenticating Wolsey's seal. *Reg. Campeggio*, fol. 82r.

[**85**] Letter of Cardinal Wolsey as legate *a latere* dispensing Reginald Sandys, professed regular priest of the observant Friars Minor,[78]

[75] This follows an ordination list including an entry recording the promotion of Holland, deacon, Worcester dioc., as priest to the title of Maiden Bradley Priory, [OSA], Salisbury dioc., under letters dimissory and this dispensation, on 20 February 1528/9.

[76] Ralph Whitehede, Coventry and Lichfield dioc., was fellow of King's Hall, Cambridge, 1500–1519; its seneschal, 1502–1503 and 1513–1514; and BA of Cambridge University, obtaining a grace there in 1503–1504 that study in Arts for six years, civil law for three and canon law for two suffice for entry in civil law. He was ordained as priest on 12 March 1502; held numerous ecclesiastical benefices, including canonries at St John's Chester, Lichfield, and Gnosall (Staffs.); and was admitted as chancellor of Lichfield on 21 July 1520, till death. He was dead by March 1535 (*BRUC*, 634–635). Doubtless the Ralph Whitehead, Ely dioc. (which included Cambridge), who obtained a papal dispensation in 1 Leo X (1513–1514) to hold a plurality of incompatible benefices; *CPL*, XX, no. 833 (rubricella of lost letter).

[77] ? = Appendix 3. **166**. Recorded in the section of the register concerning Coventry archdeaconry. On fols 16v–17r also in this section follows a letter of Clement VII licensing Whitehed as canon of Gnosall, Coventry and Lichfield dioc., BCn & CL, to hold Brinklow (*Brynklow*) par. ch., Coventry and Lichfield dioc., in union with his canonry and the prebend of Chilternall (*Chylturnhall*); dated at Bologna, 27 March 1536 [*recte*, 1526/7], with a notary's mark certifying this as a copy of the original. He was admitted as prebendary of Chilternhall, in Gnosall, on 12 May 1527, till death (*BRUC*, 635); Emden does not record Brinklow among his benefices.

[78] The Franciscan Observants had six houses in England: Canterbury; Greenwich; Newark; Newcastle-upon-Tyne; Richmond; Southampton (Knowles & Hadcock, 230–231).

resident in his legation, to receive and retain an incompatible benefice with or without cure of souls and be absent from it while studying at a university, wear his habit under secular priest's garb and with his superior's consent serve at divine offices, exercise the cure of souls, hear confessions, administer sacraments and do all things in that benefice which secular priests can do. Dated at our residence near Westminster, 10 December 1528. Below: 'Io. Hughes' (right); note signed 'T. Candell' (with notarial sign) authenticating Wolsey's seal. *Reg. Campeggio*, fol. 84v.

[**86**] Letter of Cardinal Wolsey as legate *a latere* dispensing Henry Russell, rector of Great Somerford (*Summerford Matravers*) par. ch., Salisbury dioc., to receive and retain an additional incompatible benefice with cure of souls and be absent from any of his benefices while resident in another or studying at a university. Dated at our residence near Westminster, 20 December 1528. Below: 'Io. Hughes' (left); note signed 'T. Candell' (with notarial sign) authenticating Wolsey's seal. *Reg. Campeggio*, fol. 82v.

[**87**] Letter of Cardinal Wolsey as legate *a latere* dispensing Henry Daniell, perpetual vicar of St Michael's par. ch., Whitwell (*Whyghtwell*), Norwich dioc., under a papal faculty, to receive and retain an additional incompatible benefice and be absent from any of his benefices while resident in another or studying at a university. Dated at our residence near Westminster, 20 February 1528/9. In margin: 'Copia dispensacionis magistri Henrici Daniell'. *Reg. Nykke, 4*, fols 112v–114r.

[**88**] Letter of Cardinal Wolsey as legate *a latere* dispensing Robert Knyght, Norwich dioc., subdeacon, from defect of age, being in his twenty-fourth year, so that he may be promoted by any Catholic bishop to holy, deacon's and priest's orders and minister in them, and granting a licence and faculty to that bishop to promote him thus. Dated at our residence near Westminster, 26 April 1529. *Reg. Nykke, 4*, fol. 107r.

[**89**] Letter of Cardinal Wolsey as legate *a latere* dispensing John Storke, deacon, Salisbury dioc., from defect [of age], he being in his twenty-third year, so that he may be ordained to the holy order of the priesthood by any Catholic bishop and minister in it, and conceding a licence and faculty to any bishop to ordain him thus. Dated at our residence near Westminster, 15 May 1529.[79] Below: 'Io. Hughes' (on left); 'Edmundus Bonerus legum doctor / et datarius reverendissimi

---

[79]This follows an ordination list on fol. 66v including an entry recording Storke's promotion as priest under this dispensation to the title of Vale Royal [Abbey, OCist], near(?) Oxford, on 18 September 1529; Thomas Candell is recorded in the heading to this list as a notary present at the ordinations recorded there. Probably not the John Storke

Cardinalis Eboracensis predicti' (on right); note signed 'Tho. Candell' authenticating Wolsey's seal. *Reg. Campeggio*, fol. 67r.

[**90**] Letter of Cardinal Wolsey as legate *a latere* dispensing Edward Popelay, scholar, York dioc., by apostolic authority from defect of birth, he being born of an unmarried man and an unmarried woman, so that he may be promoted to all, even holy and priest's, orders by any Catholic bishop whom he wishes and minister in them, and obtain a benefice even with cure of souls, and conceding a licence and faculty to that bishop to ordain him thus. Dated at our residence near Westminster, 13 May 1529. Signed above plica: 'Io. Hughes' (left); 'Edmundus Bonerus legum doctor / et datarius reverendissimi Cardinalis Eboracensis predicti' (right). 33.8 × 17.5 cm. Partial red wax seal depicting St Peter with keys (left) and St Paul with sword (right) framed in Renaissance-style arches, with cardinal's hat and Wolsey's coat-of-arms below, on pendant metal mandorla (11.5 × 7.5 cm) laced to the document with olive and beige silk cords.[80] University of Texas at Austin, Harry Ransom Center, Medieval and Early Modern Manuscripts HRC 212 (original).

[**91**] Letter of Cardinal Wolsey as legate *a latere* dispensing John Nabbys, BA,[81] Coventry and Lichfield dioc., so that he may be promoted by any Catholic bishop to all, even holy and priest's, orders on any Sundays or feasts *extra tempora a iure statuta*, even two on the same day, and minister in them, and granting a licence and faculty to any bishop to promote him thus. Dated at our residence near Westminster, 15 June 1529.[82] *Reg. Nykke, 4*, fol. 109v.

[**92**] Letter of Cardinal Wolsey as legate *a latere* dispensing Henry Pole and Joan Crosvener, Coventry and Lichfield dioc., so that they might marry in the third degree of consanguinity and in *cognatio spiritualis* arising from the fact that Henry's mother acted as godparent at Joan's baptism, with legitimation of future issue. Dated at our residence near Westminster, 7 July 1529. Below on right: 'Io. [*recte*, Edmundus] Bonerus legum doctor / datarius'. Note signed by Gregory Stonyng (with notarial sign) certifying this as a copy of the original. *Reg. Blythe*, fol. 47r.[83]

[**93**] Letter of Cardinal Wolsey as legate *a latere* dispensing Nicholas Pleben' *alias* 'de burgo diocesis civitatis Sepulchri(?)' [Borgo San

(diocese unspecified) who obtained a papal dispensation in 1 Leo X (1513–1514) to hold a plurality of incompatible benefices; *CPL*, XX, no. 839 (rubricella of lost letter).

[80]York Minster, Wolsey's archiepiscopal see, was dedicated to these saints. I am grateful to Dr Patrick Zutshi for bringing this document to my attention and to Andrew Gansky of the HRC for supplying photographs of it.

[81]Possibly John Nabs, BA of Cambridge University by 1526–1527 (Venn, III. 232).

[82]? = Appendix 3. **144**.

[83]Recorded in the section of the register concerning Salop archdeaconry.

Sepolcro], priest and professed of OFM resident in his legation, to receive and retain any incompatible benefice with or without cure of souls and wear his habit under secular priest's garb. Dated at the manor 'de le More', 7 September 1529. *Reg. Wolsey (Winchester) ed.*, pp. 65–6.[84]

[**94**] Incomplete letter of Cardinal Wolsey as legate *a latere* for life dispensing Thomas Waterman, rector of St Michael's par. ch., Geldeston (*Goldeston*), Norwich dioc., BCnL, under a papal faculty, to hold an additional incompatible benefice; [no date].[85] *Reg. Nykke, 4*, fol. 101r–v.

[84] The Italian Franciscan Nicholas de Burgo probably joined the convent of the Oxford Grey Friars in *c.*1517; was appointed as public praelector of theology in Cardinal College, Oxford, in 1525, resigning by 1535, and lector in divinity in Magdalen College, Oxford, in 1525–1526, still in 1529–1530; was BTh of Paris, incorporated at Oxford University on 18 February 1523, and incepted as DTh at Oxford on 11 August 1524, after seventeen years of study in theology and seven years of lecturing at Oxford. He obtained letters of denization on 25 January 1530; was admitted to the canonry and prebend of Timsbury in Romsey Abbey (Hants.) on 31 January 1530 by virtue of this dispensation, and still held these in 1536; and helped in the search for Henry VIII's papal divorce. He left Oxford in 1531 for the London Grey Friars before returning to Italy. Styling himself "Nicolaus Florentinus" he wrote a letter to Henry VIII on 20 October 1535, after his return to Italy, referring to his fellowship at Oxford and benefice in England of £25 a year which he hoped to retain (*BRUO, 1501–1540*, 85–86; *Letters and Papers*, IX, no. 645; *Reg. Wolsey (Winchester) ed.*, pp. 63–65, on his admission to Timsbury prebend).

[85] Probably the same letter as **55** above.

II

THE LIMITS OF CONFORMITY IN LATE ELIZABETHAN ENGLAND: A PLEA FOR A PRIEST

Edited by Michael Questier

II

THE LIMITS OF CONFORMITY IN LATE ELIZABETHAN ENGLAND: A PLEA FOR A PRIEST

Edited by Michael Questier

HISTORICAL INTRODUCTION

The Elizabethan settlement of religion of 1559 required that the queen's subjects, whatever their disposition in religion, should conform to specific statute-based aspects of that settlement. The consensus among scholars nowadays seems to be that the 1559 ecclesiastical legislation was relatively limited in its scope although the Elizabethan acts of supremacy and uniformity served as the groundwork for much of the subsequent, and more wide-ranging and coercive, law relating to the established Church.

The regime's conformist agenda went through a series of step changes in the 1560s, 1570s and 1580s with a number of acts which extended the law of treason and also the penalties for separatism. The best survey of the development of Catholic separatism/recusancy as a legal topic and offence is Hugh Bowler's introduction to his volume on the 1592–1593 exchequer recusancy roll, and it would be superfluous to replicate his conclusions here.[1] The leading work on the evolution of the law of treason in Elizabeth's reign remains in typescript: the PhD thesis of Leslie Ward. She demonstrates how, in the statutes of 1563, 1571 and 1581, a number of new offences were defined as treason.[2]

Since, however, this is very substantially the topic of the document I have edited and here discuss, it may be worth setting out in some detail the regulatory structure which the writer of the manuscript reproduced here was seeking to subvert, and the way in which the relevant legislation phrased the link between Catholicism and treason.

The 1571 act (13 Eliz. c. 2) was formulated in the context of the rebellion in the North during late 1569 and early 1570. That episode had seen Catholic clergy offering absolution from the sin of schism to

---

The MS of 'A plee for a prieste . . .' is to be found in the Archives of the Archdiocese of Westminster, Series A, VII, no. 104.

I am very grateful to Michael Bowman for discussions of this topic. Without his sage advice, based on years of legal training and practice, it would have been virtually impossible to take this project to a conclusion.

[1] H. Bowler (ed.), *Recusant Roll No. 2 (1593–1594)*, Catholic Record Society, 57 (London, 1965), vii–cxiv.

[2] L.J. Ward, 'The law of treason in the reign of Elizabeth I 1558–1588', PhD thesis, Cambridge, 1985, ch. 1.

those who had taken part in the rising, and the enterprise had received papal endorsement via the notorious papal bull of excommunication of Elizabeth (*Regnans in Excelsis*). As Ward points out, the 1571 statute was derived from the act of supremacy of 1559 and from 5 Eliz. c. 1 of 1563, though its penalties were much more stringent and it created five new treasons, including reconciling to or being reconciled to Rome. The principal feature of the act was that it connected the carrying or promulgation of papal bulls or edicts (i.e. assertions of papal authority) directly with 'absolution or reconciliation'. After the publication of the 1570 bull of excommunication, 'conversion implicitly involved withdrawal of obedience from the queen to the papacy' and so 'to use any bull for any purpose' or even 'to . . . possess a bull, or to convert the queen's subjects, constituted outward aid to the papacy' and this was an extension of the 1352 treason act which defined treason as adhering to an enemy of the crown.[3]

The 1571 statute was made 'agaynste the bringing in and putting in execution of bulls and other instruments from the sea of Rome'. The statute claimed that some 'seditious and very evell disposed people', disregarding their duty to God and the queen, had conspired, 'as it should seeme, verye seditiously and unnaturally' to bring the realm and crown into 'thraldome' to Rome and 'also to estraunge and alienate the myndes and hartes of sundry her majesties subjectes from their . . . obedyence, and to raise and stirr sedition and rebellion within this realme'. To do this they had procured written instruments from the bishop of Rome 'the effect wherof hath ben and is to absolve and reconcile all those that wilbe contented to forsake their due obedyence' to the queen, 'and to yeld and subjecte themselves to the said fayned, unlawfull and usurped aucthoritie, and by color' of the same written instruments to practise 'in such partes of this realme where the people for want of good instruccion are moste weake, simple and . . . ignorant, and thereby fardest from the good understanding of their duties towardes God' and the queen. The result was that those persons had 'been contented to be reconcyled to the saide usurped aucthoritie of the sea of Rome and to take absolution at the handes of the said naughtie and subtill practysers'. In this fashion, there had 'growne greate dysobedience and boldnesse in manye, not onely to withdrawe and absent themselves from all dyvyne service nowe moste godly set forth and used within this realme' but such people had also 'thought themselves dyscharged of and from all obedyence, duetie and allegiaunce to her majestie, whereby most wycked and unnaturall rebellyon hath ensued, and to the further daunger of this realme is hereafter very lyke to be renewed yf the ungodly and wycked

---

[3]Ward, 'Law of treason', 50–53, 54.

attemptes in that behalf bee not by severitie of lawes in tyme restrayned and brydeled'. Anyone reconciling or reconciled to the see of Rome in these circumstances 'shalbe deemed and adjudged highe traytors'.[4] The 1581 statute (23 Eliz. c. 1) was a response to the interventions made by the Jesuits Edmund Campion and Robert Persons after they arrived in England in mid 1580. It clarified the 1571 statute. As Ward phrases it, this new act, relying on 13 Eliz. c. 2, created three treason offences in extension of the earlier measure. It became high treason to 'possess, feign to have, or to practise by any means, the power to absolve, influence, or withdraw any of Elizabeth's subjects from their due obedience and the established religion', that is to the religion of the Church of Rome; secondly to 'persuade any subject to profess allegiance to the papacy or to any other foreign ruler . . . or to accomplish the same by any open action'; thirdly, voluntarily to convert or withdraw 'obedience to the crown' and to affirm 'allegiance to the papacy or any power other than the queen'.[5] The 1581 statute stated that

> divers evell affected persons have practised contrarye to the meaninge of the said statute, by other meanes than by bulles or instrumentes written or

---

[4]A. Luder et al. (eds), *Statutes of the Realm*, 11 vols, (London, 1810–28) [*SR*], IV, 528–529. The statute provided that 'to prevent the greate myscheefes and inconvenyences that thereby maye ensue',

> yf any person or persons after the fyrste daye of July next comming shall use or put in ure in any place within this realme or in any the queenes domynions any suche bull, wryting or instrument, written or prynted, of absolution or reconciliation at any tyme heretofore obtayned and gotten, or at any tyme hereafter to be obtayned or gotten, from the said bysshop of Rome or any his successors, or from any other person or persons aucthorized or clayming aucthoritie by or from the said bysshop of Rome, his predecessors or successors, or sea of Rome; or yf any person or persons after the said fyrste daye of July shall take upon him or them by color of any such bull, writing, instrument or aucthoritie to absolve or reconcyle any person or persons, or to grante or promisse to any person or persons within this realme or any other the queenes majestyes dominions, any suche absolution or reconciliation by any speache, preaching, teaching, writing or any other open deede; or yf any person or persons within this realme or any the queenes domynions after the said fyrste daye of Julye shall wyllingly receave and take any suche absolution or reconciliation; or els yf any person or persons have obtayned or gotten synce the laste daye of the parliament holden in the fyrst yere of the queenes majestyes raigne, or after the said fyrst daye of July shall obtayne or get from the said bysshop of Rome or any his successors or sea of Rome any maner of bull, writinge or instrument written or prynted, contaynyng any thinge, matter or cause whatsoever; or shall publishe or by any waies or meanes put in ure any suche bull, writyng or instrument; that then all and every suche acte and actes, offence and offences, shalbe deemed and adjudged by the aucthoritie of this acte to be hyghe treason.

> *SR*, IV, 529

[5]Ward, 'Law of treason', 59–60.

printed, to withdrawe divers the queenes majesties subjectes from their naturall
obedience to her majestie, to obey the said usurped aucthoritie of Rome, and
in respecte of the same to perswade great nombers to withdrawe their due
obedience to her majesties lawes.

To remedy this problem, it was now declared that

> all persons whatsoever which have, or shall have, or shall pretend to have
> power, or shall by any wayes or meanes put in practise to absolve, perswade or
> withdrawe any of the queenes majesties subjectes or any within her highenes
> realmes and dominions from their natural obedience to her majestie, or to
> withdrawe them for that entent from the relygeon nowe by her highenes
> aucthoritie established within her highenes domynions to the Romyshe
> religeon, or to move them or any of them to promise any obedience to any
> pretended aucthoritie of the sea of Rome, or of any other prince, state or
> potentate, to be had or used within her dominions

should be adjudged traitors, as would those who 'by any meanes
be willinglye absolved or withdrawne as aforesaid, or willinglye be
reconciled, or shall promise any obedience to any suche pretended
aucthoritie, prince, state or potentate as ys aforesaid'.[6]
The other principal class of offence which became treason in this
period was the action of returning into the realm following ordination
abroad, that is as a Roman Catholic priest. The 1585 statute, 27 Eliz.
c. 2, entitled 'An Act againste Jesuites Semynarie Priestes and such
other like disobedient Persons', caused 'to be adjudged a traytor' 'any
Jesuite, seminarie priest . . . or [any] religious or ecclesiasticall person
whatsoever, being borne within this realme or any other her highnesse
dominions', ordained by Rome's authority, who should 'come into, be
or remayne in any parte of this realme'.[7]
Predictably, these coercive measures triggered a debate about how
far the legal formulae in them could really define as treasonable
what Catholics themselves claimed were matters which lay exclusively
within the forum of the individual conscience and not within that
which properly belonged to the temporal power of the queen and
parliament.[8]
This redrawing of the law was so controversial, however that, in late
1581, when the Jesuit Campion and a number of co-defendants were

[6] *SR*, IV, 657.
[7] *SR*, IV, 706–707. See also the royal proclamation of 1 April 1582, P.L. Hughes and J.F.
Larkin (eds), *Tudor Royal Proclamations*, 3 vols (London, 1969), II, no. 660; J. Bellamy, *The
Tudor Law of Treason* (London, 1979), 72.
[8] See, e.g., William Allen, *An Apologie and True Declaration of the Institution and Endevours of
the two English Colleges . . .* (Rheims, 1581); William Cecil, *The Execution of Justice in England*
(London, 1583).

put on trial, they were arraigned under the fourteenth-century treason legislation rather than the 1581 statute, even though that statute had been drafted and passed in response to the challenge represented by these clergy, and under which they could have been indicted.[9]

William Allen's *True, Sincere, and Modest Defence of English Catholiques of 1584* (his reply to Lord Burghley's *Execution of Justice in England*) runs through recent martyrdoms and condemns for example the conviction of Everard Hanse 'only upon a statute made in the last parliament . . . by which it is made a crime capital to persuade any man to the Catholic religion'. According to Allen, the martyr priests Richard Kirkman, James Thomson, William Hart and Richard Thirkeld who had been executed in York were 'never charged nor suspected of any other treasons than of hearing confessions, absolving and reconciling sinners to the favour of God and to the unity of the Catholic Church . . . which both in the priest that absolveth and in the party that is absolved they have made to be the crime' of treason 'under this false and most unjust pretence: that all parties so reconciled are assoiled of their obedience to the queen and do adhere to her enemy, and admit foreign jurisdiction, power and authority, which is exercised in confession for remission of sins'.[10]

Technically, after the passage into law of the 1585 statute mentioned above, the proof of the fact of a defendant's ordination, as long as he was one of the queen's subjects, was enough for prosecuting counsel to secure a conviction. Though most of the trials where the indictment was framed according to the 1585 statute were not, as far as I am aware, recorded in detail, the chances are that counsel for the crown made the case against the accused, if he was a seminary priest, also in part by reference to his alleged treasonable purposes and intentions, that is in addition to the fact of his ordination. On at least one occasion, at Chichester in 1588, we can find crown counsel arguing that the new statute was in effect a piece of enabling legislation rather than a legal novelty. The attorney Thomas Bowyer declared to the jury on this occasion (the trial of four seminary priests, indicted under the 1585 statute):

> the treasons whereof they were to be convicted were in ded treasons by the commen lawes of the realme, and that [*sic*] verie same treasons were mencyoned in the statut of 25 E. 3 as the adhearinge to her Majesties enemyes, compassinge

[9]Ward, 'Law of treason', 248–251.

[10]William Allen, *A True, Sincere, and Modest Defence of English Catholics . . .* (London, 1914), ch. 1, 12, 13–14. For the arguments over this issue at James Bell's trial in 1584, see J.H. Pollen (ed.), *Unpublished Documents relating to the English Martyrs 1584–1603*, Catholic Record Society, 5 (London, 1908), 75, 77. For Hanse's indictment, which Ward argues was under the 1571 treason statute for uttering traitorous words, see Ward, 'Law of treason', 299–300.

and imagining the deprivation of the queen from her regall authorit[i]e and lyfe was not to be doubted to be theyr entent and purpose, which intent and treasons were sufficyent to prove the partie guyltye though the act were not executed because yt would be to[o] late to punnyshe the offence after the act [was] executed.

Bowyer added that 'this entent of theirs by the commen lawe is to be proved by the overt fact, and only for the ease and satisfaction of the country at tryall to prove the overt fact this statut was made'. No one could doubt that the pope was the queen's 'capitall enemy'. The defendants, by going out of the realm and 'there adhering to the pope and by or under his authorit[i]e taking an order of priesthood and returninge to wynne the queenes subjectes to their factyon were without any question even by the commen lawe to be adjudged traytours, all which by their owne severall examinatons appered to be true'.[11]

The State's case was, in other words, that the fact of ordination and the facts, as far as they were known, of the other offences of those indicted could not be kept logically separate. Questions such as these were almost certainly debated on each and every occasion that a clergyman and his patrons and harbourers were indicted under the new statute law. In early 1590, on trial, the priest Christopher Bales challenged the judges as to whether St Augustine of Canterbury, sent to England by Pope Gregory, was a traitor and, if not, why should he (Bales) be one since he came for no other purpose than Augustine had done.[12] At Winchester in mid 1591, Roger Dickenson was told 'thou wilt perswade poor soules from Gods religion' and he answered that 'he never did anything but to use my office and that I hope was no offence'. To this, the court replied: 'thou art made a priest beyond the sea according to the Church of Rome', only for Dickenson to retort that 'I was made a priest as other priests are and have been before me'.[13]

The Jesuit Robert Southwell argued at his trial in 1595 that it was impossible for it to be treason to be a priest *per se*, but Sir Edward Coke replied that the provable treasons of separatist Catholic clergy showed that the 1585 statute 'was not made but upon urgent cause'. Southwell's argument here was the same as appeared in his work entitled 'An Humble Supplication', a reply to the royal proclamation of 18 October 1591. (It circulated in manuscript, and did not appear in print until five

---

[11] The National Archives (TNA), SP 12/217/1, fo. 3^r; Ward, 'Law of treason', 290; R.B. Manning, *Religion and Society in Elizabethan Sussex* (Leicester, 1969), 145.

[12] Pollen, *Unpublished Documents*, 178; R. Challoner, ed. J.H. Pollen, *Memoirs of Missionary Priests* (London, 1924), 160.

[13] Archivum Britannicum Societatis Jesu (ABSJ), Stonyhurst MS Collectanea M, 146^b.

years after the regime executed him.) 'All Christendome', Southwell said, 'hath these fifteene hundred yeeres honoured for pastours and governours of their soules those that nowe are more than unfavourably termed traytors'. For 'if they that harbour, relive or receive any such be worthy to bee deemed fellons, then all the glorious saintes of this lande whose doctrine and virtue God Almightie confirmed with many miracles were no better than traitours and their abettours fellons'. Thus (the same point that Bales had made) 'Saint Augustine and his companions that converted our realme in Saint Gregories time were' themselves within 'the compasse of treason' since 'theyr functions and ours were all one equally' derived 'from the sea of Rome'. Southwell imagined the coming of the 'day of general resurrection in your Majesties time', as it might do, and he conjured up the astonishment of 'so many millions of prelates, pastours and religious people . . . that . . . honoured and blessed this kingdome with the holiness of their life and excellencie of their learning'; they would be 'amazed to see their relikes burned, their memories defaced', and their monasteries either destroyed or desecrated, 'but more would they muse to find their priesthood reckoned for treason, and the releefe of priesthood condemned for felonie, these being the two principall testimonies of devotion that theyr ages were acquainted with'. The see of Rome was 'in the selfe-same state' as before, and 'indued with the same authoritie, and neither the manner of our creation, or priesthood it selfe is any thing altered from that it was'. So 'why should it be more treasonable to be made priestes in the midsomer day of your first yeare than the next day before, or the last of Queene Maries reigne?'[14]

Henry Walpole likewise insisted in 1595 that ordination was not treason; priesthood was 'a dignity and office instituted by our Lord Jesus Christ, and given by Him to his apostles, who were priests, as were also the holy fathers and doctors of the Church who converted and instructed the world', as too were those who first brought the gospel to England. In reply, the trial judge Francis Beaumont conceded that 'merely being a priest or Jesuit' was not treason but the additional facts of, in Walpole's case, returning into the realm (which was all that was necessary for a conviction under the statute) and in addition his having been 'with the king of Spain' and his conversing with Robert Persons, William Holt and 'other rebels and traitors' were sufficient.[15]

---

[14]Pollen, *Unpublished Documents*, 334; Robert Southwell, *An Humble Supplication to her Maiestie* (n.p., 1595 (printed secretly in England, 1600–1601)), 53–56.

[15]Challoner, *Memoirs*, 225. John Aveling suggests that there was a 'clear tendency' at the treason trials in the North Riding in 1582–1583, i.e. after the 1581 statute but before that of 1585, 'to argue that ordination overseas or receiving or reconciliation by authority from

In 1601 Mark Barkworth rhetorically asked the lord chief justice 'can any one maintain that to be a priest is treason?' for 'was not our Saviour a priest according to the order of Melchisidech?'; and 'will anyone say that He was a traitor?'[16]

The regime's proceedings were, however, informed by a sense that ordination and reconciliation were expressions of ideological commitment that could be validly regarded as treasonable. How far that was the case in practice is not easy to say. In April 1591, a young man called Robert Weston (whose father was a noted London Catholic lawyer) was arrested and confessed that there was, as Lucy Underwood describes it, 'a public rite, with set formulae' for reconciling someone to Rome. Those to be reconciled had to make certain statements, on oath, about sensitive political issues; they had to deny the royal supremacy and they then swore, *inter alia*, that 'our byshopps, preachers and mynisters are lymes of the devill permitted by God to tempte his electe'. Then 'this question is demaunded of the preist to hym, if anie dissention . . . should arise' between the queen and the Church of Rome, 'which parte' would he take? And 'upon his oath he must confesse to spend his lyffe and goodes in defence of theire church'. He also had to confirm that there were seven sacraments and that the pope could not only 'forgive sinnes' but also 'excommunicate princes', and so on, after which the priest can reconcile the penitent. Depending on how far one credits Weston's statement (Underwood suggests that Weston was 'probably mingling truth, lies and hearsay'), this might be reckoned to be close enough to the claims made by government officials about the treasons involved in the supposedly spiritual ministrations of the seminarist clergy.[17]

The line taken by the regime's own apologists and pamphleteers was expressed by Francis Bacon in an unpublished piece (which probably circulated in manuscript) written in reply to Richard Verstegan's *A Declaration of the True Causes* . . . of 1592. Ventriloquizing the position of Lord Burghley, he argued that seminary priests were sent to 'reconcile' the queen's 'subjects from their obedience' and that this turned Catholics from papists of conscience into 'papists of faction'. Bacon

---

Rome was tantamount to breach of the act of 1559 and of the old treasons acts', J.C.H. Aveling, *Northern Catholics* (London, 1966), 138.

[16] Challoner, *Memoirs*, 254.

[17] TNA, SP 12/238/126, i–iv, quotations at no. iv, fo. 189[r]; L. Underwood, 'Persuading the Queen's Majesty's subjects from their allegiance: Treason, reconciliation and confessional identity in Elizabethan England' (forthcoming in *Historical Research*, 2015). I am grateful to Dr Underwood for allowing me to see this paper in draft. For John Hambley's rather different account of (his) reconciliation to Rome by the priest John Ballard in London in 1583, see TNA, SP 12/192/46, i, fo. 71[r–v].

linked this directly to Catholic separatists' refusal to attend church.[18] In other words, becoming a recusant was a visible sign of precisely this kind of otherwise invisible conspiracy. This was the argument made at the trial of James Bird at Winchester. Here the presiding judge, Sir Edmund Anderson, claimed that the fact of Bird's recusancy was enough to prove that he had been reconciled to Rome in the manner delineated by the current law of treason. Anderson allegedly said that 'a recusant is one who refuses to go to church. This no one does except those who have been reconciled to the Church of Rome; but he that is reconciled to the Church of Rome is a rebel and a traitor' and in effect ordered the jury to convict, which they did. (It was presumably known that Bird had, as Challoner says, been a seminarist at Rheims.)[19]

The eventual execution of Bird (on 25 March 1593) may in fact have been a response to the passing of anti-sectary legislation in the 1593 parliament at more or less precisely that point.[20] On and after 11 March, the puritan separatists Henry Barrow and John Greenwood, with others, had been proceeded against under the 1581 act against seditious words. This was undoubtedly shocking for some Protestants since that statute had been formulated in response to Catholic critiques of the regime. Barrow and Greenwood were convicted and executed, and their executions, evidently against the will of Lord Burghley, were provoked in part by puritan protest in the Commons against the new anti-sectary law, that is as it touched puritans.[21] The Winchester trial may have been staged in order to reinforce the claim that the extant law against offences committed by Catholic separatists should not be applied to puritans, and puritanism should under no circumstances be equated with popery.

Bird's conviction and execution were possibly also a response to the expression of harder-line Catholic opposition to occasional conformity, of exactly the sort that we know was being pumped out by the Jesuit Henry Garnet in opposition to the likes of the seminarist

---

[18] Francis Bacon, 'Certain Observations made upon a Libel published this Present Year, 1592', in J. Spedding, R. Ellis and D. Heath (eds), *The Works of Francis Bacon*, 14 vols, London, 1857–1874), VIII, 179–180, cited in P. Lake, *Bad Queen Bess* (forthcoming), ch. 15; V. Houliston, *Catholic Resistance in Elizabethan England: Robert Persons's Jesuit Polemic, 1580–1610* (Aldershot, 2007), 53.

[19] Pollen, *Unpublished Documents*, 231–232; Challoner, *Memoirs*, 188.

[20] The presiding judge Sir Edmund Anderson's hostility to Catholic separatism was, it seems, the product of religious conservatism; he was equally hostile, by turns, towards both Catholics and puritans; *ODNB*, *sub* Anderson, Edmund (article by D. Ibbetson).

[21] W. Richardson, 'The religious policy of the Cecils, 1588–1598', DPhil, Oxford, 1993, 100–111. They had been imprisoned under 23 Eliz. c. 1, i.e. for refusing to attend church, *ODNB*, *sub* Barrow, Henry (article by P. Collinson).

Thomas Bell who had himself recently gone over to the Church of England.[22]

Exactly how controversial the Bird case was may be deduced from the long delay between verdict and execution of sentence. The significance of the case locally can be picked up from the memory of the argument that Bird had with the sheriff seconds before death when he tricked him into appearing to admit that he, Bird, was being hanged only because he refused to go to church. There was a story in circulation too that Bird's severed head had bowed to his father, a conformist Winchester office holder, which proved that Bird junior knew what true obedience was.[23]

At John Rigby's trial in 1600 the crucial issue was, again, the interpretation of the statute law on reconciling. Rigby rehearsed several of the reasons why he could not be found guilty. He alleged that

> whereas I am charged in my indictment that I was reconciled – it is very true; to God Almighty so I was, and I think lawfully might be; and, as I remember, it is also allowed in your book of common prayer, in the visitation of the sick, that if any man find himself burthened in conscience he should make his confession to the minister, which confession manifesteth a breach between God and his soul, and by this humble confession he craveth pardon of his sins, and reconciliation to God again, by the hands of his minister.

And, secondly, 'whereas I am charged, that I was reconciled from my obedience' to the queen 'and to the Romish religion, I will depose the contrary; for I was never reconciled from any obedience to my princess, for I obey her still; nor to any religion, for although I sometimes went to church against my will, yet was I never of any other religion than the Catholic, and therefore needed no reconciliation in religion'. Thirdly,

> whereas, in my former answers, I said I went to church, it is true, for fear of temporal punishment I so did, but never minded to fall from the old religion, and therefore needed no reconciliation.

Fourthly he suggested to the judges that they should 'explicate the meaning of the statute to the jury: if the meaning thereof be to make it treason for a man fallen into the displeasure of God, through his sins, to be reconciled to God again, by him to whom God hath committed the authority of reconciliation, if this be treason, God's will be done'.

---

[22] P. Lake and M. Questier, *The Trials of Margaret Clitherow* (London, 2011), chs 7, 8.
[23] Pollen, *Unpublished Documents*, 231–232; Challoner, *Memoirs*, 188; Underwood, 'Persuading'.

'Then', said both the judges, 'it was by a Romish priest, and therefore treason'. Rigby answered that it was

> by a Catholic priest, who had the liberty of the prison, and was free for any man to come to him to relieve him; and, therefore, by the statute, no treason. Again, my lords, if it be not inquired of within a year and a day, there can be no advantage taken against me by this statute, if you wrong me not. Whereto replied one that sat under the judge; all this will not serve thy turn, for the jury must find it treason,

as indeed they did, although Justice Gaudy tried to persuade Rigby to conform.[24]

All of these issues were publicly brought together by the trial and execution of the priest Robert Drury and of the alleged murderer Humphrey Lloyd in 1607. Drury argued, 'at the barre', that 'if it were treason in him to be a priest, then it was the like in Saint Augustine, S. Bernard, and other reverend fathers of the Church, who received their priesthood by authority from God, and so did he presume to have doone the like'. To this the court replied that there was a great difference between his priesthood and that of the fathers of the Church, 'yet priesthood solie was not imputed to him for treason, for that profession, (though neither liked nor allowed by us) he might use and exercise in the parts beyond the seas, keeping himselfe there'. But it was not allowable, having been ordained in the Roman communion, 'to com home again into this land, and (in meere contempt of the king and his lawes) to reconcile, seduce and alienate loyall subjects harts, from love, just regard and dutie to their soveraigne'.[25]

This argument continued under the Tyburn triangular cross beam itself. Drury alleged his conviction was only for his ordination while a

[24]Challoner, *Memoirs*, 240–241 (Challoner's narrative is based on Thomas Worthington, *A Relation of Sixtene Martyrs: glorified in England in twelve monethes: With a Declaration: That English Catholiques suffer for the Catholique Religion: And that the Seminarie Priests Agree with the Iesuites* (Douai, 1601), sigs A2ʳ–C7ʳ). Protestant polemicists of course denied the validity as much as the lawfulness of sacramental reconciliation to Rome; see, e.g., Lewis Bayley, *The Practise of Pietie*, 11th edn (London, 1619), 763–765.

[25]*A True Report of the Araignment, Tryall, Conviction, and Condemnation, of a Popish Priest, named Robert Drewrie* (London, 1607), sigs A4ʳ–Bʳ. For similar arguments at the trials in 1610 of Roger Cadwallader and John Roberts, see Challoner, *Memoirs*, 300–301; J.H. Pollen (ed.), *Acts of English Martyrs* (London, 1891), 151–153. As Challoner relates it in Cadwallader's case, Bishop Robert Bennett 'seemed much to insist upon this one point, that Christ was the only sacrificing priest of the New Testament, in that proper signification of the name, priest, which is not common to all Christians; so to free himself from being a priest. Which made the blessed martyr return him this witty answer: "make that good, I pray you, my lord, for so you will prove that I am no more a priest than other men, and consequently, no traitor or offender against your law" ', Challoner, *Memoirs*, 300–301.

Protestant minister present 'shewed some papers', allegedly signed by Drury, to prove, that it was for treason more conventionally understood. Once Drury had been hanged and dismembered, 'the minister told the people they should now heare his horrible treason for which besides his refusing the oath of alleageance . . . he was worthily executed' and he pulled 'out his papers to reade' but then said there really was not time, 'others being to suffer', that is to hang for other offences; 'neither would it be greatly material because they should see very shortly in printe the whole discourse of all his treasons', that is the printed pamphlet which is the principal source for the regime's prosecution of Drury; he then 'putt up his papers againe into his pocket, whereat the people laughed and one gentl[e]man amongst the rest sayd alowde, "By God, thou hast made one of the foolishest speeches that . . . ever was made at Tyburn." '[26]

These papers were the basis for the *True Reporte of the Araignment, Tryall, Conviction, and Condemnation, of . . . Robert Drewrie.* One of the clinching pieces of evidence which the pamphlet cited for the bad mind and treasonable intentions of the priest was his pronouncing absolution over Humphrey Lloyd, who was hanged on the same day. According to the pamphlet, on 18 January 1607, Lloyd had met Thomas Morris in Aldersgate Street. Morris was 'one of the ordinary yeomen of his majesties guarde'. They drank in the Half Moon tavern and 'some speeches concerning religion passed betweene them, wherein Morris touched Lloyd to be a dissembler'. The long and the short of it was that subsequently they met again and quarrelled, and Lloyd killed Morris. Although the pamphlet more or less admitted that there was fault on both sides, it stressed Lloyd's 'cruell and bloodie hatred' and claimed that he had been involved in recent Catholic conspiracies, including the Gunpowder Plot.[27]

But the 'other' side of the story, as it were, was narrated by the Jesuit Richard Blount. Blount claimed that Morris had 'sayd' that 'papists were traytors' and Lloyd 'answered that they were as good subjects as any the king had'. Morris drew his sword and Lloyd killed him 'in his owne defence'. Lloyd 'had served the State in warrs many yeares very faithfully and had great friends', yet he was hanged 'because he professed himselfe Catholick and would not yield to goe to church', even though the renegade priest John Scudamore, a client of Archbishop Richard Bancroft, came and tried to persuade him to conform.[28]

[26] ABSJ, Stonyhurst MS Collectanea M, 99[b], 100[a].
[27] *True Report of . . . Robert Drewrie*, sig. B2[r]–3[v].
[28] ABSJ, Stonyhurst MS Collectanea M, 100[a].

The Present Document and its Origins

This manuscript position paper ('A Plea for a Priest') which is reproduced here in its full and often tedious entirety is essentially a series of legal cases, questions and quibbles, argued if not by a lawyer then by someone with at least some experience in thinking about statutory interpretation. It makes several of the arguments advanced by clergy and their harbourers when they were indicted under the new treason legislation, although, perhaps surprisingly, it does not mention any specific instance of a recent treason trial.

I should point out that I have not established the author of this piece.[29] Nor have I worked out the exact date of, or reason for, its composition. Since it refers to Lord Burghley as the 'late lord treasurer' it must have been written after Burghley's death on 4 August 1598; and, obviously enough, it was written before the end of Elizabeth's reign on 24 March 1603. It is located therefore somewhere in the middle of the disputes among, and the toleration petitioning by, Catholics in the late 1590s and up to the accession which we tend, for short hand purposes, to refer to as the Archpriest (or Appellant), controversy, and which anticipated the accession of James VI of Scotland as James I of England and Great Britain. In that one can conjecture at all about the purpose of its composition, the author seems to say that he is writing it as a position paper for someone else to use (pp. 550–551), perhaps in debates among Catholics on these topics.[30] There are

[29]Michael Bowman suggests that, since the only precedent cited in this text is *Hambleton's Case*, perhaps the author had a civil-law rather than a common-law training, though, as he remarks, there were very few precedents of any use to defendants in treason trials anyway. Mr Bowman suggests also that this text might have been compiled in connection with actual legal defences in court of indicted Catholics. Successful defences in treason trials were rare, and none is recorded on the basis of the arguments advanced here. On the other hand, although there were very few precedents of any use to a defendant on a charge of treason, a treason trial was one of the occasions when the court might grant the right to counsel – in other criminal trials the defence had no right to call witnesses and a defendant might be represented by a barrister only on questions of law. Mr Bowman advises (and this seems absolutely right) that even if the arguments advanced in the text were were unlikely to be successful while the trial was in progress, their real usefulness might be as a basis for a plea for clemency.

[30]Thomas McCoog has shown that on 3 June 1598, there was a meeting of Catholics in London. They wished to take advantage of the recent Franco-Spanish peace negotiations and they discussed which of the penal statutes should be abolished if France and Spain imposed on Elizabeth sufficiently to grant toleration. I am grateful to Dr McCoog for alerting me to this fact and to the relevant manuscript citation (Archivio Segreto Vaticano, Segr. Stato Nunz, Diverse 264, fo. 233^v: 'Quae Catholici Anglicani ex suorum jurisconsultorum consilio petunt ne nominatim revocentur a Regina in concedenda religionis Catholicae tollerantia'). Obviously this meeting predated the composition of the manuscript printed below, but it may be that this manuscript and its summary of the case against the penal

certainly echoes of these arguments in the pamphlet literature in and around the Archpriest dispute and the toleration agitation of the same period. For example, Richard Broughton's *An Apologicall Epistle* of 1601 argues that, 'as appeareth by our auntient lawes of King Edward the third' 'nothing is remembred' to be treason 'but that which tendeth either to the betraying of the king or countrey'. The character of priesthood has not changed: 'nothing is, or can be changed in that sacrament, howsoever the mindes and proceedings of Protestants doe change. The same priesthoode which was given to Saint Peter, and the apostles, the same which Saint Augustine, and his associates hadde that converted England, the same which hath beene so honored of al English kings since then, is the same'. Unless 'the state of England bee not the same it was', priesthood must still 'be honourable'. Moreover,

> there is not any poynt of civill regiment in that sacrament, being wholie spirituall and supernaturall, nothing concerning a temporall commonwealth, no renouncing or deniall of any authority in England, no conspiracie to prince, no betraying of a kingdome, of whome no one worde or mention is made, or can bee intended; no matter given in charge, no authoritie communicated, but to offer sacrifice, to pray, to preach, minister sacraments, and such priestly functions,

and precisely as the writer of 'A Plee for a Prieste . . .' argues, these things are 'but such as the ministers of England imitate the like'. Broughton insists that the functions of reconciling and excommunicating cannot be *per se* treasonable, since the Catholic diaconate is also treasonable under the Elizabethan statute of 1585.[31]

After the regime had radically changed course, in the run-up to the parliament of 1604, over how far Catholics might enjoy royal tolerance, Thomas Morgan wrote to Sir Robert Cecil on 26 April on behalf of the loyalist priest Jonas Meredith and remarked that 'thordre of priestehoode (what accompte so ever your lordship makethe thereof) is so ancient in Christes Churche and of that force as it will have

---

code against aspects of Catholic separatism came out of the same speculation about the possibility of some form of regime-sponsored tolerance.

[31] Richard Broughton, *An Apologicall Epistle serving as well for a Praeface to a Booke entituled, A Resolution of Religion: as also, containing the Authors most lawfull defence to all estates, for publishing the same* (Antwerp (imprint false, printed secretly in England), 1601), 95–96. Andrew Willet answered Broughton that Catholics' denial of the ecclesiastical supremacy is enough to constitute treason; even under the treason statute of Edward III, papist clerics 'that maintaine a forraine potentate, a knowne enemie to prince and countrie, are found to be traytors: for they which are adherent "to the kings enemies in his realme, giving them ayde and comfort within the realme, or elsewhere", are by that statute judged traytors', Andrew Willet, *An Antilogie or Counterplea to an Apologicall (he should have said) Apologeticall Epistle published by a Favourite of the Romane Separation, and (as is supposed) one of the Ignatian Faction: Wherein two hundred Untruths and Slaunders are discovered . . .* (London, 1603), 222–223.

continuance to the worldes ende notwithstandinge any humaine devise to the contrarie' that it would do no good to keep deporting them out of their native country'.[32]

During the Archpriest dispute, the claim had been that the Jesuits and their friends had, through their questionable political activities, made all Catholics more liable to become targets of the new laws. But, some argued, if the power of the Society of Jesus and its patrons could be hacked back or even rooted out completely then the state would have little reason to engage in a persecution of the, as the appellants claimed, majority of Catholics who were not by any stretch of the imagination a danger to the queen and the state. Of themselves, these were not particularly new arguments. One imagines that something like them must have been in circulation ever since the relevant legislation passed onto the statute book.[33] The question of how far the function of the (Catholic) clergy, properly understood and performed, was a purely spiritual one was, therefore, central to the *fin-de-siècle* debates about religious toleration and conformity.

It seems certain that this manuscript was intended as a contribution to these debates even though it does not touch directly on the issues generated by the Archpriest controversy. The author's principal claim is that existing statute law does not automatically condemn as treasonable the functions of the English Catholic clergy even though some Protestants had always said that they were. After a good deal of preliminary discussion of technical legal points as to how a Catholic may evade an indictment, its core argument is that Catholics can, even under the extant law, be reckoned to have a defence against some of the charges brought against them under the new treason statutes.

Thus, for example, the author declares that the current statutes, even as they stand, have been misconstrued; they do not mean what the judges often take them to mean, for example over the question of sacramental reconciliation. The argument here is that reconciliation is no different in its import from baptism or absolution from excommunication pronounced in an ecclesiastical court; these things are accomplished by the power of the ordained priest which

---

[32] TNA, SP 78/51, fo. 150ʳ; M. Questier, *Catholicism and Community in Early Modern England: Politics, Aristocratic Patronage and Religion, c.1550–1640* (Cambridge, 2006), 271–272.

[33] As far back as May 1586 we can find the loyalist priest Edward Gratley arguing to Sir Francis Walsingham that 'reconciliation imports' no more than 'a change of a man's mind from a state of sin to a state of grace, by contrition, and purpose of amendment, with submission to the authentical power of a true priest, authorized by Christ to remit sins'. Anyone who suggested that 'reconciliation binds one to the pope or Rome, excluding obedience to the prince or governor' was 'either grossly blinded or maliciously incensed', R. Lemon and M.A.E. Green (eds), *Calendar of State Papers, Domestic Series*, 12 vols [for 1547–1625] (London, 1856–1872), *Addenda 1580–1625*, 178 (TNA, SP 15/29, fo. 165ʳ).

is derived directly from God and not from the royal supremacy.[34] The 1571 statute itself 'doth shewe there be dyvers absolutions and reconciliations; or at leaste more than one'.[35]

The advice falls, then, roughly into two parts. In the first section, it argues that statutory prohibitions of Rome's clergy in England rest on a flawed definition of papal ecclesiastical primacy. The legal foundations of the English national Church cannot be taken to exclude the conventional understanding of a much broader Christendom. In effect, the author argues that the clergy who minister in the Church of England are part of this wider Church. The authority to perform their clerical functions cannot be derived solely from the exercise of the royal supremacy. If so, the carrying out of the Catholic clergy's functions cannot be treasonable *per se*. All bishops within the Catholic apostolic Church have authority to ordain priests. That ordination confers a priesthood the character of which is not derived in the first instance from the see of Rome.[36]

The writer maintains that the English state recognizes these arguments, whatever some of its spokesmen said. This was in part because all the relevant legislation, passed since the Henrician break with Rome, treated the different aspects of papal authority disjunctively, defining the pope as bishop of Rome but rejecting his additional assertion of papal authority. The writer contends also that the Roman Catholic clergy in England are not necessarily exponents of papal assertions of ecclesiastical primacy, at least as it is now interpreted by English statute law (pp. 515–521).

In the second part, relying on the disjunctive definitions of ecclesiastical authority in the first part, the writer says that the exercise of the Roman Catholic clergy's functions in England, principally the action of reconciling sacramentally to Rome, does not fall automatically within the scope of the treason statutes of 1571 and 1581 because by that action there is no intention, of itself, to withdraw from their allegiance her majesty's subjects, which intention the writer argues is required for a conviction under these statutes.

In the context of the 1590s, of course, much of this case seems highly artificial. But there are real echoes here not just of some of the more radical appellants' claims about the ways in which there might be confessional coexistence in England but also of the

---

[34] Archives of the Archdiocese of Westminster [AAW], A, VII, 526.

[35] AAW, A, VII, 527.

[36] There is an obvious compatibility here with the contemporary arguments which were deployed in order to make the case for *jure divino* episcopacy even though defenders of what one might term a high version of the supremacy would, obviously, argue that powers conferred by ordination were not ones that were to be exercised by the monarch; see e.g. J.P. Sommerville, *Politics and Ideology in England 1603–1640* (London, 1986), 208–210.

campaign (associated particularly with the appellant programme) for Rome to institute direct domestic episcopal government over English Catholics, where the principal claim was that the function of such bishops would be spiritual only and would not be in any sense a challenge to monarchical authority. It may also be possible, if rather speculatively, to draw a line between all this and the origins of what scholars have discerned (using a range of terms – everything from avant-garde conformity to 'Arminianism *avant la lettre*'[37]) as a more aggressive reaction inside the Church of England to the problem of puritanism. We can see, for example, some of these Catholic ideas and arguments surfacing in the 1614 conversion motives pamphlet of the royal chaplain Benjamin Carier, someone who is often taken as an outlier for the expression of so-called Arminian opinions in the mid-Jacobean period. Carier reminded King James that he recognized 'the Church of Rome to be mother Church, and the bishop of Rome to be the chiefe bishop or primate of all the westerne Churches, which I doe also verily believe; and therefore I doe verily thinke he hath, or ought to have, some spirituall jurisdiction in England'. Carier implied that a certain sort of Church of England cleric had always had doubts about the doctrine of the supremacy 'although, in my yonger dayes, the fashion of the world made me sweare as other men did (for which I pray God forgive me) yet I ever doubted, and am now resolved, that no Christian man can take that oath with a safe conscience'. There was also a 'statute . . . made by Queene Elizabeth', confirmed by King James, 'that it is death for any English man to be in England, being made a priest by authoritie derived, or pretended to be derived, from the bishop of Rome'. But Carier said: 'I cannot believe that I am a priest at all, unlesse I be derived by authority from Gregory the Great, from whence all the bishops in England have their being, if they have any being at all'. There was 'another statute in like manner made and confirmed that it is death to be reconciled by a Catholike priest to the Church of Rome', but Carier was 'perswaded that the Church of Rome is our mother Church and that no man in England can be saved that continues wilfully out of the visible unitie of that Church, and therefore I canot choose but perwade the people to be reconciled thereunto, if possibly they can'. Of course, by the stage that this pamphlet was written, Carier had formally separated from the national Church and we cannot be sure how far these views expressed in print really reflect his former opinions. But, if they were, then it may be that he was taking reasonably familiar Catholic positions on the statute law which had helped to define the independence of the

[37] See e.g. N. Tyacke, *Anti-Calvinists: The Rise of English Arminianism c.1590–1640* (Oxford, 1987), 5–7.

English Church but was pushing them further than the author of this 'Plea for a Priest' was prepared to do.[38]

Even if there is no straight line between late sixteenth-century arguments for toleration and, say, the rise of (as some scholars term them) avant-garde conformity, Arminianism and even Laudianism, the claims advanced here are far from nonsense. There was always a sense that the Elizabethan additions to the treason law had, as it were, pushed the envelope and that, in many instances, the case made by the prosecution at treason trials was highly controversial. While, as we have already remarked, there is in fact no sound legal basis for the arguments set down in this document, or at least, as far as we know they were never accepted as such in a court of law, they may have reflected the sense and direction of a strand of public opinion (and not necessarily an exclusively Catholic one) which was not fully convinced by the mid and late Elizabethan regime's defence of the queen and state by reference to the threat from popery.[39]

[38]Benjamin Carier, *A Treatise written by M'. Doctour Carier* . . . (Brussels, 1614), 11–12. For George Hakewill's reply to Carier, see George Hakewill, *An Answere to a Treatise* . . . (London, 1616), esp. at sigs F3^V–H4^V. See also M. Questier, 'Crypto-papism, anti-calvinism and conversion: The enigma of Benjamin Carier', *Journal of Ecclesiastical History*, 47 (1996), 45–64. There is a family likeness between Carier's arguments here and the case made by other Jacobean converts, notably Theophilus Higgons who, we know, had links with another alleged 'Arminian', Humphrey Leech; see Theophilus Higgons, *The First Motive of T. H. Maister of Arts, and lately Minister, to suspect the Integrity of his Religion* . . .(Douai, 1609); Humphrey Leech, *A Triumph of Truth, Or, Declaration of the Doctrine concerning Evangelicall Counsayles* . . . (Douai, 1609); Questier, 'Crypto-papism', 59–60.

[39]For this issue, see, e.g., P. Lake and M. Questier, 'The public politics of regime change: Thomas Digges, Robert Parsons and Sir Francis Hastings contest the religio-political arithmetic of the Elizabethan *Fin de Siècle*' (forthcoming in *Historical Journal*).

A PLEE FOR A PRIESTE: AND A PLEE TO PROVE, THAT TO ABSOLVE ONLY FROM HERESY, SCHISME, AND SINNE TO RECONSILE MERELY TO THE UNITIE OF THE HOLY CATHOLIKE CHURCHE, AND TO PERSWADE TO THE HOLY CATHOLIKE AND APOSTOLYKE ~~CHURCHE~~ RELIGION, OR TO THE ROMAN OR ROMISHE RELIGION MERELY AND ONLY FOR RELIGION, IS NOT TREASON ACCORDING TO THE LAWES, PROMULGATE BY HYR MAJESTIE.

[Archives of the Archdiocese of Westminster, Series A, VII, no. 104[1]]

The question ordreth, by what is ment by the sea of Rome, and howe the subjectes of this land are bound by the lawes of the land to beleve one holy Catholyke and apostolyke Churche, which is to be represented by some cleregy, which Church or cleregy may make priestes withowt daunger of the lawe; and whether Clemens 8° be only pope, or only bischop of Rome,[2] or both pope and bischop of Rome; that having diverse dignities, he hath different aucthorities; of the difference betwene episcopus, papa with pontifex; the difference betwene jus and lex; and by comparing other statutes with the statute in anno 27 of hyr majestie cap 2°,[3] yt is to be taken particulerly and not generally; and howe the woordes absolution, reconciliation and persuading to the Romishe religion are to be understoode in some sorte treason, in other sorte not treason. [p. 506]

---

[1] In the editing of this text I have modernized capitalization and punctuation (but not spelling except for the regularization of the use of i and j, and u and v) and I have silently expanded most contractions. I have printed marginal annotations in the body of the text, though only where the material in them adds to rather than merely repeats the text. Words that are struck out are indicated ~~thus~~ and interpolated words appear <thus>.

[2] Clement VIII, elected 30 January 1592, died 3 March 1605.

[3] 'An Act against Jesuites Semynarie Priestes and such other like disobedient Persons', *SR*, IV, 706–707. For the drafting and passing of the bill, see Ward, 'Law of treason', 62–5.

Fyrst is to be considered and learned by what warrant and mittimus every priest prisoner is committed,[4] for according to that is he and his ayders and helpers (yf he escape) none. Whether he be by the terme of traytor, or only (which is lykelyest) by the terme of semenary prieste; and whethere any which have, or may escape, be before his escape indicted uppon that statute capitally ye or no. But yf he be not, and that he be committed by the terme of semenary prieste, then may there be some hope of helpe; and then lett the prisoner at arrainement crave a coppy of the indictment, but yf yt can not be obtained then to crave that yt may be redde in Latin as yt is: for clarkes having the forme of indictment in there heades,[5] do runne over errors in Englishe, which will not so soone be in Latin.[6] And Hambletons case was one woorde wanting in hys indictment, althoughe he were found ghiltie of murder, yett judgment could never be geven on yt against hym.[7] And that errors in indictmentes may be, the second chapter in the parliament in anno 29° of hyr majestie doth sufficiently shewe the same [*in margin*: anno 29 Eliz. that no records of attainder for high treason of any persone where the partie hath bene executed, shall by the heire &c, shall not be reversed, &c for any error whatsoever.[8]] Nowe every formall indictment is a perfect silogisme: the woordes of the statute as the major: Si [?] &c in the indictment the minor; and the witnesses produced or prisoners confession, do prove the conclusion. So that those thre muste concurre, as the adjectyve with

---

[4]See W. Sheppard, *A Grand Abridgment of the Common and Statute Law of England*, 3 vols (London, 1675), II, 438. The 'mittimus' warrant was, inter alia, the authority by which the accused would be brought before the grand jury at the assizes. Its wording would be used for drawing up the bill of indictment presented to that jury (ex inf. Michael Bowman).

[5]Ward, 'Law of treason', 162: for treason cases which originated in the provinces and were tried there, the clerks of the assizes were reponsible for preparing the indictment (whereas, for treason trials in the central courts, the indictments were generally drawn by the crown's law officers, often assisted by the privy council and sometimes by senior judges).

[6]Most indictments were drafted in Latin; this was done for the sake of precision; 'certain essential legal phrases' were required for a valid indictment, without which it was liable to be voided, J.S. Cockburn, *Calendar of Assize Records: Home Circuit Indictments: Elizabeth I and James I: Introduction* (London, 1985), 76–77; cf. C. Viner, *A General Abridgment of Law and Equity*, 2nd edn, 24 vols (London, 1791–1794), XVIII, 259. It is possible that the practice of, occasionally, voiding for misspelling was rather to allow the judges to stop the progress of an indictment where substantial injustice might result after an arraignment. See also Ward, 'Law of treason', 169.

[7]The court of King's Bench in 1604 ruled that the clerk's spelling of '*burglariter*' as '*burgariter*' in a felony indictment was sufficient to void it, Cockburn, *Calendar of Assize Records: Home Circuit Indictments: Elizabeth I and James I: Introduction*, 76. The case of *Hambleton* has not been located; see also Ward, 'Law of treason', 169–170.

[8]'An Acte concerninge Errors in Recordes of Attayndors of Highe Treason', *SR*, IV, 767.

A PLEE FOR A PRIESTE: AND A PLEE TO PROVE, THAT TO ABSOLVE ONLY FROM HERESY, SCHISME, AND SINNE TO RECONSILE MERELY TO THE UNITIE OF THE HOLY CATHOLIKE CHURCHE, AND TO PERSWADE TO THE HOLY CATHOLIKE AND APOSTOLYKE ~~CHURCHE~~ RELIGION, OR TO THE ROMAN OR ROMISHE RELIGION MERELY AND ONLY FOR RELIGION, IS NOT TREASON ACCORDING TO THE LAWES, PROMULGATE BY HYR MAJESTIE.

[Archives of the Archdiocese of Westminster, Series A, VII, no. 104[1]]

The question ordreth, by what is ment by the sea of Rome, and howe the subjectes of this land are bound by the lawes of the land to beleve one holy Catholyke and apostolyke Churche, which is to be represented by some cleregy, which Church or cleregy may make priestes withowt daunger of the lawe; and whether Clemens 8° be only pope, or only bischop of Rome,[2] or both pope and bischop of Rome; that having diverse dignities, he hath different aucthorities; of the difference betwene episcopus, papa with pontifex; the difference betwene jus and lex; and by comparing other statutes with the statute in anno 27 of hyr majestie cap 2°,[3] yt is to be taken particulerly and not gcnerally; and howe the woordes absolution, reconciliation and persuading to the Romishe religion are to be understoode in some sorte treason, in other sorte not treason. [p. 506]

---

[1] In the editing of this text I have modernized capitalization and punctuation (but not spelling except for the regularization of the use of i and j, and u and v) and I have silently expanded most contractions. I have printed marginal annotations in the body of the text, though only where the material in them adds to rather than merely repeats the text. Words that are struck out are indicated ~~thus~~ and interpolated words appear <thus>.

[2] Clement VIII, elected 30 January 1592, died 3 March 1605.

[3] 'An Act against Jesuites Semynarie Priestes and such other like disobedient Persons', *SR*, IV, 706–707. For the drafting and passing of the bill, see Ward, 'Law of treason', 62–5.

Fyrst is to be considered and learned by what warrant and mittimus every priest prisoner is committed,[4] for according to that is he and his ayders and helpers (yf he escape) none. Whether he be by the terme of traytor, or only (which is lykelyest) by the terme of semenary prieste; and whethere any which have, or may escape, be before his escape indicted uppon that statute capitally ye or no. But yf he be not, and that he be committed by the terme of semenary prieste, then may there be some hope of helpe; and then lett the prisoner at arrainement crave a coppy of the indictment, but yf yt can not be obtained then to crave that yt may be redde in Latin as yt is: for clarkes having the forme of indictment in there heades,[5] do runne over errors in Englishe, which will not so soone be in Latin.[6] And Hambletons case was one woorde wanting in hys indictment, althoughe he were found ghiltie of murder, yett judgment could never be geven on yt against hym.[7] And that errors in indictmentes may be, the second chapter in the parliament in anno 29° of hyr majestie doth sufficiently shewe the same [*in margin*: anno 29 Eliz. that no records of attainder for high treason of any persone where the partie hath bene executed, shall by the heire &c, shall not be reversed, &c for any error whatsoever.[8]] Nowe every formall indictment is a perfect silogisme: the woordes of the statute as the major: Si [?] &c in the indictment the minor; and the witnesses produced or prisoners confession, do prove the conclusion. So that those thre muste concurre, as the adjectyve with

[4]See W. Sheppard, *A Grand Abridgment of the Common and Statute Law of England*, 3 vols (London, 1675), II, 438. The 'mittimus' warrant was, inter alia, the authority by which the accused would be brought before the grand jury at the assizes. Its wording would be used for drawing up the bill of indictment presented to that jury (ex inf. Michael Bowman).

[5]Ward, 'Law of treason', 162: for treason cases which originated in the provinces and were tried there, the clerks of the assizes were reponsible for preparing the indictment (whereas, for treason trials in the central courts, the indictments were generally drawn by the crown's law officers, often assisted by the privy council and sometimes by senior judges).

[6]Most indictments were drafted in Latin; this was done for the sake of precision; 'certain essential legal phrases' were required for a valid indictment, without which it was liable to be voided, J.S. Cockburn, *Calendar of Assize Records: Home Circuit Indictments: Elizabeth I and James I: Introduction* (London, 1985), 76–77; cf. C. Viner, *A General Abridgment of Law and Equity*, 2nd edn, 24 vols (London, 1791–1794), XVIII, 259. It is possible that the practice of, occasionally, voiding for misspelling was rather to allow the judges to stop the progress of an indictment where substantial injustice might result after an arraignment. See also Ward, 'Law of treason', 169.

[7]The court of King's Bench in 1604 ruled that the clerk's spelling of '*burglariter*' as '*burgariter*' in a felony indictment was sufficient to void it, Cockburn, *Calendar of Assize Records: Home Circuit Indictments: Elizabeth I and James I: Introduction*, 76. The case of *Hambleton* has not been located; see also Ward, 'Law of treason', 169–170.

[8]'An Acte concerninge Errors in Recordes of Attayndors of Highe Treason', *SR*, IV, 767.

A PLEE FOR A PRIESTE: AND A PLEE TO PROVE, THAT TO ABSOLVE ONLY FROM HERESY, SCHISME, AND SINNE TO RECONSILE MERELY TO THE UNITIE OF THE HOLY CATHOLIKE CHURCHE, AND TO PERSWADE TO THE HOLY CATHOLIKE AND APOSTOLYKE ~~CHURCHE~~ RELIGION, OR TO THE ROMAN OR ROMISHE RELIGION MERELY AND ONLY FOR RELIGION, IS NOT TREASON ACCORDING TO THE LAWES, PROMULGATE BY HYR MAJESTIE.

[Archives of the Archdiocese of Westminster, Series A, VII, no. 104[1]]

The question ordreth, by what is ment by the sea of Rome, and howe the subjectes of this land are bound by the lawes of the land to beleve one holy Catholyke and apostolyke Churche, which is to be represented by some cleregy, which Church or cleregy may make priestes withowt daunger of the lawe; and whether Clemens 8° be only pope, or only bischop of Rome,[2] or both pope and bischop of Rome; that having diverse dignities, he hath different aucthorities; of the difference betwene episcopus, papa with pontifex; the difference betwene jus and lex; and by comparing other statutes with the statute in anno 27 of hyr majestie cap 2°,[3] yt is to be taken particulerly and not generally; and howe the woordes absolution, reconciliation and persuading to the Romishe religion are to be understoode in some sorte treason, in other sorte not treason. [p. 506]

---

[1] In the editing of this text I have modernized capitalization and punctuation (but not spelling except for the regularization of the use of i and j, and u and v) and I have silently expanded most contractions. I have printed marginal annotations in the body of the text, though only where the material in them adds to rather than merely repeats the text. Words that are struck out are indicated ~~thus~~ and interpolated words appear <thus>.

[2] Clement VIII, elected 30 January 1592, died 3 March 1605.

[3] 'An Act against Jesuites Semynarie Priestes and such other like disobedient Persons', *SR*, IV, 706–707. For the drafting and passing of the bill, see Ward, 'Law of treason', 62–5.

Fyrst is to be considered and learned by what warrant and mittimus every priest prisoner is committed,[4] for according to that is he and his ayders and helpers (yf he escape) none. Whether he be by the terme of traytor, or only (which is lykelyest) by the terme of semenary prieste; and whethere any which have, or may escape, be before his escape indicted uppon that statute capitally ye or no. But yf he be not, and that he be committed by the terme of semenary prieste, then may there be some hope of helpe; and then lett the prisoner at arrainement crave a coppy of the indictment, but yf yt can not be obtained then to crave that yt may be redde in Latin as yt is: for clarkes having the forme of indictment in there heades,[5] do runne over errors in Englishe, which will not so soone be in Latin.[6] And Hambletons case was one woorde wanting in hys indictment, althoughe he were found ghiltie of murder, yett judgment could never be geven on yt against hym.[7] And that errors in indictmentes may be, the second chapter in the parliament in anno 29° of hyr majestie doth sufficiently shewe the same [*in margin*: anno 29 Eliz. that no records of attainder for high treason of any persone where the partie hath bene executed, shall by the heire &c, shall not be reversed, &c for any error whatsoever.[8]] Nowe every formall indictment is a perfect silogisme: the woordes of the statute as the major: Si [?] &c in the indictment the minor; and the witnesses produced or prisoners confession, do prove the conclusion. So that those thre muste concurre, as the adjectyve with

---

[4]See W. Sheppard, *A Grand Abridgment of the Common and Statute Law of England*, 3 vols (London, 1675), II, 438. The 'mittimus' warrant was, inter alia, the authority by which the accused would be brought before the grand jury at the assizes. Its wording would be used for drawing up the bill of indictment presented to that jury (ex inf. Michael Bowman).

[5]Ward, 'Law of treason', 162: for treason cases which originated in the provinces and were tried there, the clerks of the assizes were reponsible for preparing the indictment (whereas, for treason trials in the central courts, the indictments were generally drawn by the crown's law officers, often assisted by the privy council and sometimes by senior judges).

[6]Most indictments were drafted in Latin; this was done for the sake of precision; 'certain essential legal phrases' were required for a valid indictment, without which it was liable to be voided, J.S. Cockburn, *Calendar of Assize Records: Home Circuit Indictments: Elizabeth I and James I: Introduction* (London, 1985), 76–77; cf. C. Viner, *A General Abridgment of Law and Equity*, 2nd edn, 24 vols (London, 1791–1794), XVIII, 259. It is possible that the practice of, occasionally, voiding for misspelling was rather to allow the judges to stop the progress of an indictment where substantial injustice might result after an arraignment. See also Ward, 'Law of treason', 169.

[7]The court of King's Bench in 1604 ruled that the clerk's spelling of '*burglariter*' as '*burgariter*' in a felony indictment was sufficient to void it, Cockburn, *Calendar of Assize Records: Home Circuit Indictments: Elizabeth I and James I: Introduction*, 76. The case of *Hambleton* has not been located; see also Ward, 'Law of treason', 169–170.

[8]'An Acte concerninge Errors in Recordes of Attayndors of Highe Treason', *SR*, IV, 767.

the substantyve; or as a chequere talee which being joyned muste [word illegible] in name and somme, in shere & yere.[9] The statute is in anno 27° Eliz. cap. 2°:[10] Whosoever being [p. 507] borne subjecte &c made priest &c by any aucthoretie or jurisdiction derived, chalendged or pretended from the sea of Rome, by or of what name, title or degre soever, the same shalbe caulled or knowne to come into &c. Here may growe a question: whethere these wordes, by or of what name &c be to be referred to the sea of Rome, or to the persone religiouse or priest; yf yt be to the priest (as I take yt to be by the woordes degree, and to come into) althoughe the woorde name or title are doubtfully, then the more advauntage for the prisoner, yf to Rome, then the lesse.

By a statute in anno 1° Eliz. ca[p] 2°[11] yt is ordeyned that whatsoever persone shall &c speake &c in derogation &c of the booke of Common preyer, or of any thing there in conteyned, or any parte thereof shall incurre. In that booke there is the apostles creede, St Athanasius Creede, and the Nicene creede, which Nicene, (or Constantinopolitane creede, for that yt was made at Constantinople, and approved at the Nicene Councell), hath lardger woordes for the purpose than the reste, albeyt to vowe in baptisme the apostles creede were sufficient, wherein every Christian bindeth hymselfe to beleve the hooly Catholyke Churche which is a company of men. Butt the Nicene creede sayth, one holy Catholyke and apostolyke Churche, so that every subject of this land (being a Christian) is bounde by the lawes promulgate by hyr majestie, to beleve one universall Churche, lyke to the apostles in aucthoritie, or pertaining to an apostle. For eythere the woorde apostolyke is to be understoode according to the Englishe woorde lyke to an apostle, as lordlyke and ladylyke, lyke to lorde and lady; or according to the Latin apostolicus, -ca, -cum, pertaining to an apostle, as Elias Anthonius [p. 508] Nebrissensis in his dictionarie doth declare;[12] albeyt that Barrett[13] and Legate[14] with

---

[9]Revenue paid into the receipt of the exchequer was registered in the teller's office by notches on tally sticks equivalent to the sum entered on the teller's bill, and split down the middle, M.S. Giuseppi (ed.), *Guide to the Contents of the Public Record Office*, 2 vols (London, 1963), I, 98.

[10]For the drafting and passing of the bill, see Ward, 'Law of treason', 62–65.

[11]'An Acte for the Uniformitie of Common Prayoure and Dyvyne Service in the Churche, and the Administration of the Sacramentes', *SR*, IV, 356.

[12]Antonio de Lebrixa (Antonio de Nebrija 1441–1552), *Dictionarium Latinohispanicum et Vice Versa Hispanicolatinum, Aeolio Antonio Nebrissensi Interprete* . . . (Antwerp 1570), sig. Bvi[v].

[13]John Barret, *An Alvearie or Quadruple Dictionarie, containing foure sundrie tongues* (London, 1580), 507.

[14]Thomas Thomas, *Dictionarium Linguae Latinae et Anglicanae . . . Cantabrigiae: Ex Officina Iohannis Legatt* . . .(London, 1589), sig. E[v]–2[r]. John Legate (d. 1620 ?) possessed an exclusive

other moderne wryters in there dictionaries do omitte the woorde, yt may be because yt ymporteth the same.

Nowe yf the Church which we are bound to beleve, by the lawes of the land be lyke the apostles, then hath yt aucthorities not only to forgeve synnes but also to make priestes; for St Paule [Titus 1] dyd not only make priestes; but also ordeyned that Titus should constitute priestes.[15] Or yf yt be taken to pertaine to an apostle, then can not the Churche of England be only yt. For take the first tyme of our conversion in King Lucius dayes,[16] wrought by Fuganus and Damanus with others, from St Eleutherius pope and martyr; and there is no knowledge of any the apostles to be then alive. And for St John the Evangelist, which is holden to lyve the longest, yett made he his aboade in Asia which is in the Easte; and not in England, which is in the Weste; and albeyt yt is sayd that Joseph of Aramathia dyed at Glassenbury,[17] yett was he no apostle, or had he bene as there were xii besydes St Paule and Barnabas, yett that counsell at Nicea[18] determined but one apostolyke Churche, and at suche tyme as that counsell was holden this country was over-runne with infidelitie againe some 30 yeres before and so continewed some 300 yeres untill St Gregorie, pope and doctor of the Churche, who sent and wrought the second conversion of this our country, or at leaste the laste from paganisme. And therefore England <may be a parte> of the apostolyke [p. 509] Churche. But only yt, yt can not be.

In anno 25° Henr. 8 cap. 21°[19] for as muche as your majestie is supreme hed of the Churche of England, as the prelates and cleregy of your realme representing the seyd Churche in there synodes and convocations have recognized the same; and by a statute in anno 24° Henr. 8 cap. 12°[20] yt hath the body spirituall &c without the entirmedling of any exteriour persone or persones to determine all doubtes &c.

And in the sayd statute in anno 25° cap. 21° provyded allwayes that this acte nor any thing or thinges therein conteyned shalbe hereafter interpreted or expounded that your grace, your nobles and subjectes intend by the same to declyne or vary from the congregation of

right to publish the Latin dictionary compiled by Thomas Thomas, who was his predecessor as printer to the University of Cambridge.

[15] Titus 1:5.

[16] H.A. MacDougall, *Racial Myth in English History* (Montreal, 1982), 9, 32.

[17] MacDougall, *Racial Myth*, 14.

[18] First Council of Nicea, AD 325.

[19] 'An Acte for the Exoneracion frome Exaccions payde to the See of Rome', *SR*, III, 464–471.

[20] 'An Acte that the Appeles in suche Cases as have ben used to be pursued to the See of Rome shall not from hensforth had ne used but wythin this Realme', *SR*, III, 427–429.

Christes Churche in any thinges concerning the very articles of the Catholyke fayth of Christiandome &c. Which two statutes, albeyt they were repealed by a statute made in annis primo et secundo Phi. & Mary,[21] so were the same statutes revived by a statute in anno primo Eliz. cap. 2°. Then is the Churche of England a Churche represented by the cleregy of England without any exterior persone whosoever, not varieng from the congregation of Christes Churche in any thinges touching the very articles of the Catholyke fayth of Christiandome.

By this the lawes of the land do geve us to understand that Christe hath his Churche besydes the Churche of England [p. 510] and our Saviour having [sic] but one Churche, and England being a Churche without any exteriour person. So that yf England be not his Churche as by those statutes yt may be supposed, nor a parte of his Churche, excluding every other persone, then eythere the communion of saintes muste only be in England, or England they have sequestred out of the communion of saintes.

Nowe England to be only the Churche of Christe, this were greatly to ympare the principallytie and signurie of our Saviour, he which gave his lyfe for his Churche, and his lyfe have he gave for all the world, and all men in the state of grace are members of his misticall body, which is his Churche.

Nowe yf the Churche of England be not that mysticall body, what derogation were that to hyr majestie, that should be intitled suche a member of that Churche, which is not the body of Christe.

Nowe yf the Churche of England be represented by the cleregy of England, then no doubte but the holy Catholyke and apostolyke Church is represented by the cleregy of that holy Catholyke and apostolyke Churche; which Churche of Christ hath (as St Paule sayth) [Acts 20; Titus 1] [22] bischops; and bischops have aucthoritie to make priestes; which priestes made by bischops of the holy Catholyke and apostolyke Churche he thinketh dishonorably of hyr majestie and magistrates that understandeth the lawes of the land to include them as daungerous members of this common weale [p. 511] which are made priestes by the aucthoritie of that holy Catholyke and apostolyke Churche; yt being apparaunt that the lawes of this land do hold that there is one holy Catholyke and apostolyke Churche and that hyr majesties subjectes are bound to beleve yt.

---

[21] 'An Acte repealing all Statutes Articles and Provisions made against the See Apostolick of Rome since the xx[th] yere of King Henry theight, and also for thestablishment of all spyrytuall and ecclesiasticall Possessions and Hereditamentes conveyed to the Layetye' (1 & 2 Philip and Mary, c. 8), *SR*, IV, 246–254.

[22] Acts 20:28; Titus 1:5.

By a coppy of an indictment a man might partely yf not apparauntly perceave whethere the woordes 'by' or 'of what name' &c had relation to the prieste, or to the sea of Rome. The woordde 'sea' is sedes in Latin, that is seate, which is taken to be the Church of Rome; which sea, seate, bischopricke or Churche is to be represented by some man or men; which at this day is holden to be Clemens 8° papa. So they will have Clemens 8° to be episcopius Rom[a]e, and not Romanus pontifex, nor papa.

Then lett the question be whethere he be only pope, or only bischop of Rome, or bothe pope and bischop of Rome. Yf they will have him to be only episcopius Rom[a]e, then as every bischop hath his archbischop, primate, metrapolitan or patriarche, then would I gladly know who is the bischop of Rome his archebischop, primate, metrapolitane or patriarche; and, withall, who was the firste bischop of Rome; for that may as easily be knowne as any bischop of England. Some do suppose that St Silvester was the firste; others, Leo decimus; for Guychardin in his Italien cronacle[23] geves Leo 10[us] and his predecessors the title or terme of il papa, and il pontifice; and not vescuovo, that is bischop. And that he recompteth [p. 512] that Luthere woold that Leo 10[us] woold content hymselfe with his episcopate di Roma, that is with his bischoprick of Rome; and not to extend his jurisdiction into other bischoprickes, and that in the statutes made in the 25 yere of Henry the 8th, and after in his tyme, he goeth by the title or terme of bischop of Rome, otherwise caulled the pope. And John Stowe in the somary of his cronicle sayth in the 26 yere of Henry the 8th in November was held a parliament wherein the bischop of Rome with all his aucthoritie was cleane banished this realme, and commaundement geven that he should no more be caulled pope, but bischop of Rome.[24] So that with the Italians there is greate difference betwene il papa, il pontifice and vescuovo, and therefore at the election of the pope Guichardine sayth: gli vescuovi et gli baroni Romani, that is the bischops and Romaine lordes or barons, do guarde the conclave (which is more than to any bischop in Christiandome) and with Englishmen, betwene pope and bischop of Rome, ells woold not that title or terme [have] bene countremaunded by the kinges commaunde.

---

[23]Francesco Guiccardini's history of Italy (*Storia d'Italia*).

[24]John Stow, *The Summarie of Englishe Chronicles: (Latelye collected and published) abridged and continued til this present moneth of November in the yeare of our Lord God 1567*(London, 1567), fo. 148[v]: 'in November [26 Henry VIII] by a parliamente the byshop of Rome with al his authoritie was cleane banished this realme, and commaundement geven that he should no more be called Pope but bishop of Rome, and that the king should be reputed as supreme head of the Church of England'.

Some, as aforeseyd, say that St Silvester the pope, was the first bischop of Rome, and his predecessors only popes: and the raison they yeld is: because that Constantine the greate after he became Christian, and geving the tenth parte of his empyre to the Churche [p. 513] for thythe [i.e. tithe], and yelding hys emperyall seate of Rome to St Silvester, then pope, and translating hys empyre or emperiall seate to Constantinople was since by couler of that, of late, caulled bischop of Rome. But yf he were not, nor his predecessors before hym, bischops of Rome, howe could he be then: as thoughe the emperour could make hym bischop of Rome, who had more humilitie and religion in hym than to take uppon hym suche aucthoritie? For St Silvester his pontificall jurisdiction was not any more by that augmented, albeyt his habilitie was thereby mightily amended. For instance, the bischop of Ely, for the tyme being, hath royaltie in the Ile of Ely, and not in the reste of Cambridge shere as there; and yet, for his episcopall jurisdiction, yt is as greate in Cambridge shere as there, and no greater in the Ile, then ells where in Cambridge shere.[25] Semblably the pope, albeyt for his temporall estate he hath principalitie in Rome, Romania and other landes geven to the Romane Churche and not ells where. But for his pontificall dignitie or jurisdiction, as greate ells where in the holy Catholyke Churche, as there.

Nowe as the termes of pope and bischop of Rome are caulled into question in these dayes, the true definition or signification of them are necessarie to be knowne.

First: Episcopius; according to John Veron his dictionary corrected 1575 a bischop, which hath superintendance of some place, which [p. 514] watcheth and hath an eye to, or governance of, some people.[26] Barrett in his dictionarie dedicated to the late lord tresorer:[27] episcopius, a bischop, an espye, an overseer.[28] Elius Anthonius Nibrissen in his dictionarie: episcopius, a bischop a prelate of the Churche, and episcopos, an espye.[29] So that Nibrissen makes a difference between episcopius and episcopos; for papa and pontifex, they are in the opynion of some all one, and therefore Guichardin, with the Italians, il papa, and il pontifice, is all one.

Nibrissen sayth that papa is pontifex maximus vel summus.[30]

---

[25] The bishop of Ely was also custodian of the liberty of Ely and so exercised secular as well as spiritual power over those parishes, though not the rest of his diocese in Cambridgeshire, M.J. Ingram, *Church Courts, Sex and Marriage in England, 1570–1640* (Cambridge, 1987), 352.

[26] John Veron, *A Dictionarie in Latine and English, heretofore set forth by Master Iohn Veron, and now newlie corrected and enlarged* (London, 1584), sig. Pvi[r].

[27] Sir William Cecil, Lord Burghley (d. 4 August 1598).

[28] Barret, *Alvearie*, sig. Gvi[r].

[29] Lebrixa, *Dictionarium*, sig. I.ii[v].

[30] Lebrixa, *Dictionarium*, sig. Tv[r].

Legate in his dictionarie to the late lord tresorer sayth: papa a father, the pope.[31]

Veron sayth pontifex is a minister of holy thinges, a bischop.[32]

Barrett sayth pontifex, a chiefe bischop, a prelate, and pontifex maximus, a highe bischop.[33]

Legate sayth: pontifex, a bischop, a prelate, and pontifex maximus, the pope, the chiefest bischop.[34]

The Councell helden at Tridentum dyd commend the approbation and correction of there actions, Romanus pontifici, and not episcopo de Roma.

And in Leviticus 21° chapter, pontifex, id est sacerdos [p. 515] maximus.[35]

Nowe yf the sea of Rome be but only the sea of a bischop, what aucthoritie of jurisdiction can he have over any other bischop, and much lesse over archbischops and patriarches in Fraunce, Spayne and Germanie, or any other parte of Christiandome? But yf Clemens 8° not only be bischop of Rome, but Romanus pontifex, or papa, and such priestes as come over are made by bischops, [and] deryve there aucthoritie from Romanus pontifice or papa, this is nothing offensyve to the lettre of the lawe; for there is as muche difference betwene episcopus Rom[a]e, and Romanus pontifex, or papa, as is betwene rex Francorum, and rex Francie and, betwene these, there is as muche, as is betwene treason and not treason. For whosoever Englishe subjecte shall say, that Henry of Burbon, that nowe is, is Rex Francie, is in case of high treason, but not so in caulling hym rex Francorum; and therefore without daunger he may be caulled the Frenche kinge, but not the kinge of Fraunce.[36] The objection [an objection] which may be made is that the bischop of Rome and the pope is all one man, and therefore all included in the same aucthoritie.

[The answere] Admitt he be all one man, yett yf yt [be] two dignities, then are there different aucthorities.

But first yf he be pope, and that name or dignetie ymporte or [p. 516] signifie so muche, howe can he be an inferior bischop, no more

---

[31]Thomas, *Dictionarium*, sig. Pp8[r].

[32]Veron, *Dictionarie*, sig. Ii.iiii[r]. Veron was a Huguenot Protestant, and it is probably significant that the author here selects instances from a Reformed work to support his case against hostile Protestant scrutiny.

[33]Barret, *Alvearie*, sig. Gvi[r].

[34]Thomas, *Dictionarium*, sig. Tt3[v].

[35]Leviticus 21:10.

[36]By the act 13 Eliz. c. 1, it was treason directly to 'publish, declare . . . or saye' that Elizabeth was not or should not be queen of England, France and Ireland, Ward, 'Law of treason', 20–21; *SR*, IV, 526. In mid 1585 Mark Wiersdale was indicted for saying that Elizabeth was not queen of France or Ireland, Ward, 'Law of treason', 182–183.

then hyr majestie can be dutchez of langkaster, yt being incorporate into the crowne? And then yt is as easye to fynde a duke of Langkaster since Henry the 4th, a duke of Yorke since Edward the 4th, or a duke of Gloscester since Rycherd the 3[d] as to fynde a bischop of Rome. That there is a pope, yt is clerely to be inferred by the lawes of the land. For yf there be popishe recusantes, then there is a pope; but popishe recusantes there are [a° 35° Eliz. cap. 2°].[37] Ergo there is a pope. The maior proved, the minor foloweth.

But lett yt be that Clemens 8° be both bischop of Rome and pope. Then by his papacy he hath pontificall dignitie, and by his bishoprick of Rome but diocesan jurisdiction; and so different auctorities. Els the bischop of Winc[h]ester is parsone of E[a]st Meade.

Nowe suppose the case that a lawe were made to frustrate all leasez made by all the parsones of the land; and the bischop of Winc[h]ester had as well made leasez of his bishoprick landes as of his parsonage of E[a]st Meade. Woold the lawe be understoode to avoyde all his leasez made of his bishoprick lands? I thinke [p. 517] not, for he makes ministers as bishop of Winc[h]ester and not as parsone of E[a]st Meade; and he is of the higher howse of parliament, not as parson of East Meade, but as bischop of Winc[h]ester.

The shryve [sheriff] of Huntingdon and Cambridge sheres is all one man, but different aucthorities, for yf the quenes writt be directed to hym for Huntingdon shere, can he execute the same in Cambridge shere? I take yt not.

Henry the last king of Portingall,[38] being cardinall, could aswell performe priestly founction as kingly aucthoritie, which was more than Saule or Jeroboam, kinges of Israell, or Ezras, king of Juda, could do for that they receaved reproche and punishment of God for intruding themselves into the sacerdotale dignitie. Then in the carde[n]all kinge there was different aucthorities, yett all one man.

Melchizadeck, being king and prieste, had in hym different aucthorities, for yf they were relatyve, that is one depending uppon the other, then the messias, being foretold, to be a priest for ever after the ordre of Melchizadeck, should have bene king of Salem to[o]; and so to have had a kingdome of this woorld, which our Saviour hymselfe dyd disclame before Pylate.

Nowe yf Clemens 8° be but bischop of Rome, then other bischops and muche lesse archebischops <and patriarkes> can no more deryve there aucthorities from hym than he from them, and [p. 518]

---

[37]'An Acte against Popishe Recusantes', *SR*, IV, 843–846.
[38]Henry (1512–1580), king of Portugal and the Algarves (1578–1580), and cardinal of the Church of Rome (1545).

then suche priestes as are made by them, without daunger of the lawe.

Butt yf Clemens 8⁰ be papa or pontifex, and that to be taken as in the 21 of Leviticus, for other bischops are written by the woorde 'episcopus', and he only Romanus pontifex; then suche priestes as are made by bischops, deryving there aucthoritie from the papacy or pontificall dignitie are not included within the compas of the statute.

Or yf they be made priestes by the bischops or bischop representing the apostolike Churche, muche lesse can they be indaungered when the lawes of this land do bind us, or at leste protecte us, to beleve that Churche.

Nowe eyther the apostolyke Churche and sea of Rome are bothe represented by one bischop and cleregy, or they are not. Yf they be, then are the subjectes of this land in harde case to be bound by the lawes to beleve them; and capitally to be indaungered in receaving them. Yf they be not bothe one, then without daunger (I hope) I may receave those whom hyr majesties lawes do binde me to beleve.

That the lawe is to be taken, according to the lettre of the lawe; Elius Anthonius Nebrissenses, maketh this difference betwen jus and lex: jus the facultie [p. 519] or power of every one, the right which interpreteth the lawe; lex for the lawe, generally of the verbe lego, legis.[39]

Barrettt in his dictionarie sayth, lawe, right: jus a jussu deducit, nihil enim aliud est jus, quam quod vel natura, vel civitas aut populus, vel gens, vel consuetudo jubet[.][40] Differt autem jus a lege, quod jus generale est, lex vere ejus est species. Jus etiam ad non scripta pertinet, ut jus naturale et jus gentium lex tantum ad jus scriptum refertur.[41]

And our Saviour hymselfe, to the lawyere which tempted hym, sayd in lege quid scriptum est quomodo legis.

Nowe yf the lawe to be taken and understoode, as yt is written; according to the opynion humane and aucthoritie divine. Then lett us see whatt the law sayth. The lawe [anno 27 Eli[z]][42] sayth, as aforeseyd, whosoever shalbe made prieste &c by any aucthoritie &c from the sea of Rome shall &c.

---

[39] Lebrixa, *Dictionarium*, sigs Nvii[r], Oiii[r].

[40] In his text Barret, *Alvearie*, sig. Nniiii[v] inserts 'Loy, droit'.

[41] Barret, *Alvearie*, sig.Nniiii[v].

[42] i.e. 'An Act againste Jesuites Semynarie Priestes and such other like disobedient Persons', *SR*, IV, 706–707.

Butt John at Style was made priest &c from the hooly Catholyke and apostolyke Churche.[43] Therefore not ghiltie yf obiection should be made that you meane the Sea of Rome.

To that may be answered: yf Christ his Churche were begune in Hierusalem presently after his passion [Acts 9], before any Englishe men were members of yt, is [sic] to be Catholyke and apostolyke, that is universall, and lyke, or pertaining to, an apostle; then the Churche of England can not be yt, and then muste you needes [p. 520] graunte yt to be some where, and syth our Saviour hymselfe hath not designed yt locall, and his apostles pronounced yt to be universall; and the hooly councell at Nicea determined yt to be both universall and apostolicall; for my parte, as one of the meanest members of Christ his Churche, I dare not restraine yt to be provinciall or nationall.

Hadde this statute runne with suche lardge or generall woordes, as some other statutes doe, then had yt bene more daungerous; as, for example, in anno 23 Elizabeth Regine,[44] whosoever shall withdrawe &c to any pretended aucthoritie of the sea of Rome, or of any other state or potentate.

[Anno 24 H8 ca. 12] There the termes are from the sea of Rome, or any forraine courtes or potentates of the woorld &c.[45]

From or to the sea of Rome or from or to any other forraine court or courtes &c.

Make provision to the sea of Rome or ells where for any thing &c.

[Anno 25 H8 ca. 20] By the bischops of Rome, otherwyse caulled the pope and sea of Rome.[46]

[cap. 21] By the bischop of Rome, otherwyse caulled the pope and sea of Rome &c.[47]

Wherein the bischop of Rome, not as to the observauntes of the lawes of any forraine prince, potentate or prelate &c.

To the use of the seyd bischop of Rome or of the sea of Rome, which he caulleth apostolyke. Sue to the seyd bischop of Rome, caulled the pope, or to the sea of Rome. Obtained at the courte of Rome. [p. 521]

---

[43] For the function of juries in exonerating the indicted person by identifying fictitious individuals as the guilty party, see E. Hanson, 'Torture and truth in Renaissance England', *Representations* 34 (1991), 53–84, at 81 n. 38, citing L. A. Knafla, 'John at Love killed her: The assizes and criminal law in early modern England', *University of Toronto Law Journal* 35 (1985), 314–317; cf. Cockburn, *Calendar of Assize Records: Home Circuit Indictments: Elizabeth I and James I: Introduction*, 113.

[44] 'An Acte to reteine the Queenes Ma^tes Subjectes in their due Obedience' (23 Eliz. c. 1), *SR*, IV, 657–658.

[45] *SR*, III, 428.

[46] 'An Acte restraining the Payment of Annates, &c', *SR*, III, 462–464.

[47] *SR*, III, 464–471.

[cap. 22] By raison whereof the bischop of Rome and sea apostolyke &c from the courte of Rome.[48]

[Anno 28 H8 cap. 16] Of the bischop of Rome for the tyme being, or by the aucthoritie of the sea of Rome.[49]

[Anno 25 H8 ca. 14] Made by the popes or bischops of Rome, which statute,[50] albeyt yt was repealed in anno 1° Edwardi 6 cap. 12,[51] yett yt expresseth popes and buschops of Rome in the disjonctyve. Therefore different aucthorities.

Nowe, had the statute of making priestes gon with suche generall termes as these doe, then had there bene lesse helpe; and these going by diverse termes do ymporte different aucthorities.

Nowe yf the letter of the lawe be to be observed, and these shewe differ[e]nt aucthorities, and but one aucthoritie countremaunded by the lawe, then are the reste free.[52]

Howe the woordes absolution, reconsiliation and persuading to the Romishe religion are to be understoode aswell not treason, or treason according to the statute in a° 23° Eliz Regine cap. primo.

[Anno 23 Eliz ca. 1°] The preamble of the statute sayth: where practize hath bene by other meanes than by bulles &c to withdrawe diverse the quenes subjectes from there naturall obeydience to hyr majestie to obey the usurped aucthoritie of Rome, and in respecte of the same to persuade great nombers to withdrawe there due obeyience to hyr majesties lawes established for the due syrvice of almightie God.[53]

This statute hath relation to a statute in anno 13° Eliz. cap 2°.[54] This of 13° hath reference to anno 5° of hyr majestie cap. 1°; that statute in anno 5° hath designment to a statute made in anno [p. 522] primo of hyr majestie cap. 1°[55] which, being so, lett us begin at the first and so drawe downe to 23 Eliz. cap. 1°.

[Anno Eliz. cap. 1°] First the statute in anno 1° sayth in the preamble thereof that, in the tyme of Henry the 8, diverse statutes were made

---

[48] 'An Acte for the Establishement of the Kynges Succession', *SR*, III, 471–474.

[49] 'An Acte for the Release of suche as have obtained pretended Lycenses and Dispensacions from the See of Rome', *SR*, III, 672–3.

[50] 'An Acte for Punysshement of Heresye', *SR*, III, 454–455.

[51] 'An Acte for the Repeale of certaine Statutes concerninge Treasons, Felonyes, &c', *SR*, IV, 18–22.

[52] Michael Bowman points out that this is a sound line of legal argument. If a statute distinguishes between several different categories of authority and specifies that only one is unlawful, then the silence concerning the others means that they are presumed to be lawful and valid.

[53] *SR*, IV, 657.

[54] 'An Acte agaynste the bringing in and putting in execution of Bulls and other Instruments from the Sea of Rome', *SR*, IV, 528–531.

[55] Ward, 'Law of treason', 50–53: 13 Eliz. c. 2 was derived from the act of supremacy of 1559 and from 5 Eliz. c. 1 of 1563.

for the extinguishment &c of all forraine aucthorities &c owt of the realme; as also for the restoring and uniting to the ymperiall crowne of the realme the auncient jurisdiction &c, and to the intent that all usurped and forraine power &c may be extinguished, be yt enacted that no forraine prince, prelate &c spirituall or temporall shall at any tyme &c use or exercize within this realme &c any manner of power of jurisdiction &c spirituall or ecclesiasticall &c.

The reformation of heresiez &c to be united and annexed to the imperiall crowne.

Yf any persone &c dwelling &c within this realme &c shall hereafter by wryting &c maintaine and defend &c any jurisdiction spirituall or ecclesiasticall of any forraine prince, prelate &c whatsoever heretofore claimed, used &c, whosoever shall doe yt shall forfett all there goodes and cattelles for there first offence and yf he be not woorth 20^{li} then to ly in prison for a yere. For the second offence praemunire. For the third offence treason.[56]

[Anno 5° Eliz. ca. 1°] The jurisdiction and power unjustly claimed and usurped within the realme &c: whosoever shall maintaine or defend &c in case of praemunire.[57] [p. 523]

The statute in anno 13° cap. 2° sayth, for the abolishing of the usurped power and jurisdiction of the bischop of Rome and of the sea of Rome, heretofore unlaufully claymed &c within the realme &c, and yett neverthelesse diverse seditiouse and very evill disposed people without &c, or of the fayth and allegiaunce which they ought to beare and have to hyr majestie, or feere &c of the seyd statutes but mynding, as yt should seeme very seditiously and unnaturally not only to bring this realme &c into thraldome &c of the jurisdiction &c claymed by the sea of Rome, but also to estraunge and alyenate the myndes and hartes of sundry hyr majesties subjectes from there dutifull obeydience, and to raise and stirre sedition and rebellyon within this realme &c have lately procured and obtained to themselves from the seyd bischop of Rome and his seyd sea diverse bulles &c, the effecte whereof hath bene and is to absolve and reconcile all those that wilbe contente to forsake there due obeydience to hyr majestie, and to yelde and to subjecte themselves to the seyd aucthoritie &c. By couler [by couler, not by vertue] of which bulles &c, suche persones secretly and seditiously in some partes of the realme where the people are moste weake, simple and ignoraunte &c have by theyr subtill practisez &c not only to withdrawe themselves from dyvine service established &c but

[56]Ward, 'Law of treason', 44–45; no one was prosecuted for treason under the Elizabethan act of supremacy.

[57]'An Acte for thassurance of the Quenes Ma^{tes} royal Power over all Estates and Subjectes within her Highnes Dominions', *SR*, IV, 402–405.

also have thought themselves dischardged of and from all obeydience, dutie and allegiaunce to hyr majestie, whereby unnaturall rebellion hath ensued.

For remedy &c be yt enacted &c that yf any persone &c shall use &c any suche bull &c of absolution or reconsiliation &c or yf any persone &c shall take uppon hym by couler of any suche bull &c to absolve or reconsile any persone &c or promyse &c to any persone any suche absolution or reconciliation by speche &c or yf any persone &c shall willingly receave &c any suche absolution or reconsiliation, or yf any persone &c have obtained &c any manner of bull &c containing any matter or thinge whatsoever &c in case of treason.[58] [p. 524]

By the statute in anno primo et quinto Eliz. there the matter tendes but merely of defending &c of jurisdiction claimed by the sea of Rome, but as that sea claimed not royall aucthoritie but in the persone of the pope pontificall jurisdiction, so the penalties were not highe treason, albeyt for the third offence in the first yere yt was. So was yt lesse for the first offence than in the 5 yere, which made yt merely premunirie.[59]

The statute in 13°, treating of royall dignitie, inflicteth, for the same, highe treason. But as the same statute sayth that some ignoraunte, weake and simple subjectes have bene not only withdrawen from religion established but thoughte themselves fre from there alledgiaunce, howe this may be wrested out of the symple, or easely ignorauntly graunted, when as they come before some uncharitable magistrate that will not lett to saye: you can not be of the popes religion but you must yeld him obeydience. So that not only the simple but also others of ordenary witt may easely be intrapped by some uncharitable cleregie (in especiall) magistrates who fynd themselves farre able to defend there doctryne by the penall statutes than by St Paules or the reste of the apostles epistles; for that they woold drawe all absolution, reconsiliation or persuation to the Catholyke religion, or as they terme yt the Romish religion, to be no lesse than treason,[60] and that they take the statute in anno 23° of hyr majestie, cap. 1° no lesse; wherein they shewe themselves as sufficient

---

[58] *SR*, IV, 528–529.

[59] This somewhat unclear paragraph apparently compares the penalties of the 1563 statute (directed against those who maintained the jurisdiction of the pope) with those of the 1559 supremacy act, 1 Eliz. c. 1 (*SR*, IV, 350), which restored the rights of the imperial crown against the claims to jurisdiction of the papacy and made it high treason on the third offence to defend 'by any means the authority or religious jurisdiction of any forreine prince . . . or potentate'. The 1563 treason act stipulated the penalties of praemunire for the first and of treason for the second refusal to take the oath of supremacy (though only certain persons were to be subject to demands to take it a second time, and Elizabeth prevented its tender a second time in any case), Ward, 'Law of treason', 44–49.

[60] *SR*, IV, 528–529; see Ward, 'Law of treason', 50–53.

in the understanding the lawes of the land as they do holy [p. 525] writt, and bothe alike, and that absolution, reconsiliation and persuation to the Romaine, or Romishe religion only, and for no other intent but merely for religion, is not treason, and that [is] easye to be conceaved. For the preamble of the statute sayth: where sythence the statute made in anno 13° of hyr majestie, cap. 1°,[61] diverse have practized otherwyse than by bulles &c to withdrawe diverse [of] hyr majesties subjectes from there naturall obeydience to hyr majestie &c for reformation whereof and to declare the true meaning of the seyd lawe in anno 13°. So that, howsoever subtelly or sinisterly the woordes of absolution or reconsiliation were taken by some, yett the grave and sage magistrates dyd and do knowe that neyther hyr majestie, the lawe, nor intent of the lawe was to have absolution, reconsiliation and persuation to the Romaine or Romishe religion merely and only for religion to be treason. And therefore yt sayth in the seyd statute in anno 23° Eliz.: be yt enacted by the aucthoritie of this present parliament that all persones whatsoever, which have, shall have or pretend to have power &c to absolve, persuade, or withdrawe any [of] hyr majesties subjectes &c from there naturall obeydience to hyr majestie, or to withdrawe them for that intent from the religion &c nowe established &c to the Romishe religion, or to move them, or any of them, to promyse any obeydience to any pretended aucthoritie of the sea of Rome, or of any other prince, state or potentate, to be used within hyr dominions, or shall doe any overt acte to that intent or purpose, shalbe in case of treason. So that lett hym be Catholyke, or as they caulle hym papist, protestant or puritan that shall take uppon hym to withdrawe from [p. 526] naturall obeydience, he shalbe in case of treason. And yf he persuade to the Romishe religion for that intent, yt is treason. Yf the woordd 'intent' had byne omitted in the statute, then only the persuation to the Romishe religion had bin treason, but the woorde 'intent' hath relation unto the woordes 'from naturall obeydience'.[62]

Yt is an ordenary objection of the adversarie that yt a Catholyke have gone to churche within these 20 yeres, or [is] younge and therefore baptized in this quenes tyme, and frequented the religion established by hyr highnesse, that suche a Catholyke can not but

[61] The writer is actually referring to 13 Eliz. c. 2 (*SR*, IV, 528–531); the general treason act of 1571, 13 Eliz. c. 1 (SR, IV, 526), provoked by the rising in 1569 and associated plots defined a number of new offences, in form very similar to the Henrician treason statute of 1534, Ward, 'Law of treason', 16–23.

[62] Cf. Richard Burn, *Ecclesiastical Law*, 6th edn, 4 vols (London, 1797), III, 145, citing the decision of the judges, after Campion's indictment, that 'if any person shall have power to absolve, though he move none with an intent to draw them from their obedience; or shall move any with an intent to draw them from their obedience, though he pretend not to have power to absolve', both these acts are treason under the statute.

be absolved and reconsiled and so by consequent from his naturall obeydience, and so drawe the simple and insufficient (which knowe not the distinction) into daunger of treason.

Butt that every absolution and reconsiliation is not treason may thus be proved. First according to the sacred Scripture: 'vade et reconciliare fratri tuo'; againe, 'reconciliatti sumus deo per Jesum Christum dominum nostrum'. And the child baptized, what is he but reconciled to God by absolution in baptisme from originall synne, yett not from his naturall obeydience? And besydes this, the comissarie protestant, for any one which is excommunicate, before he be admitted or receaved into there congregation, is he not to be absolved or reconsiled and doth not the commissarie saye eyther to the partie or persone, or by proxie (laying his hand on his hed): by vertue of the aucthoritie the Church hath geven to me, I do absolve the[e] from all thy synns in the name of the Father and of the Sone and of the holy ghoste, which woordes he speketh in Latin? And doth the Catholyke prieste say any more to the partie confessed? [p. 527]

Then yf he doth not (as he doth not, in dede) is there any word which importeth absolution from there naturall obeydience, or any reconciliation to any forrain prince, prelate, or potentate &c? The statute in anno 13° of hyr majestie doth shewe there be dyvers absolutions and reconciliations, or at leaste more than one, for that yt sayth any suche absolution or reconciliation, by any speche, preaching &c which what is ment thereby, before in the same statute yt sheweth for that yt sayth not only the aucthoritie claimed by the sea of Rome but also to estraunge and alyenate the myndes and hartes of sundry subgettes &c of and from all dutie and allegiaunce to hyr majestie; which wordes to the prudent are plaine enough. Yett yf some simple Catholykes be not hable to answere yt sufficientlye and some forwarde protestant redy to further the disfavour of them, by meanes of there insufficiency hereby are they brought into obliquy, and then the communaltie they cry 'crucifige'.

Yett as the statute in 13° is easie enoughe to be understode of any magistrate that woold deale charitably with the ignoraunte, whom they fynd to have more zeale than sapyence, there should not so many have bene indaungered, as there have bene.

Butt yett some in especiall of the ecclesiasticall magistrates (I will not say all, for I have knowne Catholykes which have sayd that they have bene aswell entreated before them as any other) which seeme to wrest the statute in anno 23° contrary to the true meaning thereof; and that statute is to declare the true meaning of the statute in 13°.

Butt yt seemeth that they leerned all there lodgick where the pretended pope Johanne gott all hyr learning, which is sayd to be in Athens some 200 yeres after that universitie was dissolved,[63] and the studientes there, in the end, came into Fraunce, [p. 528] and the succession of them, are the Sorbonites in Paris.

For take the tyme of Heraclius [anno domini 630] the emperor,[64] making warres into Persia, and having Mahomett, generall of the Sarrasins (his mercenary souldyers), and the muteny made by Mahomett, uppon the retourne from those warres (that shortly after he became lord of that parte of the world) [anno domini 634] and take the tyme of the pope poetically pretended [circa anno domini 847] which was supposed to be betwene Leo 4us and Benedictus 3us. So that then Athens was a fitt universitie for such a pope. So some according to the sufficiencie of there silogismes seeme to have learned there lodgick and lawe in lyke universitie[s]. For yf yt be drawen into a perfecte silogisme, eyther major holdeth not with minor, or minor with the major, and then of that no good conclusion can be had as to the purpose. The statute in anno 23° sayth all persones whatsoever, which have, or shall have, or shall pretend to have power, or shall by any wayes or meanes put in practize to absolve, perswade or withdrawe any the quenes majesties subjectes, or any within hyr highnesse realmes or dominions from there naturall obeydience to hyr majestie, or to withdrawe them for that intent from the religion nowe by hyr highnesse aucthoritie established within hyr highnesse dominions to the Romishe religion, or to move them, or any of them, to promise any obeydience to any pretended aucthoritie of the sea of Rome, or of any other prince, state or potentate to be had or used within hyr highnesse dominions, or shall doe any overt acte to that intent or purpose and every of them shalbe to all intentes adjudged traytors. Here is the major, and in every indictment [p. 529] for such causez, this is the preamble of the indictment, or ells the indictment muste have relation unto this preamble. Nowe because I meane to discourse by yt selfe of absolution and reconciliation and after by yt selfe of persuation to the Roman religion, I will nowe sett downe the minor, to the major, only concerning absolution & reconciliation.

Butt John att Style priest hath absolved Rycherd Doe the quenes subject from his naturall obeydience to hyr majestie. Ergo John at Style hath committed treason. This is the minor to the major so farre as yt serveth for absolution; and this is the parte of the indictment which

---

[63] *Pope Joan: A Dialogue between a Protestant and a Papist; manifestly proving, That a Woman, called Joan, was Pope of Rome; against the Surmises and Objections made to the Contrary, by Robert Bellarmine and Caesar Baronius, Cardinals; Florimondus Raemondus, N.D. and other Popish Writers, impudently denying the same: By Alexander Cooke,* repr. in *Harleian Miscellany,* 10 vols (London, 1808–1813), IV, 121–123.

[64] Flavius Heraclius Augustus, eastern Roman emperor 610–641.

muste have relation to the preamble of the statute: or first placed in the indictment, and have reference to yt.

To this John at Style priest denieth the minor, which to the indictment is to pleade not ghiltie. Richerd Doe is the only man which is to be produced as witnesse against the priest, which yf he became Catholike only but to intrappe the priest, he can say no more but that he, making his confession to the priest of his synnes, he gave hym absolution, but in forme aforeseyd, as the comissarie protestant or Catholyke priest useth, which is from his sinnes only and not from natural obeydience to hyr majestie.

Yf objection should be made that yt includeth or inferreth from naturall obeydience to hyr majestie, answere ~~made~~ may be made: why were not those woordes then 'from naturall obeydience to hyr majestie' left out of the statute? For lett them to be left out of the indictment, and then woold there be error sufficient in yt. And why in the statute in 13° of hyr majestie is yt there sayd, any suche absolution [p. 530] which importeth ~~suche~~ some speciall absolution, and not to be taken for absolution generally?

For yf they woold (as some of them doe) say that they can not be papistes (contrary in religion to there sovereigne) and loyall subjects, these which are thous conceipted, yt may be that they measure other mens conditions by there owne dispocitions, that had they bene in Quene Maryes dayes, or yf hyr majestie should doe as Henry the Frenche kinge for the change of his religion hath done,[65] the which Catholykes prayers to God for hyr highnesse in good tyme hyr majestie may. For I see no reason in the woorld but the Catholyk subjectes of this realme may have as greate hope of hyr highnesse, as when yt was there was had of the Frenche kinge for the same. And therefore for my parte I will neythere presume of any, nor dispare of any, syth the hartes of kinges are in the handes of God.

Butt yt may be doubted that men so conceipted woold do there endevour to be of distourbant demeanour [?]. Butt to retourne, yf he can not be in religion contrary, and withall in loyaltie; in what case then were the apostles and Christians in the primatyve Churche, yea and the Jues to[o], being (before our Saviour his passion) the people of God? For what emperours or kinges were of there religion? For from the tyme that the Romans had conquered Pallestine, and devyded the kingdome [p. 531] of Judea into tetrarchies, then not only the Jues but also there petie kinges, and muche more Kinge Herod (being a proselite, that is of a gentile become circumcised) and thereby in profession a Jue, were all traytors for that they were ~~of~~ different in religion from there liege lord. Butt this is straunge to be

---

[65] i.e. Henry IV of France who converted to the Church of Rome in 1593.

considered, that the emperours being heathens, and there presidentes pagans, accepted of there tribute and quiett behavior in the common weale, and left there religion to themselves as a thing not depending uppon the state. So farre forthe as when the Jues made [it] a matter of religion or conscience not to entre into the pretorie or princely pallace in regarde of there pasche, the president Pylate came forthe to them. And lykewyse the president Festus [Actes 25] concerning St Paull, uppon the surmisez or objections his accusers made, sayd he suspected no evill in him, but questions (as he termed them) of his superstition. So that for his religion, nor his accusors (being Jues) both different and dissonant from the emperor, Festus never made doubt, as matter of state, estraunging there allegiaunce from there liege lord. Yf yt can not be but the Catholyke or papist is out of his allegiaunce by meanes of his religion only, then no doubte those which suffred in Quene Maryes dayes for religion only were out of there allegiaunce by meanes of there contrary religion to hyr highnesse. Those which will nedes hold the one against the papistes nowe, muste nedes graunte the other [p. 532] against the protestantes then. And then, according to Aristotle [Arist[otle], Retor], yf that which she dyd were juste and right, then that which they recaved and suffred was juste and right which, yf they had forsaken there allegiaunce to there sovereign, they demerited no lesse.

Butt yf these opynions and conclusions be holden for good, then our Savyour tooke the straungest course that the somme [?] of sapyens could doe, to plant or ordaine a religion that those which should professe yt should renounce there allegiaunce to there lord or kinge. For to his apostles he not only gave them commission to goe into all the woorld to preache and baptyse &c, and withall whosoever ~~whose~~ woold not here the Churche, lett hym be as an heathen or publicaine; but also sayd he woold dispose of them a kingdome, as his father had dispoosed of hym. And St Peeter to saye, you are a kinglyke priesthoode [Actes 9]. And when the Churche was fyrst planted and did increase, what emperour, kinge, or prince was of yt, so that Christ could have his primatyve Churche without any potentate or the woorld member of yt? And further St Peter with St James, together with the priestes at Hierusalem [Actes 15] to hould a councell and decree precepts. And also St Paule, not only for devulging therin but also for saying [Actes 20] attend you &c for the hooly ghoste hath placed you bischops to rule the Churche of God. And not only this but also to say obedite propositis vestris et subjacete [p. 533] eos &c. Nowe men which are of conceipte that the subjecte can not be of a different religion from his sovereign and a true subject, eythere lett them reverse there judgementes, or there may be inferred that had they encountred the primatyve churche and had had warrauntes to there will, licencez to there beliefe, or commissions to there conceiptes, that they woold no otherwyse have entreated our Saviour, his apostles and martyrs than they were delt withal.

For the other parte concerning persuation: the statute [anno 23 Eliz.] sayth whosoever shall withdrawe them, for that intent, from the religion nowe by hyr highnesse aucthoritie established to the Roman religion; so that this woorde intent muste have relation ~~from~~ to the words 'there naturall obeydience'.

Then is yt to be: whosoever shall withdrawe any [of] the quenes subjectes from the religion established to the Romishe religion from there naturall obeydience, shalbe in case of treason. Butt John at Style hath withdrawen Rycherd Doe the quenes subjecte from the religion established to the Romische religion from his naturall obeydience. Ergo in case of treason.

To this John at Style pleadeth not ghiltie to the indictment, which is, he denyeth the minor.

Rycherd Doe, produced for witnesse, sayth that John at Style told hym that he muste hold praying to sainctes and beleve the reall presence in the sacrament, where is wrought transubstantiation &c.

Yf this be all Rycherd Doe can say against John at Style, here is but opynion not persuation, and this is lyke as yf [p. 534] a chirurgian lay a sovereigne plaster uppon ded fleshe; or the phisitian to geve mutrative medecine before he woorketh evacuation of corrupte humours. For Aristotle [Aristotle, Retor] sayth the arte of retorick or persuation is first to disable the one, and after commend the other: and yeld raisons negatively and affirmatively. So that had John at Style spoken in derogation of the religion established, and sayd praying to sainctes is to be by this raison, that [Genesis 48] Jacob gave in chardge that Josephes children should invocate his name and the names of the fathers Abraham and Isaack, which were before departed this woorld, and he then redy to dye, what ells is this but to pray to the sainctes departed? And lykewyse yf he had sayd for the reall presence in the sacrament, yf the sonne of god were hable by his woorde to woorke transubstantiation of the creatures of stones, and make them breade, then the sonne of God was hable by hys woorde to woorke transubstantiation of the creatures of breade and wyne and make them his body and bloudde. Butt he could do the one; ergo he could do the other. The devill graunting the major, he can not chuse but be woorse than the devil which denyeth the minor. This had bene persuation to the Catholyke, Romaine or Romishe religion, yett from no naturall obeydience. Nowe for so muche as the lawe is more laudable by [p. 535] howe muche the more yt is by raison probable. Then comparing somme other statutes with yt, we shall see what absourdities

For admitt the case, that a Catholyke or popishe recusant should persuade any hyr majesties subjecte [p. 539] to the Romishe religion that were a recusant, viz Jue, pagan or apostata (yf any suche there be) purytan or Brownist or any other sectarie (I will not say atheistes for they will goe to any religion pro forma rather than they will suffre any punishment for profession of fayth) which doth forbeare going to the religion established. This can not be treason, because he was not withdrawen from the religion established. For yt can not be sayd a man to be withdrawen from that company or congregation whereof he is non[e]; and a man to dissuade any from one religion, when they both professe other, yett diverse, were as ridiculous as yf a man should dissuade his friend from maryeng some speciall mayde or wydowe when the partie is in love and maryed to an other. And yett yf he should persuade or withdrawe any such pagan, Jue, apostata &c (being a subjecte) from his naturall obeydience to hyr majestie, althoughe he persuaded hym not to the Roman religion, yett by the same woordes preceding in the same statute yt is treason.

Nowe yf an Italyan, Frenchman or Fleming &c within the realme or dominions (no fre denizen) frequenting the religion established &c should by a Catholyke or popishe recusant [be] persuaded to the Romishe religion, can this be treason? Not unlesse he can thereby be withdrawen from his naturall obeydience to [p. 540] hyr majestie, and yf he can not be withdrawen from his naturall obeydience to hyr majestie, because he is no naturall borne subject, nor made fre denizen, nor naturalized by parliament, can religion and allegiaunce, or naturall obeydience be relative? And yf by this consequence they can not, then may John at Style persuade the subjecte (being pagan, Jue, apostata, puritan or Brownist &c) to the Roman religion, because he professeth not the religion established; and lykewise the forriner frequenting the religion established, because he can not be persuaded from naturall obeydience, yf he owe non to hyr majestie.

The speciallest objection which may be made (in my simple opynion) to pretend to prove religion and naturall obeydience to be relatyve is thus: yf the persuading to the Romishe religion of any within hyr highnesse dominions &c for the intent aforeseyd muste be from naturall obeydience, or not treason, then where some Italians, Frenchmen and Flemings &c are within hyr highnesse dominions (being forreners), and yf therefore they owe no naturall obeydience to hyr majestie; and yett suche forrener frequenting the religion established &c, [p. 541] which forryner John at Style hath withdrawen from the same to the Romishe religion, then that can not be for the intent, from his naturall obeydyence, yf the forryner owe non; and the woordes being 'any within the dominions' &c, and this forriner being one, therefore the persuading to the Romishe religion merely or only for religion is treason, which objection may thus be answered.

These woordes 'any within hyr highnesse dominions' muste ~~have~~ have aswell reference to the future, or woordes following 'naturall obeydyence' as the words 'for that intent' muste have relation to the same words 'naturall obeydyence' precedent. And then the woorde 'any' muste be understood [as] any such as oweth naturall obeydyence to hyr majestie (for can a man withdrawe that from any other which is not owing to hym?). Nowe yf all within the realme (forryners not excepted) do owe naturall obeydience to hyr majestie, then any whosoever or whatsoever within the realme may be withdrawen from the one or the other. Butt yf forryners (within the dominions) doe owe no naturall obeydience to hyr majestie, then the woorde 'any' muste be understode of any within hyr dominions which are denizens, or naturalysed by parliament, for suche have made themselves hyr majesties subjectes, and so admitted and allowed hyr highnes there liege lady. Yf this be thus [p. 542] then some within the realme or dominions (being forryners) frequenting the religion established &c may be withdrawen from the same to the Romishe religion without daunger of treason, because they can not be withdrawen for that intent, that is from there naturall obeydyence, yf they owe non. Then by this, religion and allegiaunce, or naturall obeydience, are not relative.

Or yf to persuade from the religion established &c to the Romishe religion any within the realme &c is ment by the statute aswell of any forryner as of any denizen; and yf forryners owe no allegiaunce nor naturall obeydience to hyr majestie, then to persuade any suche from the religion established to the Roman religion can not be treason, unlesse yt be for moving them or any of them to promyse any obeydience to any pretended aucthoritie of the sea of Rome &c as in the same statute in anno 23° yt followeth. And eyther this is to be the true meaning of this statute, or elles this statute standeth more nede of a statute to explaine this difficultie in yt. Then had the statute in 13° nede of the statute in 23° to expresse or declare the true meaning of that. And then withall, where is the booke of the execucion of justice in England,[70] not for religion, but for treason.

Nowe as the puritauntes, presiciandes[71] and Brownistes, or what title or terme suche sectaries have, are start up in England, since hyr majesties reigne, and so by consequent are withdrawen from the religion established, the which abandoning is eythere of themselves,

---

[70] Cecil, *The Execution of Justice.*
[71] Precisians, i.e. puritans.

or by the persuation of others; which, yf yt be, may yt be justly [p. 543] sayd that they have or can absolve themselves from there naturall obeydience to hyr majestie, or yf they be receaved into the congregation of any such sectaries by there superintendent or elder, shall yt be holden that they are reconsiled to any forrayn prince, state or potentate &c which is in unitie of opynion with them? But in the woorld there ~~wilbe~~ can not be found any. And my raison is, lett there wryters be examined effectually; and they no doubt will be proved to dissent in essentiall pointes.

Nowe yf the starte upp sectarie may abandon the religion established and persuade others to assosiate hymselfe with others to be received into there congregations without being reconsiled to any forrain prince &c because there be non, may not the Catholyke or papist do the lyke without being reconsiled to some forraine prince &c, althoughe (thankes be to God) there be many of there religion? Yf all or any sectaries may, and Catholykes or papistes may not, then is there case muche lyke to the apostles which were prohibited [Actes 5] only to speake in the name of Jesus. Butt Saduzes were not which denyed the resurrection, yett the apostles muste, which proved the same.

Nowe whosoever shall take uppon them to absolve, reconcile or persuade, or to be absolved, reconciled or persuaded from his naturall obeydyence to hyr majestie, or shall persuade to the Romishe religion; for that intent [he is] in case of treason. Butt yf a Protestant excommunicate submitt hymselfe to the ordenary, yf he presumeth to geve hym absolution without any protestation of reconsiliation to hyr majestie, and so lykewyse whosoever is receaved into the unitie of the Catholyke Churche hath only absolution from hys synnes which he confesseth without any manner of protestation of absolution from his allegiaunce to hyr majestie, or reconciliation to any forrain prynce, prelate, state or potentate whosoever or whatsoever by name, directly or indirectly, [p. 544] nowe yf only to forsake the profession Protestant, and to come to be in unitie of the holy Catholyke Churche (or as they terme yt of the Romishe religion) were to be a traytor, then lesse daunger were yt for newe-become Catholykes, (before they come to be convicte[d] for recusancie) for then [anno 35° Eliz. ca. 2°] they are to geve in there names to be restrained, and to retaine themselves or incurre the daunger of the lawe; and there confinement is a confession of there fayth, and passyvely a profession of religion, to extoll the aucthoritie of the bishop of Rome claymed; for that were only praemunire; which, albeyt yt be a wonderfull greate punishment, yett of two evells I take yt to be farre lesse to loose utterly all my goodes and during my lyfe my landes and libertie, the which offence is to be founde within the yere, or not at all; and yett for the same offence there is no corruption of bloodde, no disinheriting my heire, nor prejudice to my wyfes dowry, and besydes charitably to be receaved in prison without daunger to them whome suche persone shall relieve, which in case of praemunire generally is not admitted. This I saye is farre more tolerable than the other, to be drawen, hanged and quartered, with losse to my heire and wyfe of all my landes and goodes for ever. I do not speake this to ymbolden any man to attempte the one, but to shew the insufficiencie, or lacke of charitie of those, which so woold wreste the other.

Butt yf suche conclusions shall stand for good, and the sacred Scripture thus to be interpreted, in what case are many Christians in, and then better to be [p. 545] a wooman than a man, for our Savyour saith, whosoever looketh on a wooman to luste after hyr hath committed advoutry in his harte. But John at Style hath looked on a wooman, ergo he hath committed advoutry. Yf this were a true silogisme, who but borne-blinde men are fre from advoutry. But ad the woordes luste after hyr, and then, with Godes grace, millions of men. Semblably, Catholykes to persuade to the Catholyke religion I hoope there be many, but to persuade to yt from naturall obeydience to hyr majestie I woold be sory that there should be any. Lykewyse the prophett Esay sayth [Esay 10 ver. 1] v[a]e qui conduit leges iniquas. But what kinges have not made lawes (yf they have lyved any tyme). Ergo all kinges are cursed, not, unlesse the woorde wicked be joyned to there laws. The prophett Hieremy [Hierem. ~~23 ver.~~ 22 ver. 13] sayth, v[a]e qui edificat domum suam in injustitiam. Yf there conclusion may hold, all builders of howsez are cursed; but lett them putt to in injustitiam, and then I hope in God full many are free. Further the same prophett sayth [Hierem. 23 ver. 1] v[a]e pastoribus qui disprodunt et dilacerent gregem pastue meae. Yf that hold, then all spirituall pastors are cursed, but ad to, the spoleters and tearers of the flock, and then no doubte all shall not.

The prophett Ezechiell sayth [Ezechiel 13 ver. 3] v[a]e prophetis insipientibus qui sequntur spiritum suum et nihil vident; yf this of there conclusion be true, the prophett Ezechiel hath not let to cry for vengeaunce to hym selfe and to all the prophettes of God. But lett the minor concurre with the major, and then non but [p. 546] foolishe prophettes, suche as followe there owne fancie, are accursed, the which, who are the lyklyest to be suche, at this day, eyther Catholyke priestes or Protestant ministers, I persuade my selfe of the one, that they were content the matter were committed to a jury of gentills and Jues to be censured by them.

The same prophett [Ezech. 34 ver. 2] sayth v[a]e pastoribus Israell, qui pascebant semetipsos: nonne greges a pastoribus pascuntur. Here lykewyse they woold have all spirituall pastours cursed because some peradventure which only feede themselves do fynde by the prophett to be cursed.

The prophett Amos [Amos 6] sayth, v][a]e qui opulenti estis in Sion. Yf there conclusion be true the woorde wealt[h]ie being left out, and then all in Syon are cursed, and yf Syon here be taken for the holy Catholyke Churche (as in dyverse placez of the prophettes yt is) then, in regarde of there ritchez, they are content to kepe themselves out because they woold not as they thinke be cursed.

The prophett Nathan sayth [Nathan 3], v[a]e civitas sanguinum &c, yf there conclusion may hold, which leaving out bloudy, then all cities are cursed. The prophett Habacuck [Habacuck 2] sayth, v[a]e qui multiplicat non sua; leave out non sua, and all good husbandes are cursed which were propre doctrine for young gentlemen to persuade them to prodigality. Againe the prophett Esay [Esay 5] sayth, v[a]e qui consurgitis mane ad ebrietatem sectandam et petandum usque ad vesperam &c; lett the periodde be made at mane in the minor, and a good argument for sloughtfull servauntes to defend there long lyeng in [p. 547] bedd and yett is yt aswell to be made in this, as in the argument persuading to the Roman religion, leaving out 'for that intent', which muste be understoode from naturall obeydience.

In Ecclesiasticus [Ecclesiasticus 41] yt ys written, v[a]e vobis viri impii qui derelequistis legem domini altissimi. Lett the periodde be made in the minor at viri; and then all men are cursed, but lett yt be at his propre place, and then lett any man looke to hymsclf whethere he be not included in the company of those which have forsaken the law of the moste highe lord.

St Jude in his Epistle sayth, v[a]e illis qui in via Cain alicrunt, et errore Balaam &c, et in contradictione Core perierunt. Howe can any omission be here made, unlesse yt be at illis, and then is yt uncertaine who is cursed, but lette yt runne to his full pointe, and murderers, holders of errors, and scismatiks are all accursed. For Caine slew his brother Abell. Balaam was a false prophett, and Chore intruded hymselfe (being a suborderdenate [sic] prieste) into the sacerdotale dignitie, or chiefe priestes office [Numbers 16] for the which he was ingulphed into hell. And for so muche as not only he but all his complices or company, lett every man looke to hymselfe to avoyde assosiation with sectaries.

Yf these were framed into formall silogismes and compared with the woordes of the statute [anno 23° Eliz] of the withdrawing from the religion established to the Roman religion, then eythere those can not be true silogismes or that not treason. [p. 548]

An other way to prouve that persuasion to the Romishe religion only for religion is not treason may thous [sic] be proved: lett John at Style say whether doth not this courte hold that heresy and veritie are contradictorie (the which no doubt will be graunted) but not any point which hath byn declared against hym is heresy. Then is yt veritie and, yf they be not untruethes, will the lawe drawe John at Style to be a traytor for uttering to any man the truyth?

Here will ryse a newe question: whethere yt be heresy ye[a] or no? Butt neyther that, nor any pointe of doctryne or fayth, which the hooly Catholyke, Romain or Romishe Churche holdeth or teacheth is not, nor can not any wayes be proved heresy: and then veritie; and, yf yt be true, shall yt be treason? This were absurde and dishonorable to the country. Butt that no pointe thereof is heresy thous [*sic*] I prove yt.

In anno primo of hyr majestie cap 1°, yt sayth [?] these words: the reformation and determination of all manner of errors, heresies, scismes, abusez &c shalbe united and annexed to the emperiall crowne of this realme, provyded alwayes and be yt enacted &c that suche persone or persones to whom your highnesse &c shall hereafter by [p. 549] lettres patentes under the greate seale of England geve aucthoritie to have or execute any jurisdiction, power or aucthoritie spirituall, or to visit, order or correcte any errors, heresies scismes, abusez or enormities by vertue of this acte, shall not in any wyse have aucthoritie or power to determine &c any matter or cause to be heresye but only suche as heretofore have bene determined &c heresy by the aucthoritie of the canonicall Scriptures, or by the first foure generall councelles, or by any of them, or by any other generall counselles wherein the same was declared heresy by the expresse and plaine woordes of the sayd canonicall Scripture or suche as hereafter shalbe determined &c to be heresy by the highe courte of parliament of this realme with the assent of the cleregy in there convocation. But the pointes which John at Style delyvered to Rycherd Doe, nor any other pointe of doctryne or fayth holden by the hooly Catholyke apostolyke, Romain or Romishe Churche are not holden to be heresye or herysies not by any determination aforeseyd. Ergo no heresye, and then veritie, for what pointe of fayth or doctryne do the papistes of England hold at this day that was not holden the first 600 yeres or at leaste not condempned for heresye then?

Nowe to recapitulate the statutes and the distinctions of the causez [anno 23° and 29° Eliz.]: whosoever forbeareth going to the churche monthly, 20^{li}, and this not [p. 550] only to Catholykes but also to Protestauntes suche as forbeare goyng to churche.

Whosoever is convicted for recusancie, being a popishe recusant [anno 35° Eliz. ca. 2°], (that is to be in unitie of fayth and religion with the pope) he is to be restreined to the distaunce of fyve myles from the place he will seate hymelfe at.

Whosoever shall extoll &c the aucthoritie claimed by the bischop of Rome within the realme, to be in praemunire [anno 5° Eliz.], albeyt in anno 1° Eliz. yt was made for the fyrste tyme, yf not woorthe 20^{li}, a yeres ymprisonment; for the 2 tyme praemunire, and the 3 tyme treason.

Whosoever shall persuade to forbeare comming to churche [anno 35° Eliz ca. 1°], or to be present at any unlawfull assemblies under couler of religion contrary to hyr majesties lawes yf a ~~Catholyke~~ popishe recusant, be the persuader, he is to ly in prison untill he conforme hymselfe. [This statute was but to continewe, to the end of the next parliament, and there not continewed, therefore not in force.]

Whosoever shall absolve or be absolved, from naturall obeydience, reconcile or be reconciled to any forrain prince &c or persuade to the Romishe religion, for that intent [anno 13° and 23° Eliz.], in case of treason.

Thus according to the meanesse of my witt, I have acquainted you with my conceipte. My [*sic* for 'I'] desyre you in all charitie that yf you thinke good to lett this passe further that you will have yt perused and penned [p. 551] by grave and mature advise and deliberacion. For I accompte my selfe but as a labourer which hath hewen yt out of the rock and so leave yt, for some [word illegible] freemason to square and carve yt, according to his skill, beseeching our blessed lady, that she will be an intercessor to hyr sonne, our Saviour Jesus Christe, that yt may prove to as good effecte, as I do desyre.

Deo gracias.

PERSONAL AND PLACE NAME INDEX TO APPENDICES 2–4

Places are named here in their modern form with their pre-1974 English or Welsh county. Owing to the complications surrounding naming conventions in this period, all people are listed primarily by their first names. English equivalents of Latin Christian names are given where their bearers are from English dioceses, but unusual Christian names are italicized and not translated. Where Christian names or patronymics refer to people from Welsh dioceses, the standard Welsh forms are used (e.g. Ieuan, not John, for Iohannes; Gwilym, not William, for Willelmus; etc.). Welsh patronymics are not listed separately from the full names of their bearers; surnames are listed separately, but with cross-references to their bearers' full names, in keeping with the indexing of Welsh personal names, and are spelled as in the sources. The numbers of entries in texts in Appendices (Apps) 2, 3 and 4 are indicated in bold. Peter Clarke's introduction and Apps 1a and 1b are not indexed below, nor are references to Wolsey himself in any of the texts edited. Place names in the dating clauses of texts in App. 4 are not indexed either, as Wolsey's letters calendared there are usually dated at Westminster, and papal letters at St Peter's, Rome.

Abell, *see* Robert (alias Mailand)
Abergwili (Carmarth.), canonry App. 2. **29**n
Aberporth (Cardigans.) App. 3. **159**n
Abbot, Laurence App. 2. **12**
Abingdon Abbey (Berks.), *see* D. Thomas Rouland (abbot of)
Acton Burnell (Salop) App. 3. **59**n
Adam More App. 3. **92**
Adrian VI, Pope App. 4. **13**, **14**
Agille, John App. 2. **102**
Aglionby, Thomas App. 3. **12**
Agnes Amyse App. 2. **46**
Agnes Batt App. 3. **65**
Agnes Baynley App. 2. **106**
Agnes Bedle App. 2. **105**
Agnes verch Dd App. 3. **49**
Agnes Ingham App. 2. **97**
Agnes Molls App. 2. **43**
Agnes Rutter App. 3. **148**
Agnes Smyth' App. 2. **47**
Agnes Wasshington' App. 3. **90**
Alan Percie (Percy) App. 3. **4**
Alcoke, John App. 4. **72**

Alconbury (Hunts.) App. 3. **45**n
Alen, Catherine App. 2. **11**
Alen, John, M., DCn & CL App. 4. **50**
Alexander Boston, MA App. 4. **7**
Alexander Colyns App. 4. **22**, **23**
Alexander VI, Pope App. 2. **27**n
Aleynton', Richard App. 2. **50**
Alice Berriman App. 3. **93**n
Alice Broke App. 3. **46**
Alice Colombe App. 2. **44**
Alice Hawkyns App. 2. **50**
Alice Hoggerson' App. 2. **13**
Alice Relf App. 3. **98**
Alice Swallow App. 3. **63**
Alice To(ur)ner App. 2. **101**
Alice Wenscerley App. 3. **149**
Alice Weyrhorne App. 2. **39**
All Saints', Bristol (Gloucs.): Kalendars chantry App. 4. **10**n; Kalendars provost App. 4. **36**n
All Saints', Cricklade (Wilts.), par. ch. App. 4. **40**n
All Saints', Kimcote (Leics.) App. 4. **60**